James Henry Fillmore

New Christian Hymn and Tune-Book

A Selection of Hymns and Tunes for Christian Worship

James Henry Fillmore

New Christian Hymn and Tune-Book
A Selection of Hymns and Tunes for Christian Worship

ISBN/EAN: 9783337289805

Printed in Europe, USA, Canada, Australia, Japan

Cover: Foto ©Thomas Meinert / pixelio.de

More available books at **www.hansebooks.com**

NEW CHRISTIAN

HYMN AND TUNE-BOOK:

A SELECTION OF

HYMNS AND TUNES FOR CHRISTIAN WORSHIP.

IN TWO PARTS.

————

Speaking to yourselves in psalms and hymns and spiritual songs, singing and making melody in your heart to the Lord.—Eph. v. 19.

————

ST. LOUIS:
JOHN BURNS, PUBLISHER.
1882.

PREFACE.

THE space usually given to preface will be found filled with music; but some few features call for mention.

The book is divided into two parts, which, roughly speaking, contain—the old, standard hymns and tunes, in the first; and the later, popular hymns, of the "Gospel Songs" variety, in the second.

The style, here adopted, of placing the hymn at the right of its tune, in many cases, instead of always below it, will find favor with music-readers, after a short experience. This plan has great advantages in making up such a work.

In announcing a hymn, I take the liberty to recommend that it be done solely by the *number*, without mention of the page. It will also be well to name the tune, as, usually, the music on pages facing each other is adapted to all the hymns on those pages.

The Analytical Index is arranged on the best model known to me. I hope it will be found very serviceable.

Among many to whom this work is greatly indebted, I desire to especially recognize Messrs. J. H. ROSECRANS, J. P. POWELL, J. R. MURRAY, E. S. LORENZ, T. C. O'KANE, and my brother FRED—musical friends; and also Elder L. H. JAMESON, to whose authorship and proficiency, both in letters and music, I am under many obligations. These, and a multitude of correspondents, will pardon, for the sake of brevity, this slight acknowledgment of numerous and signal favors.

With these few indications, the public will dismiss my editorial labors, and forget them in the wealth of sacred song which it has been my privilege to select from the vast treasure-house of Christian psalmody. Trusting that the selection will meet the approval of all who desire pure, fervent congregational worship, I commit it to the blessing of the Father and the favor of His children.

JAS. H. FILLMORE.

CINCINNATI, *July* 20, 1882.

NOTE.—I have not intentionally omitted any proper credits in these pages, and shall be glad to hear from any one who finds the recognition incorrect or unsatisfactory.

ELECTROTYPED AT
FRANKLIN TYPE FOUNDRY,
CINCINNATI.

NEW CHRISTIAN

HYMN AND TUNE-BOOK.

PART I.

DUKE STREET. L. M.   JOHN HATTON.

Awake, my tongue, thy trib - ute bring   To him who gave thee power to sing;

Praise him who is all   praise a - bove,   The source of wis-dom and of love.

1

AWAKE, my tongue, thy tribute bring
To him who gave thee power to sing;
Praise him who is all praise above,
The source of wisdom and of love.

2 How vast his knowledge! how profound!
A deep where all our thoughts are drowned;
The stars he numbers, and their names
He gives to all those heavenly flames.

3 Thro' each bright world above, behold
Ten thousand thousand charms unfold;
Earth, air, and mighty seas combine
To speak his wisdom all divine.

4 But in redemption, O what grace!
Its wonders, O what thought can trace!
Here, wisdom shines forever bright;
Praise him, my soul, with sweet delight.
JOHN NEEDHAM.

2

JEHOVAH reigns; his throne is high;
His robes are light and majesty;
His glory shines with beams so bright
No mortal can sustain the sight.

2 His terrors keep the world in awe;
His justice guards his holy law;
His love reveals a smiling face;
His truth and promise seal the grace.

3 Thro' all his works his wisdom shines,
And baffles Satan's deep designs;
His power is sovereign to fulfill
The noblest counsels of his will.

4 And will this glorious Lord descend
To be my Father and my Friend?
Then let my songs with angels join;
Heaven is secure, if God be mine.
ISAAC WATTS.

3

NEW CHRISTIAN

OLD HUNDRED. L. M.

GUILLAUME FRANC.

Be - fore Je - ho - vah's aw - ful throne, Ye na - tions, bow with sa - cred joy;

Know that the Lord is God a - lone; He can cre - ate, and he de - stroy.

3

BEFORE Jehovah's awful throne,
Ye nations, bow with sacred joy;
Know that the Lord is God alone;
He can create, and he destroy.

2 His sovereign power, without our aid,
Made us of clay, and formed us men;
And when like wandering sheep we strayed,
He brought us to his fold again.

3 We are his people, we his care—
Our souls, and all our mortal frame;
What lasting honors shall we rear,
Almighty Maker, to thy name?

4 We'll crowd thy gates with thankful songs,
High as the heavens our voices raise;
And earth, with her ten thousand tongues,
Shall fill thy courts with sounding praise.

5 Wide as the world is thy command;
Vast as eternity thy love;
Firm as a rock thy truth shall stand,
When rolling years shall cease to move.
ISAAC WATTS.

4

FROM all that dwell below the skies,
Let the Creator's praise arise;
Let the Redeemer's name be sung
Through every land, by every tongue.

2 Eternal are thy mercies, Lord;
Eternal truth attends thy word;
Thy praise shall sound from shore to shore
Till suns shall rise and set no more.
ISAAC WATTS.

5

THEE we adore, eternal Lord;
We praise thy name with one accord;
Thy saints, who here thy goodness see,
Thro' all the world do worship thee.

2 To thee aloud all angels cry,
The heavens and all the powers on high;
Thee, holy, holy, holy King,
Lord God of hosts, they ever sing.

3 Th' apostles join the glorious throng;
The prophets swell th' immortal song;
The martyrs' noble army raise
Eternal anthems to thy praise.

4 From day to day, O Lord, do we
Highly exalt and honor thee;
Thy name we worship and adore,
World without end, for evermore.
THOS. COTTERILL.

6

KINGDOMS and thrones to God belong:
Crown him, ye nations, in your song;
His wondrous name and power rehearse:
His honors shall enrich your verse.

2 He rides and thunders through the sky;
His name, Jehovah, sounds on high;
Praise him aloud, ye sons of grace;
Ye saints, rejoice before his face.

3 God is our shield, our joy, our rest;
God is our King: proclaim him blest.
When terrors rise, when nations faint,
He is the strength of every saint.
ISAAC WATTS.

4

UXBRIDGE. L. M.   LOWELL MASON.

Ere mountains reared their forms sublime, Or heaven and earth in order stood;

Be-fore the birth of an-cient time, From ev-er-last-ing, thou art God.

7

ERE mountains reared their forms sublime,
Or heaven and earth in order stood;
Before the birth of ancient time,
From everlasting, thou art God.

2 A thousand ages, in their flight,
With thee are as a fleeting day;
Past, present, future, to thy sight
At once their various scenes display.

3 But our brief life's a shadowy dream—
A passing thought, that soon is o'er—
That fades with morning's earliest beam,
And fills the musing mind no more.

4 To us, O Lord, the wisdom give
Each passing moment so to spend
That we at length with thee may live,
Where life and bliss shall never end.
HARRIET AUBER.

UPTON. L. M.   FROM "MASONS' SACRED HARP."

God of my life, to thee belong   *Touched by thy love, each tuneful chord*
The grateful heart, the joyful song;   *Resounds the goodness of the Lord.*

8

GOD of my life, to thee belong
The grateful heart, the joyful song;
Touched by thy love, each tuneful chord
Resounds the goodness of the Lord.

2 Yet why, dear Lord, this tender care?
Why doth thy hand so kindly rear
A useless cumberer of the ground,
On which so little fruit is found?

3 Still let the barren fig-tree stand,
Upheld and fostered by thy hand;
And let its fruit and verdure be
A grateful tribute, Lord, to thee.
E. SCOTT.

9

WITH deepest reverence at thy throne,
Jehovah, peerless and unknown,
Our feeble spirits strive, in vain,
A glimpse of thee, great God, to gain.

2 Who, by the closest search, can find
Th' eternal, uncreated Mind?
Nor men, nor angels can explore
Thy heights of love, thy depths of power.

3 That power we trace on every side;
O may thy wisdom be our guide!
And while we live, and when we die,
May thine almighty love be nigh.
E. BUTCHER.

5

NEW CHRISTIAN

JOSEPH MAINZER.

Serv-ants of God, in joy-ful lays Sing ye the Lord Je-ho-vah's praise;

His glo-rious name let all a-dore, From age to age, for ev-er-more.

10

SERVANTS of God, in joyful lays
Sing ye the Lord Jehovah's praise;
His glorious name let all adore,
From age to age, for evermore.

2 Who is like God? so great, so high,
He bows himself to view the sky;
And yet, with condescending grace,
Looks down upon the human race.

3 He hears the uncomplaining moan
Of those who sit and weep alone;
He lifts the mourner from the dust;
In him the poor may safely trust.

4 O then, aloud, in joyful lays,
Sing to the Lord Jehovah's praise;
His saving name let all adore,
From age to age, for evermore.

JAMES MONTGOMERY.

11

O LOVE beyond conception great,
That formed the vast, stupendous plan,
Where all divine perfections meet
To reconcile rebellious man.

2 There wisdom shines in fullest blaze,
And justice all her right maintains;
Astonished angels stoop to gaze,
While mercy o'er the guilty reigns.

3 Yes, mercy reigns, and justice too;
In Christ they both harmonious meet,
He paid to justice all her due,
And now he fills the mercy-seat.

UNKNOWN.

12

ERE the blue heavens were stretched abroad,
From everlasting was the Word;
With God he was, the Word was God,
And must divinely be adored.

2 By his own power were all things made;
By him supported, all things stand;
He is the whole creation's head,
And angels fly at his command.

3 But, lo! he leaves those heavenly forms,
The Word descends and dwells in clay,
That he may converse hold with worms,
Dressed in such feeble flesh as they.

4 Archangels leave their high abode
To learn new mysteries here, and tell
The love of our descending God,
The glories of Immanuel.

ISAAC WATTS.

13

GOD is the refuge of his saints,
When storms of sharp distress invade;
Ere we can offer our complaints,
Behold him present with his aid.

2 Let mountains from their seats be hurled
Down to the deep, and buried there,
Convulsions shake the solid world,
Our faith shall never yield to fear.

3 Zion enjoys her monarch's love,
Secure against a threatening hour;
Nor can her firm foundations move,
Built on his truth, and armed with power.

ISAAC WATTS.

TRURO. L. M.   CHARLES BURNEY.

With one consent let all the earth To God their cheer-ful voic-es raise;

Glad homage pay, with aw - ful mirth, And sing be - fore him songs of praise.

14

WITH one consent let all the earth
  To God their cheerful voices raise;
Glad homage pay, with awful mirth,
  And sing before him songs of praise:

2 Convinced that he is God alone,
  From whom both we and all proceed;
We, whom he chooses for his own,
  The flock that he vouchsafes to feed.

3 O enter, then, his temple gate,
  Thence to his courts devoutly press;
And still your grateful hymns repeat,
  And still his name with praises bless.

4 For he's the Lord supremely good,
  His mercy is forever sure;
His truth, which always firmly stood,
  To endless ages shall endure.
                TATE AND BRADY.

15

JEHOVAH reigns; he dwells in light,
Arrayed with majesty and might;
The world, created by his hands,
Still on its firm foundation stands.

2 But ere this spacious world was made,
Or had its first foundation laid,
His throne eternal ages stood,
Himself the Ever-living God.

3 Forever shall his throne endure;
His promise stands forever sure;
And everlasting holiness
Becomes the dwellings of his grace.
                ISAAC WATTS.

16

THE Lord will come, the earth shall quake,
The hills their fixéd seat forsake;
And withering, from the vault of night,
The stars withdraw their feeble light.

2 The Lord will come, but not the same
As once in lowly form he came;
A silent Lamb to slaughter led,
The bruised, the suffering, and the dead.

3 The Lord will come—a dreadful form,
With wreath of flame, and robe of storm,
On cherub wings, and wings of wind,
Anointed Judge of human kind.

4 While sinners in despair shall call,
"Rocks, hide us! mountains, on us fall!"
The saints, ascending from the tomb,
Shall joyful sing, "The Lord is come!"
                REGINALD HEBER.

17

THE Lord is King! Lift up thy voice,
O earth! and all ye heavens, rejoice!
From world to world the joy shall ring—
"The Lord omnipotent is King!"

2 The Lord is King! Who, then, shall dare
Resist his will, distrust his care?
Holy and true are all his ways;
Let every creature speak his praise.

3 O when his wisdom can mistake,
His might decay, his love forsake,
Then may his children cease to sing
"The Lord omnipotent is King!"
                JOSIAH CONDER.

7

LEYDEN. L. M.   COSTELLO.

E-ter-nal God, ce-les-tial King, Ex-alt-ed be thy glorious name; Let hosts in heaven thy praises sing, And saints on earth thy love proclaim, And saints on earth thy love proclaim.

18

ETERNAL God, celestial King,
  Exalted be thy glorious name;
Let hosts in heaven thy praises sing,
  And saints on earth thy love proclaim.

2 My heart is fixed on thee, my God;
  I rest my hope on thee alone;
I'll spread thy sacred truths abroad,
  To all mankind thy love make known.

3 Awake, my tongue; awake, my lyre;
  With morning's earliest dawn arise;
To songs of joy my soul inspire,
  And swell your music to the skies.

4 With those who in thy grace abound,
  To thee I'll raise my thankful voice,
Till every land, the earth around,
  Shall hear, and in thy name rejoice.
                    WM. WRANGHAM.

19

Now for a song of lofty praise
  To great Jehovah's only Son;
Awake, my voice, in heavenly lays,
  And tell the wonders he hath done.

2 Sing how he left the worlds of light,
  And those bright robes he wore above;
How swift and joyful was his flight,
  On wings of everlasting love!

3 Deep in the shades of gloomy death
  Th' almighty Captive prisoner lay;
Th' almighty Captive left the earth,
  And rose to everlasting day.

4 Among a thousand harps and songs,
  Jesus, the Lord, exalted reigns;
His sacred name fills all their tongues,
  And echoes through the heavenly plains.
                    ISAAC WATTS.

PARK STREET. L. M.   FREDERICK M. A. VENUA.

Sweet is the work, my God! my King! To praise thy name, give thanks and sing; To show thy love by morning light, And talk of all thy truth at night, And talk of all thy truth at night.

LUTON. L. M.   GEORGE BURDER.

A-wake, my soul, awake, my tongue, My God de-mands the grate-ful song;

Let all my in-most powers re-cord The wondrous mer - cy of the Lord.

20

AWAKE, my soul, awake, my tongue,
My God demands the grateful song;
Let all my inmost powers record
The wondrous mercy of the Lord.

2 Divinely free his mercy flows,
Forgives my sins, allays my woes,
And bids approaching death remove,
And crowns me with indulgent love.

3 His mercy, with unchanging rays,
Forever shines, while time decays;
And children's children shall record
The truth and goodness of the Lord.

4 While all his works his praise proclaim,
And men and angels bless his name,
O let my heart, my life, my tongue
Attend, and join the blissful song!
ANNE STEELE.

21

SWEET is the work, my God! my King!
To praise thy name, give thanks and sing;
To show thy love by morning light,
And talk of all thy truth at night.

2 Sweet is the day of sacred rest;
No mortal care shall seize my breast;
O may my heart in tune be found,
Like David's harp of solemn sound.

3 My heart shall triumph in the Lord,
And bless his works, and bless his word;
Thy works of grace, how bright they shine!
How deep thy counsels! how divine!
ISAAC WATTS.

22

HIGH in the heavens, eternal God,
Thy goodness in full glory shines;
Thy truth shall break through every cloud
That vails and darkens thy designs.

2 Forever firm thy justice stands,
As mountains their foundations keep:
Wise are the wonders of thy hands;
Thy judgments are a mighty deep.

3 My God, how excellent thy grace!
Whence all our hope and comfort springs;
The sons of Adam, in distress,
Fly to the shadow of thy wings.

4 Life, like a fountain, rich and free,
Springs from the presence of my Lord;
And in thy light our souls shall see
The glories promised in thy word.
ISAAC WATTS.

23

TRIUMPHANT Lord, thy goodness reigns
Through all the wide celestial plains;
And its full streams unceasing flow
Down to th' abodes of men below.

2 Through nature's work its glories shine;
The cares of providence are thine;
And grace erects our ruined frame
A fairer temple to thy name.

3 O give to every human heart
To taste and feel how good thou art;
With grateful love and reverent fear,
To know how blest thy children are.
P. DODDRIDGE.

NEW CHRISTIAN

HARVEY'S CHANT. C. M.

Wm. B. Bradbury.

Hail! great Crea-tor, wise and good! To thee our songs we raise; Nat-ure, thro' all her various scenes, In-vites us to thy praise, In-vites us to thy praise.

By Per. Biglow & Main.

24

Hail! great Creator, wise and good!
 To thee our songs we raise;
Nature, through all her various scenes,
 Invites us to thy praise.

2 At morning, noon, and evening mild,
 Fresh wonders strike our view;
And, while we gaze, our hearts exult
 With transports ever new.

3 Thy glory beams in every star
 Which gilds the gloom of night;
And decks the smiling face of morn
 With rays of cheerful light.

4 And while, in all thy wondrous ways,
 Thy varied love we see;
O may our hearts, great God, be led
 Through all thy works to thee.
                                   Anon.

25

O God, our help in ages past,
 Our hope for years to come,
Our shelter from the stormy blast,
 And our eternal home!

2 Beneath the shadow of thy throne
 Thy saints have dwelt secure;
Sufficient is thine arm, alone,
 And our defense is sure.

3 Before the hills in order stood,
 Or earth received her frame,
From everlasting thou art God,
 To endless years the same.

4 A thousand ages in thy sight
 Are like an evening gone,
Short as the watch that ends the night
 Before the rising sun.

5 Time, like an ever-rolling stream,
 Bears all its sons away;
They fly, forgotten, as a dream
 Dies at the opening day.

6 O God, our help in ages past,
 Our hope for years to come,
Be thou our guard while life shall last,
 And our eternal home!
                              Isaac Watts.

26   [*To other tune. No. 563.*]

Jesus, thou art the sinner's friend;
 As such I look to thee:
Now in the fullness of thy love,
 O Lord, remember me.

2 Remember thy pure word of grace,
 Remember Calvary;
Remember all thy promises,
 And then remember me.

3 I own I'm guilty, own I'm vile;
 Yet thy salvation's free:
Then in thy all-abounding grace,
 O Lord, remember me.

4 And when I close my eyes in death,
 And creature helps all flee,
Then, O my great Redeemer, Lord,
 I pray, remember me.
                          Richard Burnham.

DUNDEE. C. M.

GUILLAUME FRANC.

God moves in a mys-ter-ious way His won-ders to per-form;

He plants his foot-steps on the sea, And rides up-on the storm.

27

God moves in a mysterious way
  His wonders to perform;
He plants his footsteps on the sea,
  And rides upon the storm.

2 Deep in unfathomable mines
  Of never-failing skill
He treasures up his bright designs,
  And works his gracious will.

3 You fearful saints, fresh courage take;
  The clouds you so much dread
Are big with mercy, and shall break
  In blessings on your head.

4 Judge not the Lord by feeble sense,
  But trust him for his grace;
Behind a frowning providence
  He hides a smiling face.

5 His purposes will ripen fast,
  Unfolding every hour;
The bud may have a bitter taste,
  But sweet will be the flower.

6 Blind unbelief is sure to err,
  And scan his work in vain;
God is his own interpreter,
  And he will make it plain.
                    WILLIAM COWPER.

28

Thy kingdom, Lord, forever stands,
  While earthly thrones decay;
And time submits to thy commands,
  While ages roll away.

2 Thy sovereign bounty freely gives
  Its unexhausted store;
And universal nature lives
  On thy sustaining power.

3 Holy and just in all thy ways,
  Thy providence divine;
In all thy works, immortal rays
  Of power and mercy shine.

4 The praise of God—delightful theme!—
  Shall fill my heart and tongue;
Let all creation bless his name
  In one eternal song.
                    ISAAC WATTS.

29

O THOU, whose own vast temple stands
  Built over earth and sea,
Accept the walls that human hands
  Have raised to worship thee.

2 Lord, from thine inmost glory send,
  Within these courts to bide,
The peace that dwelleth, without end,
  Serenely by thy side.

3 May erring minds that worship here,
  Be taught the better way;
And they who mourn, and they who fear,
  Be strengthened as they pray.

4 May faith grow firm, and love grow warm,
  And pure devotion rise,
While round these hallowed walls the storm
  Of earth-born passion dies.
                    W. C. BRYANT.

BROOMSGROVE. C. M.   ANON.

Songs of im - mor - tal praise be-long To my al-might-y God; He has my

heart, and he my tongue, To spread his name abroad, To spread his name abroad.

30

Songs of immortal praise belong
  To my almighty God;
He has my heart, and he my tongue,
  To spread his name abroad.

2 How great the works his hand has wrought!
  How glorious in our sight!
And men in every age have sought
  His wonders with delight.

3 How most exact is nature's frame!
  How wise th' eternal mind!
His counsels never change the scheme
  That his first thoughts designed.

4 When he redeemed his chosen sons,
  He fixed his covenant sure;
The orders that his lips pronounce
  To endless years endure.
                ISAAC WATTS.

31

I sing th' almighty power of God,
  That made the mountains rise,
That spread the flowing seas abroad,
  And built the lofty skies.

2 I sing the wisdom that ordained
  The sun to rule the day;
The moon shines full at his command,
  And all the stars obey.

3 I sing the goodness of the Lord,
  That filled the earth with food;
He formed the creatures with his word,
  And then pronounced them good.

4 Creatures that borrow life from thee
  Are subject to thy care;
There's not a place where we can flee,
  But God is present there.
                ISAAC WATTS.

ROCHESTER. C. M.   ISRAEL HOLDROYD.

I sing th' al-might-y power of God, That made the mountains rise,

That spread the flow - ing seas a - broad, And built the loft - y skies.

STEPHENS. C. M.　　　　　　　　　　　　　　　WILLIAM JONES.

Je - ho - vah, God, thy gracious power On ev - ery hand we see;

O may the bless - ings of each hour Lead all our thoughts to thee.

32

JEHOVAH, God, thy gracious power
　On every hand we see;
O may the blessings of each hour
　Lead all our thoughts to thee.

2 If on the wings of morn we speed
　To earth's remotest bound,
Thy hand will there our footsteps lead,
　Thy love our path surround.

3 Thy power is in the ocean deeps,
　And reaches to the skies;
Thine eye of mercy never sleeps,
　Thy goodness never dies.

4 From morn till noon, till latest eve,
　Thy hand, O God, we see;
And all the blessings we receive
　Proceed alone from thee.

5 In all the varying scenes of time,
　On thee our hopes depend;
Through every age, in every clime,
　Our Father, and our Friend.
　　　　　　　　　　　　JOHN THOMSON.

33

SWEET is the memory of thy grace,
　My God, my heavenly King!
Let age to age thy righteousness
　In sounds of glory sing.

2 God reigns on high, but not confines
　His goodness to the skies;
Through the whole earth his bounty shines,
　And every want supplies.

3 With longing eyes thy creatures wait
　On thee for daily food;
Thy liberal hand provides their meat,
　And fills their mouths with good.

4 How kind are thy compassions, Lord,
　How slow thine anger moves!
But soon he sends his pardoning word
　To cheer the souls he loves.

5 Creatures, with all their endless race,
　Thy power and praise proclaim;
But saints that taste thy richer grace
　Delight to bless thy name.
　　　　　　　　　　　　ISAAC WATTS.

34

BEHOLD the sure foundation-stone,
　Which God in Zion lays,
To build our heavenly hopes upon,
　And his eternal praise!

2 Chosen of God, to sinners dear,
　And saints adore the name;
They trust their whole salvation here,
　Nor shall they suffer shame.

3 The foolish builders, scribe and priest,
　Reject it with disdain;
Yet on this Rock the Church shall rest,
　And envy rage in vain.

4 What though the gates of hell withstood,
　Yet must this building rise;
'Tis thine own work, Almighty God,
　And wondrous in our eyes.
　　　　　　　　　　　　ISAAC WATTS.

ST. ANNS. C. M.   WM. CROFT.

Blest be the ev-er-last-ing God, The Fa-ther of our Lord;

Be his a-bound-ing mer-cy praised, His maj-es-ty a-dored.

35

BLEST be the everlasting God,
  The Father of our Lord;
Be his abounding mercy praised,
  His majesty adored.

2 When from the dead he raised his Son,
  And called him to the sky,
He gave our souls a lively hope
  That they should never die.

3 What though the first man's sin requires
  Our flesh to see the dust;
Yet as the Lord, our Saviour, rose,
  So all his followers must.

4 There's an inheritance divine,
  Reserved against that day;
'Tis uncorrupted, undefiled,
  And can not fade away.

5 Saints, by the power of God, are kept
  Till the salvation come;
We walk by faith as strangers here
  Till Christ shall take us home.
      ISAAC WATTS.

36

How precious is the book divine,
  By inspiration given!
Bright as a lamp its precepts shine,
  To guide our souls to heaven.

2 It sweetly cheers our drooping hearts
  In this dark vale of tears;
Life, light, and joy, it still imparts,
  And quells our rising fears.

3 This lamp, through all the tedious night
  Of life, shall guide our way,
Till we behold the clearer light
  Of an eternal day. J. FAWCETT.

BRIDGMAN. C. M.   BEETHOVEN, ARR. BY GEO. KINGSLEY.

A-wake, a-wake the sa-cred song To our in-car-nate Lord!

Let ev-ery heart and ev-ery tongue A-dore th'e-ter-nal Word!

MEDFIELD. C. M.

WM. MATHER.

Long as I live, I'll praise thy name, My King, my God of love;

My work and joy shall be the same In the bright world a-bove.

37

Long as I live, I'll praise thy name,
  My King, my God of love;
My work and joy shall be the same
  In the bright world above.

2 Great is the Lord, his power unknown,
  And let his praise be great;
I'll sing the honors of thy throne,
  Thy work of grace repeat.

3 Thy grace shall dwell upon my tongue,
  And, while my lips rejoice,
The men that hear my sacred song
  Shall join their cheerful voice.

4 Fathers to sons shall teach thy name,
  And children learn thy ways;
Ages to come thy truth proclaim,
  And nations sound thy praise.
                              Isaac Watts.

38

Awake, awake the sacred song
  To our incarnate Lord!
Let every heart and every tongue
  Adore th' eternal Word!

2 That awful Word, that sovereign power,
  By whom the worlds were made—
O happy morn! illustrious hour!—
  Was once in flesh arrayed!

3 Then shone almighty power and love,
  In all their glorious forms,
When Jesus left his throne above,
  To dwell with sinful worms.

4 Adoring angels tuned their songs
  To hail the joyful day;
With rapture, then, let mortal tongues
  Their grateful worship pay.
                              Anne Steele.

39

What glory gilds the sacred page,
  Majestic, like the sun!
It gives a light to every age;
  It gives, but borrows none.

2 The hand that gave it still supplies
  His gracious light and heat;
His truths upon the nations rise;
  They rise, but never set.

3 Let everlasting thanks be thine,
  For such a bright display
As makes the world of darkness shine
  With beams of heavenly day.

4 My soul rejoices to pursue
  The paths of truth and love,
Till glory breaks upon my view
  In brighter worlds above.
                              William Cowper.

40

Lord, let thy Spirit penetrate
  This heart and soul of mine;
And my whole being with thy grace
  Pervade, O Life divine!

2 As this clear air surrounds the earth,
  Thy grace around me roll;
As the fresh light pervades the air,
  So pierce and fill my soul.
                              Horatius Bonar.

15

NEW CHRISTIAN

NICÆA. 11s, 12s, & 10s. JOHN B. DYKES.

Ho-ly, ho-ly, ho - ly! Lord God Al-might-y! Ear-ly in the

morn-ing our song shall rise to thee; Ho-ly, ho-ly, ho - ly!

merci-ful and might-y! God o-ver all, and blest e-ter-nal-ly.

41

HOLY, holy, holy! Lord God Almighty!
Early in the morning our song shall rise to thee;
Holy, holy, holy! merciful and mighty!
God over all, and blest eternally.

2 Holy, holy, holy! all the saints adore thee,
Casting down their golden crowns around the crystal sea;
Cherubim and seraphim falling down before thee,
Who wast, and art, and evermore shalt be.

3 Holy, holy, holy! though the darkness hide thee,
Though the eye of sinful man thy glory may not see;
Only thou art holy, there is none beside thee;
Perfect in power, in love, and purity.

4 Holy, holy, holy! Lord God Almighty!
All thy works shall praise thy name, in earth, and sky, and sea;
Holy, holy, holy! merciful and mighty!
God over all, and blest eternally.

REGINALD HEBER—alt.

LYONS. 10s & 11s. HAYDN.

O worship the King, all-glorious a-bove, And grate-ful-ly sing his
D. S. Pa-vilioned in splendor and

won-der-ful love; Our Shield and De-fend-er, the An-cient of days,
gird-ed with praise.

42

O WORSHIP the King, all-glorious above,
And gratefully sing his wonderful love;
Our Shield and Defender, the Ancient of days,
Pavilioned in splendor, and girded with praise.

2 Thy bountiful care, what tongue can recite?
It breathes in the air, it shines in the light;
It streams from the hills, it descends to the plain,
And sweetly distills in the dew and the rain.

3 Frail children of dust, and feeble as frail,
In thee do we trust, nor find thee to fail;
Thy mercies, how tender! how firm to the end,
Our Maker, Defender, Redeemer, and Friend!

4 Our Father and God, how faithful thy love!
While angels delight to hymn thee above,
The humbler creation, though feeble their lays,
With true adoration shall lisp to thy praise.

ROBERT GRANT.

43

YE servants of God, your Master proclaim,
And publish abroad his wonderful name:
The name, all-victorious, of Jesus extol;
His kingdom is glorious, and rules over all.

2 God ruleth on high, almighty to save;
And still he is nigh, his presence we have:
The great congregation his triumph shall sing,
Ascribing salvation to Jesus our King.

3 "Salvation to God, who sits on the throne,"
Let all cry aloud, and honor the Son;
Our Saviour's high praises the angels proclaim,—
Fall down on their faces, and worship the Lamb.

C. WESLEY.

LANESBORO. C. M.

WM. DIXON.

Ear-ly, my God, without de-lay, I haste to seek thy face; My thirst-y spir-it

faints a - way, My thirst-y spir- it faints a - way, With-out thy cheer-ing grace.

44

EARLY, my God, without delay,
  I haste to seek thy face;
My thirsty spirit faints away,
  Without thy cheering grace.

2 So pilgrims on the scorching sand,
  Beneath a burning sky,
Long for a cooling stream at hand;
  And they must drink, or die.

3 Not life itself, with all its joys,
  Can my best passions move,
Or raise so high my cheerful voice
  As thy forgiving love.

4 Thus, till my last, expiring day,
  I'll bless my God and King;
Thus will I lift my hands to pray,
  And tune my lips to sing.
                              ISAAC WATTS.

45

COME, ye that know and fear the Lord,
  And raise your souls above;
Let every heart and voice accord
  To sing that—God is love.

2 This precious truth his word declares,
  And all his mercies prove;
While Christ, th' atoning Lamb, appears,
  To show that—God is love.

3 Behold his loving-kindness waits
  For those who from him rove,
And calls of mercy reach their hearts,
  To teach them—God is love.

4 O may we all, while here below,
  This best of blessings prove,
Till warmer hearts, in brighter worlds,
  Shall shout that—God is love.
                              G. BURDER.

GENEVA. C. M.

JOHN COLE.

When all thy mer-cies, O my God! My ris-ing soul sur-veys,

Trans- port- ed with the view, I'm lost in won- der, love and praise!

HUMMEL. C. M.   H. C. ZEUNER.

Yes, I will bless thee, O my God, Through all my mortal days,

And to e - ter - ni - ty pro - long Thy vast, thy boundless praise.

46

YES, I will bless thee, O my God,
Through all my mortal days,
And to eternity prolong
Thy vast, thy boundless praise.

2 Nor shall my tongue alone proclaim
The honors of my God;
My life, with all its active powers,
Shall spread thy praise abroad.

3 Not death itself shall stop my song,
Though death will close my eyes;
My thoughts shall then to nobler heights
And sweeter raptures rise.

4 There shall my lips, in endless praise,
Their grateful tribute pay;
The theme demands an angel's tongue,
And an eternal day.
                              O. HEGINBOTHAM.

47

LORD, while for all mankind we pray,
Of every clime and coast,
O hear us for our native land,
The land we love the most.

2 O guard our shores from every foe;
With peace our borders bless;
With prosperous times our cities crown,
Our fields with plenteousness.

3 Unite us in the sacred love
Of knowledge, truth, and thee;
And let our hills and valleys shout
The songs of liberty.

4 Lord of the nations, thus to thee
Our country we commend;
Be thou her refuge and her trust,
Her everlasting Friend.
                              J. R. WREFORD.

48

WHEN all thy mercies, O my God!
My rising soul surveys,
Transported with the view, I'm lost
In wonder, love and praise.

2 Unnumbered comforts on my soul
Thy tender care bestowed,
Before my infant heart conceived
From whom those comforts flowed.

3 When in the slippery paths of youth
With heedless steps I ran,

Thine arm, unseen, conveyed me safe,
And led me up to man.

4 Ten thousand thousand precious gifts
My daily thanks employ;
Nor is the least a cheerful heart
That tastes those gifts with joy.

5 Through all eternity, to thee
A joyful song I'll raise;
But O! eternity's too short
To utter all thy praise!
                              J. ADDISON.

DOVER. S. M.

AARON WILLIAMS.

Great is the Lord, our God, And let his praise be great;

He makes his church-es his a-bode, His most de-light-ful seat.

49

GREAT is the Lord our God,
And let his praise be great;
He makes his churches his abode,
His most delightful seat.

2 These temples of his grace,
How beautiful they stand—
The honors of our native place,
The bulwarks of our land!

3 In Zion God is known
A refuge in distress;
How bright has his salvation shone
Through all her palaces!

4 In every new distress
We'll to his house repair;
We'll think upon his wondrous grace,
And seek deliverance there.
ISAAC WATTS.

50

O BLESS the Lord, my soul!
His mercies bear in mind;
Forget not all his benefits;
The Lord to thee is kind.

2 He will not always chide;
He will with patience wait;
His wrath is ever slow to rise,
And ready to abate.

3 He pardons all thy sins,
Prolongs thy feeble breath;
He healeth thine infirmities,
And ransoms thee from death.

4 Then bless his holy name,
Whose grace hath made thee whole,
Whose loving-kindness crowns thy days;
O bless the Lord, my soul!
ISAAC WATTS.

SWABIA. S. M.

ANON.

O bless the Lord, my soul! His mer-cies bear in mind;

For-get not all his ben-e-fits; The Lord to thee is kind.

SILVER STREET. S. M.   Isaac Smith.

Come, sound his praise a-broad, And hymns of glo-ry sing;

Je-ho-vah is the sov-ereign God, The u-ni-ver-sal King.

51

Come, sound his praise abroad,
  And hymns of glory sing;
Jehovah is the sovereign God,
  The universal King.

2 He formed the deeps unknown;
  He gave the seas their bound;
The watery worlds are all his own,
  And all the solid ground.

3 Come, worship at his throne;
  Come, bow before the Lord;
We are his work, and not our own;
  He formed us by his word.

4 To-day attend his voice,
  Nor dare provoke his rod;
Come, like the people of his choice,
  And own your gracious God.
                                    Isaac Watts.

52

The Lord Jehovah reigns:
  Let all the nations fear;
Let sinners tremble at his throne,
  And saints be humble there.

2 Jesus, the Saviour, reigns;
  Let earth adore its Lord;
Bright cherubs his attendants wait,
  Swift to fulfill his word.

3 In Zion stands his throne;
  His honors are divine;
His Church shall make his wonders known,
  For there his glories shine.

4 How holy is his name!
  How fearful is his praise!
Justice, and truth, and judgment join
  In all the works of grace.
                                    Isaac Watts.

53

My soul, repeat his praise,
  Whose mercies are so great;
Whose anger is so slow to rise,
  So ready to abate.

2 High as the heavens are raised
  Above the ground we tread,
So far the riches of his grace
  Our highest thoughts exceed.

3 His power subdues our sins;
  And his forgiving love,
Far as the east is from the west,
  Doth all our guilt remove.

4 The pity of the Lord,
  To those that fear his name,
Is such as tender parents feel;
  He knows our feeble frame.

5 Our days are as the grass,
  Or like the morning flower;
If one sharp blast sweep o'er the field,
  It withers in an hour.

6 But thy compassions, Lord,
  To endless years endure;
And children's children ever find
  Thy words of promise sure.
                                    Isaac Watts.

CRANBROOK. S. M.
THOMAS CLARK.

Grace! 'tis a charm-ing sound, Har-mo - nious to the ear; Heaven with the echo shall re-

sound,
Heaven with the ech-o shall resound, Heaven with the ech-o shall re-sound, And

all the earth shall hear, And all the earth shall bear, And all the earth shall hear.
And all the earth shall hear, And all the earth,

54

GRACE! 'tis a charming sound,
Harmonious to the ear;
Heaven with the echo shall resound,
And all the earth shall hear.

2 Grace first contrived a way
To save rebellious man;
And all the steps that grace display,
Which drew the wondrous plan.

3 Grace led our wandering feet
To tread the heavenly road;
And new supplies each hour we meet
While pressing on to God.

4 Grace all the work shall crown
Through everlasting days;
It lays in heaven the topmost stone,
And well deserves our praise.
PHILIP DODDRIDGE.

CLAPTON. S. M.
WILLIAM JONES.

Give to the winds thy fears; Hope, and be un - dis-mayed:

God hears thy sighs, and counts thy tears; God shall lift up thy head.

GERAR. S. M.   LOWELL MASON.

Raise your tri-umph-ant songs To an im-mor-tal tune; Let the wide

earth re-sound the deeds Ce-les-tial grace has done.

55

RAISE your triumphant songs
  To an immortal tune;
Let the wide earth resound the deeds
  Celestial grace has done.

2 Sing how Eternal Love
  His Chief Belovéd chose,
And bade him raise our wretched race
  From their abyss of woes.

3 His hand no thunder bears,
  Nor terror clothes his brow;
No bolts to drive our guilty souls
  To fiercer flames below.

4 He shows his Father's love,
  To raise our souls on high;
He came with pardon from above
  To rebels doomed to die.

5 Now, sinners, dry your tears;
  Let hopeless sorrow cease;
Bow to the scepter of his love,
  And take the offered peace.
                ISAAC WATTS.

56

THY name, almighty Lord,
  Shall sound through distant lands;
Great is thy grace, and sure thy word;
  Thy truth forever stands.

2 Far be thine honor spread,
  And long thy praise endure,
Till morning light and evening shade
  Shall be exchanged no more.
                ISAAC WATTS.

57

GOD is the fountain whence
  Ten thousand blessings flow;
To him my life, my health, and friends,
  And every good, I owe.

2 The comforts he affords
  Are neither few nor small;
He is the source of fresh delights,
  My portion and my all.

3 He fills my heart with joy,
  My lips attunes for praise;
And to his glory I'll devote
  The remnant of my days.
                UNKNOWN.

58

GIVE to the winds thy fears;
  Hope, and be undismayed:
God hears thy sighs, and counts thy tears;
  God shall lift up thy head.

2 Thro' waves, and clouds, and storms,
  He gently clears thy way;
Wait thou his time; so shall this night
  Soon end in joyous day.

3 Far, far above thy thought
  His counsel shall appear,
When fully he the work hath wrought
  That caused thy needless fear.

4 What though thou rulest not!
  Yet heaven, and earth, and hell
Proclaim, God sitteth on the throne,
  And ruleth all things well.
                PAUL GERHARDT.

LUTHER. S. M. THOS. HASTINGS.

A-wake, and sing the song Of Mo-ses and the Lamb; Wake, ev - ery

heart and ev - ery tongue, To praise the Saviour's name; To praise the Saviour's name.

59

AWAKE, and sing the song
  Of Moses and the Lamb;
Wake, every heart and every tongue,
  To praise the Saviour's name.

2 Sing of his dying love;
  Sing of his rising power;
Sing how he intercedes above
  For those whose sins he bore.

3 Sing on your heavenly way,
  You ransomed sinners, sing;
Sing on, rejoicing every day
  In Christ, the glorious King.

4 Soon shall you hear him say,
  "You blessèd children, come!"
Soon will he call you hence away,
  And take his pilgrims home.
                    WM. HAMMOND.

60

To GOD, the only wise,
  Our Saviour and our King,
Let all the saints below the skies
  Their humble praises bring.

2 'Tis his almighty love,
  His counsel and his care,
Preserve us safe from sin and death,
  And every hurtful snare.

3 He will present our souls,
  Unblemished and complete,
Before the glory of his face,
  With joys divinely great.

4 Then all the chosen seed
  Shall meet around the throne,
Shall bless the conduct of his grace,
  And make his wonders known.
                    ISAAC WATTS.

GILCREST. S. M. J. H. ROSECRANS.

Blest are the pure in heart, For they shall see our God;

The se - cret of the Lord is theirs; Their soul is his a - bode.

CARLISLE. S. M.　　　　　　　　　　　　　　　　　　CHARLES LOCKHART.

Lord, I de-light in thee, And on thy care de-pend;

To thee in ev-ery trou-ble flee, My best, my on-ly Friend.

61

LORD, I delight in thee,
　And on thy care depend;
To thee in every trouble flee,
　My best, my only Friend.

2 When nature's streams are dried,
　Thy fullness is the same;
With this will I be satisfied,
　And glory in thy name.

3 Who made my heaven secure,
　Will here all good provide.
While Christ is rich, can I be poor?
　What can I want beside?

4 I cast my care on thee;
　I triumph and adore:
Henceforth my great concern shall be
　To love and please thee more.
　　　　　　　　　　　JOHN RYLAND.

62

BLEST are the pure in heart,
　For they shall see our God;
The secret of the Lord is theirs;
　Their soul is his abode.

2 Still to the lowly soul
　He doth himself impart,
And for his temple and his throne
　Chooseth the pure in heart.

3 Lord, we thy presence seek:
　May ours this blessing be;
O give the pure and lowly heart,—
　A temple meet for thee.
　　　　　　　　　　　JOHN KEBLE.

63

GREAT Source of life and light,
　Thy heavenly grace impart;
Thy Holy Spirit grant, and write
　Thy law upon my heart.

2 My soul would cleave to thee;
　Let naught my purpose move;
O let my faith more steadfast be,
　And more intense my love.

3 Long as my trials last,
　Long as the cross I bear,
O let my soul on thee be cast
　In confidence and prayer.

4 Conduct me to the shore
　Of everlasting peace,
Where storm and tempest rise no more,
　Where sin and sorrow cease.
　　　　　　　　　　　UNKNOWN.

64

HEIRS of unending life,
　While yet we sojourn here,
O let us our salvation work
　With trembling and with fear.

2 God will support our hearts
　With might before unknown;
The work to be performed is ours,
　The strength is all his own.

3 'Tis he that works to will,
　'Tis he that works to do;
His is the power by which we act,
　His be the glory too!
　　　　　　　　　　　UNKNOWN.

3　　　　　　　　　　25

ROCKINGHAM. L. M.

LOWELL MASON.

'Twas by an or-der from the Lord The an-cient prophets spoke his word;

His Spir-it did their tongues in-spire, And warmed their hearts with heavenly fire.

65

'Twas by an order from the Lord
The ancient prophets spoke his word;
His Spirit did their tongues inspire,
And warmed their hearts with heavenly fire.

2 Great God, mine eyes with pleasure look
On the dear volume of thy book;
There my Redeemer's face I see,
And read his name who died for me.

3 Let the false raptures of the mind
Be lost, and vanish in the wind:
Here I can fix my hope secure;
This is thy word, and must endure.

ISAAC WATTS.

66

O LOVE of God, how strong and true;
Eternal and yet ever new;
Above all price, and still unbought;
Beyond all knowledge and all thought!

2 O wide-embracing, wondrous love,
We read thee in the sky above;
We read thee in the earth below,
In seas that swell and streams that flow.

3 We read thee best in him who came
To bear for us the cross of shame;
Sent by the Father from on high,
Our life to live, our death to die.

HORATIUS BONAR.

DOXOLOGY. Irr.

ENGLISH.

67 *Ho-ly! Ho-ly! Ho-ly! Lord God of Sabaoth! Heaven and earth are full, full of thy*

glory; Heaven and earth are full, are full of thy glory; Glo-ry be to
Glo-ry be to thee,

thee, Glo-ry be to thee, to thee, to thee, O Lord, most high.
Glo-ry be to thee, Glo-ry be, etc.

CREATION. L. M. D.   HAYDN.

{ The spacious firmament on high, With all the blue, e-the-real sky, }
{ And spangled heavens, a shining frame, Their great O-rig-i-nal proclaim. }

Th' un-wearied sun, from day to day, Does his Cre-a-tor's power display,

And pub-lish-es to ev-ery land The work of an al-might-y hand.

68

THE spacious firmament on high,
With all the blue, ethereal sky,
And spangled heavens, a shining frame,
Their great Original proclaim.
Th' unwearied sun, from day to day,
Does his Creator's power display,
And publishes to every land
The work of an almighty hand.

2 Soon as the evening shades prevail,
The moon takes up the wondrous tale,
And nightly, to the listening earth,
Repeats the story of her birth :
While all the stars that round her burn,
And all the planets in their turn,
Confirm the tidings as they roll,
And spread the truth from pole to pole.

3 What though in solemn silence all
Move round this dark, terrestrial ball—
What though no reäl voice nor sound
Amid their radiant orbs be found—
In reason's ear they all rejoice,
And utter forth a glorious voice;
Forever singing as they shine,
"The hand that made us is divine."
JOSEPH ADDISON.

69

THE heavens declare thy glory, Lord;
In every star thy wisdom shines;
But, when our eyes behold thy word,
We read thy name in fairer lines.
The rolling sun, the changing light,
And nights and days, thy power confess;
But the blest volume thou hast writ
Reveals thy justice and thy grace.

2 Sun, moon, and stars convey thy praise
Round the whole earth, and never stand;
So, when thy truth began its race,
It touched and glanced on every land.
Nor shall thy spreading gospel rest,
'Till thro' the world thy truth has run;
Till Christ has all the nations blest,
That see the light, or feel the sun.

3 Great Sun of Righteousness, arise;
Bless the dark world with heavenly light;
Thy gospel makes the simple wise,
Thy laws are pure, thy judgments right.
Thy noblest wonders here we view,
In souls renewed, and sins forgiven;
Lord, cleanse my sins, my soul renew,
And make thy word my guide to heaven.
ISAAC WATTS.

27

WAVERTREE. L. M. 6 l.   WM. SHORE.

Thou art, O God, the life and light Of all the wondrous world we see;
Its glow by day, its smile by night, Are but reflections caught from thee;

Where'er we turn, thy glo-ries shine, And all things fair and bright are thine.

70

THOU art, O God, the life and light
  Of all the wondrous world we see;
Its glow by day, its smile by night,
  Are but reflections caught from thee.
Where'er we turn, thy glories shine,
And all things fair and bright are thine.

2 When day, with farewell beam, delays
  Among the opening clouds of even,
And we can almost think we gaze,
    Through opening vistas, into heaven—
Those hues that mark the sun's decline,
So soft, so radiant, Lord, are thine.

3 When night, with wings of starry gloom,
  O'ershadows all the earth and skies,
Like some dark, beauteous bird, whose plume
  Is sparkling with unnumbered dyes—
That sacred gloom, those fires divine,
So grand, so countless, Lord, are thine.

4 When youthful spring around us breathes,
  Thy Spirit warms her fragrant sigh;
And every flower that summer wreathes
  Is born beneath thy kindling eye.
Where'er we turn, thy glories shine,
And all things fair and bright are thine.
                                      THOMAS MOORE.

71

JESUS, thou source of calm repose,
  All fullness dwells in thee divine;
Our strength, to quell the proudest foes;
  Our light, in deepest gloom to shine;
Thou art our fortress, strength, and tower,
Our trust and portion evermore.

2 Jesus, our Comforter thou art;
  Our rest in toil, our ease in pain;
The balm to heal each broken heart;
  In storms our peace, in loss our gain;
Our joy beneath the worldling's frown;
In shame, our glory and our crown;

3 In want, our plentiful supply;
  In weakness, our almighty power;
In bonds, our perfect liberty;
  Our refuge in temptation's hour;
Our comfort midst all grief and thrall;
Our life in death; our all in all.
                                      CHARLES WESLEY.

72

MY PROPHET thou, my Heavenly Guide,
  Thy sweet instructions I will hear;
The words that from thy lips proceed,
  O how divinely sweet they are!
Thee, my great Prophet, I would love,
And imitate the blest above.

2 My great High Priest, whose precious blood
  Was offered once upon the cross;
Who now dost intercede with God,
  And plead the friendless sinner's cause,—
In thee I trust, thee would I love,
And imitate the blest above.

3 My King supreme, to thee I bow,
  A willing subject at thy feet;
All other lords I disavow,
  And to thy government submit;
My Saviour King this heart would love,
And imitate the blest above.
                                      UNKNOWN.

28

SELENA. L. M. 6 l.   ISAAC B. WOODBURY.

The Lord my past-ure shall pre-pare, And feed me with a shepherd's care;
His presence shall my wants supply, And guard me with a watch-ful eye:

My noonday walks he shall at - tend, And all my midnight hours de - fend.

By permission.

73

THE Lord my pasture shall prepare,
And feed me with a shepherd's care;
His presence shall my wants supply,
And guard me with a watchful eye:
My noonday walks he shall attend,
And all my midnight hours defend.

2 When in the sultry glebe I faint,
Or on the thirsty mountain pant,
To fertile vales and dewy meads
My weary, wandering steps he leads,
Where peaceful rivers, soft and slow,
Amid the verdant landscape flow.

3 Though in the paths of death I tread,
With gloomy horrors overspread,
My steadfast heart shall fear no ill,
For thou, O Lord, art with me still;
Thy friendly crook shall give me aid,
And guide me through the dismal shade.
JOSEPH ADDISON.

74

THOUGH waves and storms go o'er my head,
Though strength, and health, and friends be gone;
Though joys be withered all, and dead,
Though every comfort be withdrawn;
On this my steadfast soul relies—
Father, thy mercy never dies.

2 Fixed on this ground will I remain,
Though my heart fail, and flesh decay;
This anchor shall my soul sustain,
When earth's foundations melt away;
Mercy's full power I then shall prove,
Loved with an everlasting love.
J. A. ROTHE, TR. BY J. WESLEY.

75

MY HOPE is built on nothing less
Than Jesus' blood and righteousness;
I dare not trust the sweetest frame,
But wholly lean on Jesus' name:
On Christ, the solid rock, I stand;
All other ground is sinking sand.

2 When darkness seems to vail his face,
I rest on his unchanging grace;
In every high and stormy gale,
My anchor holds within the vail:
On Christ, the solid rock, I stand;
All other ground is sinking sand.

3 His oath, his covenant, and blood,
Support me in the whelming flood;
When all around my soul gives way,
He then is all my hope and stay:
On Christ, the solid rock, I stand;
All other ground is sinking sand.
EDWARD MOTE.

76

WHEN adverse winds and waves arise,
And in my heart despondence sighs;
When life her throng of cares reveals,
And weakness o'er my spirit steals,
Grateful I hear the kind decree,
That "as my day, my strength shall be."

2 One trial more must yet be past,
One pang—the keenest and the last;
And when, with brow convulsed and pale,
My feeble, quivering heart-strings fail,
Redeemer, grant my soul to see
That "as my day, my strength shall be."
MRS. L. H. SIGOURNEY.

NEW CHRISTIAN

Hugh Bond.

I'll praise my Maker while I've breath, And when my voice is lost in death

Praise shall em - ploy my nobler powers; My days of praise shall ne'er be past,

While life, and thought, and be-ing last, Or im - mor - tal - i - ty en-dures.

77

I'll praise my Maker while I've breath,
And, when my voice is lost in death
  Praise shall employ my nobler powers;
My days of praise shall ne'er be past,
While life, and thought, and being last,
  Or immortality endures.

2 Happy the man whose hopes rely
On Israel's God: he made the sky,
  And earth, and seas, with all their train.
His truth forever stands secure;
He saves th' oppressed, he feeds the poor,
  And none shall find his promise vain.

3 The Lord pours eye sight on the blind;
The Lord supports the fainting mind;
  He sends the laboring conscience peace;
He helps the stranger in distress,
The widow and the fatherless,
  And grants the prisoner sweet release.
                Isaac Watts.

78

I love the volume of thy word:
What light and joy its truths afford
  To souls benighted and distressed!
Thy precepts guide my doubtful way;
Thy fear forbids my feet to stray;
  Thy promise leads my heart to rest;

2 Thy threatenings wake my slumbering eyes,
And warn me where my danger lies.
  But 'tis thy blessèd gospel, Lord,
That makes my guilty conscience clean,
Converts my soul, subdues my sin,
  And gives a free, but large, reward.

3 Who knows the errors of his thoughts?
My God, forgive my secret faults,
  And from presumptuous sins restrain;
Accept my poor attempts of praise,
That I have read thy book of grace,
  And book of nature, not in vain.
                Isaac Watts.

WILMOT. 7s.   C. M. von Weber.

Ho - ly Bi - ble, book di - vine, Pre - cious treas - ure, thou art mine:

Mine to tell me whence I came; Mine to teach me what I am.

79

Holy Bible, book divine,
Precious treasure, thou art mine:
Mine to tell me whence I came;
Mine to teach me what I am;

2 Mine to chide me when I rove;
Mine to show a Saviour's love;
Mine thou art to guide and guard;
Mine to punish or reward;

3 Mine to comfort in distress,
Suffering in this wilderness;
Mine to show, by living faith,
Man can triumph over death;

4 Mine to tell of joys to come,
And the rebel sinner's doom:
O thou holy book divine,
Precious treasure, thou art mine.

             John Burton.

PRECIOUS BIBLE. 8s, 7s & 7s.   Arr. by A. D. Fillmore.

{ Pre-cious Bi - ble, what a treas-ure Does the word of God af-ford }
{ All I want for life or pleas-ure, Food and medicine, shield and sword: }

Let the world ac-count me poor, Hav-ing this, I need no more.

80

Precious Bible, what a treasure
Does the word of God afford!
All I want for life or pleasure,
Food and medicine, shield and sword:
Let the world account me poor,
Having this, I need no more.

2 Food to which the world's a stranger,
Here my hungry soul enjoys;

Of excess there is no danger—
Though it fills, it never cloys:
On a dying Christ I feed,
He is meat and drink indeed.

3 In the hour of dark temptation,
Satan can not make me yield;
For the word of consolation
Is to me a mighty shield:
While the Scripture truths are sure,
From his malice I'm secure.

             John Newton.

ANTIOCH. C. M.   HANDEL.

Joy to the world, the Lord is come! Let earth receive her King; {Let ev-ery heart pro-pare him room,}

And heaven and nature sing, And heaven and nature sing, And heaven, and heaven and nature sing.

sing,

And heaven and nature sing, And heaven and nature sing,

81

Joy to the world! the Lord is come:
  Let earth receive her King;
Let every heart prepare him room,
  And heaven and nature sing.

2 Joy to the earth! the Saviour reigns:
  Let men their songs employ;
While fields and floods, rocks, hills, and plains,
  Repeat the sounding joy.

3 No more let sins and sorrows grow,
  Nor thorns infest the ground;
He comes to make his blessings flow,
  Far as the curse is found.

4 He rules the world with truth and grace,
  And makes the nations prove
The glories of his righteousness,
  And wonders of his love.

ISAAC WATTS.

ZERAH. C. M.   LOWELL MASON.

To us a Child of hope is born, To us a Son is given: Him shall the tribes of earth obey;

Him, all the hosts of heaven: Him shall the tribes of earth obey; Him, all the hosts of heaven.

82

To us a Child of hope is born;
  To us a Son is given:
Him shall the tribes of earth obey;
  Him, all the hosts of heaven.

2 His name shall be the Prince of peace,
  For evermore adored,
The Wonderful, the Counselor,
  The great and mighty Lord!

3 His power, increasing, still shall spread;
  His reign no end shall know;
Justice shall guard his throne above,
  And peace abound below.

4 To us a Child of hope is born,
  To us a Son is given;
The Wonderful, the Counselor,
  The mighty Lord of heaven!

JOHN MORRISON.

ATHENS. C. M. D.　　　　　　　　　　　　　　F. GIARDINI.

While shepherds watched their flocks by night, All seated on the ground, The angel of the Lord came down, And glo-ry shone a-round. "Fear not," said he,—for mighty dread Had seized their troubled mind,—"Glad tidings of great joy I bring, To you and all mankind.

83

WHILE shepherds watched their flocks by night,
　All seated on the ground,
The angel of the Lord came down,
　And glory shone around.
"Fear not," said he,—for mighty dread
　Had seized their troubled mind,—
"Glad tidings of great joy I bring,
　To you and all mankind.

2 "To you, in David's town, this day
　Is born, of David's line,
The Saviour, who is Christ the Lord;
　And this shall be the sign :
The heavenly babe you there shall find
　To human view displayed,
All meanly wrapped in swathing bands,
　And in a manger laid."

3 Thus spake the seraph—and forthwith
　Appeared a shining throng
Of angels, praising God, who thus
　Addressed their joyful song:

"All glory be to God on high,
　And to the earth be peace;
Good-will henceforth from heaven to men
　Begin, and never cease!"
　　　　　　　　　TATE AND BRADY.

84

HARK, the glad sound! the Saviour comes,
　The Saviour promised long;
Let every heart prepare a throne,
　And every voice a song.
He comes, the prisoner to release,
　In Satan's bondage held;
The gates of brass before him burst,
　The iron fetters yield.

2 He comes, from thickest films of vice
　To clear the mental ray,
And on the eyeballs of the blind
　To pour celestial day.
He comes, the broken heart to bind,
　The bleeding soul to cure,
And, with the treasures of his grace,
　T' enrich the humble poor.
　　　　　　　　　PHILIP DODDRIDGE.

HERALD ANGELS. 7s. D.   MENDELSSOHN.

Hark! the herald angels sing, Glo-ry to the new-born King; Peace on earth, and mercy mild,

God and sinners reconciled! { Joy-ful, all ye nations, rise; } With th' angelic host proclaim,
{ Join the triumph of the skies; }

Christ is born in Beth-le-hem, With th' angelic host proclaim, Christ is born in Bethlehem!

85

HARK! the herald angels sing,
"Glory to the new-born King!
Peace on earth, and mercy mild,
God and sinners reconciled!"
Joyful, all ye nations, rise;
Join the triumph of the skies;
With th' angelic host proclaim,
Christ is born in Bethlehem!

2 See, he lays his glory by,
Born that man no more may die;
Born to raise the sons of earth;
Born to give them second birth.
Vailed in flesh the Godhead see;
Hail th' incarnate Deity;
Pleased as man with men to dwell,
Jesus, our Immanuel!

3 Hail the heaven-born Prince of peace!
Hail the Sun of Righteousness!
Light and life to all he brings,
Risen with healing in his wings.

Let us, then, with angels sing,
"Glory to the new-born King!
Peace on earth, and mercy mild,
God and sinners reconciled!"
                              CHARLES WESLEY.

86

BRIGHT and joyful was the morn
When to us a Child was born;
From the highest realms of heaven
Unto us a Son was given.
On his shoulder he shall bear
Power and majesty, and wear,
On his vesture and his thigh,
Names most awful, names most high.

2 Wonderful in counsel he,
Christ, th' incarnate Deity;
Sire of ages, ne'er to cease;
King of kings, and Prince of peace.
Come and worship at his feet;
Yield to him the homage meet;
From the manger to the throne,
Homage due to God alone.
                              J. MONTGOMERY.

FENNOR. 11s & 10s, with Chorus.   I. B. WOODBURY.

{ Hail the blest morn, when the great Media-tor Down from the regions of glo-ry descends! }
{ Shepherds, go worship the Babe in the manger; Lo! for your guide the bright angel attends. }
D. C. Star of the East, the ho-ri-zon a-dorn-ing, Guide where our infant Redeemer is laid.

CHORUS.   D. C.

Brightest and best of the sons of the morning, Dawn on our darkness, and lend us thine aid;

87   [First verse in the music.]

2 Cold on his cradle the dew-drops are shining,
  Low lies his head with the beasts of the stall;
Angels adore him, in slumbers reclining,
  Maker, and Monarch, and Saviour of all.—CHO.

3 Say, shall we yield him, in costly devotion,
  Odors of Edom and offerings divine—
Gems from the mountain, and pearls from the ocean,
  Myrrh from the forest, and gold from the mine?—CHO.

4 Vainly we offer earth's richest oblation,
  Vainly with gold would his favor secure;
Richer, by far, is the heart's adoration,
  Dearer to God are the prayers of the poor.—CHO.

REGINALD HEBER.

LAURA. 11s & 10s.   W. A. BARRETT.

Brightest and best of the sons of the morning, Dawn on our darkness, and lend us thine aid;

Star of the East, the ho-ri-zon a-dorn-ing, Guide where our infant Redeemer is laid.

DUANE STREET. L. M. D.   GEORGE COLES.

When, marshaled on the night-ly plain, The glittering host bestud the sky,

S.   Fine.

One star a - lone, of all the train, Can fix the sin-ner's wandering eye.
D. S. *But one a - lone the Saviour speaks,—It is the Star of Beth-le-hem.*

D. S.

Hark! hark! to God the cho-rus breaks, From ev-ery host, from ev-ery gem;

88

WHEN, marshaled on the nightly plain,
  The glittering host bestud the sky,
One star alone, of all the train,
  Can fix the sinner's wandering eye.
Hark! hark! to God the chorus breaks
  From every host, from every gem;
But one alone the Saviour speaks,—
  It is the Star of Bethlehem.

2 Once on the raging seas I rode:
  The storm was loud, the night was dark,
The ocean yawned, and rudely blowed
  The wind that tossed my foundering bark.
Deep horror then my vitals froze;
  Death-struck, I ceased the tide to stem—
When suddenly a star arose;
  It was the Star of Bethlehem!

3 It was my guide, my light, my all;
  It bade my dark forebodings cease;
And through the storm and danger's thrall
  It led me to the port of peace.
Now safely moored, my perils o'er,
  I'll sing, first in night's diadem,
Forever and for evermore,
  The Star, the Star of Bethlehem.
                               H. K. WHITE.

89

OUR Lord is risen from the dead,
  Our Saviour is gone up on high;
The powers of hell are captive led,
  Dragged to the portals of the sky.
There his triumphal chariot waits,
  And angels chant the solemn lay;
"Lift up your heads, you heavenly gates;
  You everlasting doors, give way."

2 Loose all your bars of massy light,
  And wide unfold the radiant scene:
He claims those mansions as his right—
  Receive the King of glory in.
Who is the King of glory—who?
  The Lord, who all his foes o'ercame;
Who sin and death and hell o'erthrew,
  And Jesus is the Conqueror's name.

3 Lo! his triumphal chariot waits,
  And angels chant the solemn lay:
"Lift up your heads, you heavenly gates;
  You everlasting doors, give way."
Who is the King of glory—who?
  The Lord, of boundless might possessed;
The King of saints and angels, too—
  Lord over all, forever blest.
                           CHARLES WESLEY.

36

HOSANNA. L. M. 6 l., with Chorus. New Arrangement.

Thy worth-i-ness is all our song, O Lamb of God; for thou wast slain,
And by thy blood brought'st us to God, Out of each nation, tribe and tongue:

To God hast made us kings and priests, And we shall reign up-on the earth:

D. S. Ho-san-na! ho-san-na! Ho-san-na to the Lamb of God!

Glo-ry! glo-ry! let us sing Grateful prais-es to our King:

90

THY worthiness is all our song,
O Lamb of God; for thou wast slain,
And by thy blood brought'st us to God,
Out of each nation, tribe and tongue;
To God hast made us kings and priests;
And we shall reign upon the earth.

CHO.—Hosanna! hosanna!
Hosanna to the Lamb of God!
Glory! glory! let us sing
Grateful praises to our King:
Hosanna! hosanna!
Hosanna to the Lamb of God!

2 Salvation to our God, who shines
In face of Jesus, on the throne,
The only just and merciful—
Salvation to the worthy Lamb,
With loud voice all the church ascribes;
"Amen," say angels round the throne:—Cho.

3 To him who loved us, and hath washed
Us from our sins in his own blood,
And who hath made us kings and priests
To his own Father and his God,
The glory and dominion be
To him eternally. Amen.—Cho.
UNKNOWN.

37

MENDON. L. M.   German.

Ye nations round the earth, re-joice Be-fore the Lord, your sovereign King;

Serve him with cheerful heart and voice; With all your tongues his glo-ry sing.

91

YE NATIONS round the earth, rejoice
  Before the Lord, your sovereign King;
Serve him with cheerful heart and voice;
  With all your tongues his glory sing.

2 The Lord is God; 'tis he alone
  Doth life, and breath, and being give;
We are his work, and not our own,
  The sheep that on his pastures live.

3 Enter his gates with songs of joy;
  With praises to his courts repair;
And make it your divine employ
  To pay your thanks and honors there.

4 The Lord is good, the Lord is kind;
  Great is his grace, his mercy sure;
And the whole race of men shall find
  His truth from age to age endure.
                                ISAAC WATTS.

92

AWAKE, my soul, and with the sun
Thy daily course of duty run;
Shake off dull sloth, and joyful rise
To pay thy morning sacrifice.

2 Wake, and lift up thyself, my heart,
And with the angels bear thy part,
Who, all night long, unwearied, sing
Glory to the Eternal King.

3 Glory to thee, who safe hast kept,
And hast refreshed me, while I slept!
Grant, Lord, when I from death shall wake,
I may of endless life partake.

4 Lord, I my vows to thee renew:
Scatter my sins as morning dew;
Guard my first springs of thought and will,
And with thyself my spirit fill.
                                THOMAS KEN.

93

GOD, in the gospel of his Son,
Makes his eternal counsels known;
'Tis here his richest mercy shines,
And truth is drawn in fairest lines.

2 Here sinners of a humble frame
May taste his grace and learn his name;
'Tis writ in characters of blood,
Severely just—immensely good.

3 Here Jesus, in ten thousand ways,
His soul-attracting charms displays;
Recounts his poverty and pains,
And tells his love in melting strains.

4 May this blest volume ever lie
Close to my heart, and near my eye;
Till life's last hour my soul engage,
And be my chosen heritage.
                                BENJ. BEDDOME.

94

ZION, awake, thy strength renew;
Put on thy robes of beauteous hue;
Church of our God, arise and shine,
Bright with the beams of truth divine.

2 Soon shall thy radiance stream afar,
Wide as the heathen nations are;
Gentiles and kings thy light shall view,
All shall admire and love thee too.
                                WILLIAM SHRUBSOLE.

APPLETON. L. M.   WILLIAM BOYCE.

Je-sus shall reign where'er the sun Does his suc-ces-sive jour-neys run;

His kingdom stretch from shore to shore, Till moons shall wax and wane no more.

95

JESUS shall reign where'er the sun
Does his successive journeys run;
His kingdom stretch from shore to shore,
Till moons shall wax and wane no more.

2 For him shall endless prayer be made,
And praises throng to crown his head;
His name, like sweet perfume, shall rise
With every morning sacrifice.

3 Where he displays his healing power,
Death and the curse are known no more;
In him the tribes of Adam boast
More blessings than their father lost.

4 Let every creature rise, and bring
Peculiar honors to our King;
Angels descend with songs again,
And earth repeat the loud Amen.
ISAAC WATTS.

96

REDEEMED from guilt, redeemed from fears,
My soul enlarged, and dried my tears,
What can I do, O Love Divine,
What to repay such gifts as thine?

2 What can I do, so poor, so weak,
But from thy hands new blessings seek:
A heart to feel thy mercies more,
A soul to know thee, and adore?

3 O teach me at thy feet to fall,
And yield to thee myself, my all—
Before thy saints my sins to own,
And live and die to thee alone.
H. F. LYTE.

97

GLORY to thee, whose powerful word
Bids the tempestuous wind arise!
Glory to thee, the sovereign Lord
Of air and earth, and seas and skies!

2 Let air, and earth, and skies obey,
And seas thine awful will perform;
From them we learn to own thy sway,
And shout to meet the gathering storm.

3 What tho' the floods lift up their voice,
Thou hearest, Lord, our silent cry;
They can not damp thy children's joys,
Or shake the soul, while God is nigh.

4 Roar on, ye waves; our souls defy
Your roaring to disturb their rest;
In vain t' impair the calm ye try—
The calm in a believer's breast,
CHARLES WESLEY.

98

THY footsteps, Lord, with joy we trace,
And mark the conquests of thy grace.
Complete the work thou hast begun,
And let thy will on earth be done.

2 O show thyself the Prince of peace;
Command the din of war to cease;
O bid contending nations rest,
And let thy love rule every breast.

3 Thou good and wise and righteous Lord,
All move subservient to thy word;
O soon let every nation prove
The perfect joy of Christian love.
UNKNOWN.

GILEAD. L. M.　　　　　　　　　　　　　C. H. MEHUL.

E - ter-nal Lord, from land to land Shall ech-o thine all-glo-rious name,

Till kingdoms bow at thy command, And ev-ery lip thy praise proclaim.

99

ETERNAL Lord, from land to land
　Shall echo thine all-glorious name,
Till kingdoms bow at thy command,
　And every lip thy praise proclaim.

2 Exalted high on every shore,
　The banner of the cross, unfurled,
Shall summon thousands to adore
　The Saviour of the ransomed world.

3 Thousands shall join thy pilgrim band,
　And, by that sacred standard led,
Press forward to Immanuel's land,
　Nor fear the thorny path to tread.

4 Triumphant over every foe,
　Their ransomed hosts shall move along
To that blest world, where sin and woe
　Shall never mingle with their song.
　　　　　　　　　　　　UNKNOWN.

100

THERE'S nothing bright, above, below,
From flowers that bloom to stars that glow,
But in its light my soul can see
Some features of the Deity.

2 There's nothing dark, below, above,
But in its gloom I trace thy love,
And meekly wait the moment when
Thy touch shall make all bright again.

3 The light, the dark, where'er I look,
Shall be one pure and shining book,
Where I may read, in words of flame,
The glories of thy wondrous Name.
　　　　　　　　　　THOMAS MOORE.

101

HAD I the tongues of Greeks and Jews,
And nobler speech than angels use,
If love be absent, I am found,
Like tinkling brass, an empty sound.

2 Were I inspired to preach and tell
All that is done in heaven and hell;
Or could my faith the world remove,
Still I am nothing without love.

3 Should I distribute all my store
To feed the hungry, clothe the poor,
Or give my body to the flame,
To gain a martyr's glorious name,—

4 If love to God and love to men
Be absent, all my hopes are vain;
Nor tongues, nor gifts, nor fiery zeal,
The work of love can e'er fulfill.
　　　　　　　　　　ISAAC WATTS.

102

O RENDER thanks to God above,
The fountain of eternal love,
Whose mercy firm through ages past
Has stood, and shall forever last.

2 Who can his mighty deeds express,
Not only vast, but numberless?
What mortal eloquence can raise
His tribute of immortal praise?

3 Extend to me that favor, Lord,
Thou to thy chosen dost afford:
From my transgressions set me free,
And let me ever joy in thee.
　　　　　　　　　　ISAAC WATTS.

40

BREWER. L. M.

FROM "MASONS' SACRED HARP."

How sweet the praise, how high the theme, To sing of him who rules su-preme;

Who dwells at God's right hand on high, Yet looks on us with ten-der eye!

103

How sweet the praise, how high the theme,
To sing of him who rules supreme;
Who dwells at God's right hand on high,
Yet looks on us with tender eye!

2 Th' angelic host, in countless throngs,
Recount his glories in their songs,
And golden harps salute his ear;
Yet our weak praise he deigns to hear.

3 The planets roll, their orbits round;
Unnumbered worlds, in space profound,
Are ruled by him, by him controlled;
Yet he's the Shepherd of our fold.

4 Exalted high upon his throne,
The universe is all his own;
Untold the honors he doth wear,
Yet we are objects of his care.

BENJ. SKENE.

104

Now be my heart inspired to sing
The glories of my Saviour King;
He comes with blessings from above,
And wins the nations to his love.

2 Thy throne, O Lord, forever stands;
Grace is the scepter in thy hands;
Thy laws and works are just and right,
But truth and mercy thy delight.

3 Let endless honors crown thy head;
Let every age thy praises spread;
Let all the nations know thy word,
And every tongue confess thee Lord.

ISAAC WATTS.

105

PRAISE ye the Lord! 'Tis good to raise
Our hearts and voices in his praise;
His nature and his works invite
To make this duty our delight.

2 Great is the Lord, and great his might,
And all his glories infinite;
His wisdom vast, and knows no bound—
A deep where all our thoughts are drowned.

3 He loves the meek, rewards the just,
Humbles the wicked in the dust,
Melts and subdues the stubborn soul,
And makes the broken spirit whole.

4 His saints are precious in his sight;
He views his children with delight;
He sees their hope, he knows their fear,
Approves and loves his image there.

ISAAC WATTS.

106

O, COME, loud anthems let us sing,
Loud thanks to our Almighty King;
For we our voices high should raise,
When our salvation's Rock we praise.

2 Into his presence let us haste,
To thank him for his favors past;
To him address, in joyful songs,
The praise that to his name belongs.

3 O, let us to his courts repair,
And bow with adoration there;
Down on our knees, devoutly, all
Before the Lord, our Maker, fall.

NAHUM TATE.

NEW CHRISTIAN

LINWOOD. L. M.　　　　　　　　　　　　ROSSINI.

I know that my Re-deem-er lives—What comfort this sweet sen-tence gives!

He lives, he lives, who once was dead; He lives, my ev-er-liv-ing Head.

107

I KNOW that my Redeemer lives—
What comfort this sweet sentence gives;
He lives, he lives, who once was dead!
He lives, my ever-living Head.

2 He lives, to bless me with his love;
He lives, to plead for me above;
He lives, my hungry soul to feed;
He lives, to bless in time of need;

3 He lives, to grant me rich supply;
He lives, to guide me with his eye;

He lives, to comfort me when faint;
He lives, to hear my soul's complaint;

4 He lives, my kind, wise, heavenly Friend;
He lives, and loves me to the end;
He lives, and while he lives I'll sing:
He lives, my Prophet, Priest, and King.

5 He lives, all glory to his name;
He lives, my Saviour, still the same—
O the sweet joy this sentence gives:
I know that my Redeemer lives!
SAMUEL MEDLEY.

WARE. L. M.　　　　　　　　　　　GEORGE KINGSLEY.

Fling out the ban-ner; let it float Skyward and seaward, high and wide—

The sun, that lights its shining folds, The cross, on which the Sav-iour died.

108

FLING out the banner; let it float
Skyward and seaward, high and wide—
The sun, that lights its shining folds;
The cross, on which the Saviour died.

2 Fling out the banner; angels bend,
In anxious silence, o'er the sign,
And vainly seek to comprehend
The wonder of the love divine.

3 Fling out the banner; let it float
Skyward and seaward, high and wide—
Our glory, only in the cross;
Our only hope, the Crucified.

4 Fling out the banner, wide and high,
Seaward and skyward, let it shine,
Nor skill, nor might, nor merit, ours:
We conquer only in that sign.
G. W. DOANE.

42

GERMANY. L. M.

BEETHOVEN.

To thee, my heart, e - ter - nal King, Would now its thankful trib - ute bring;

To thee its hum - ble hom-age raise In songs of ar - dent, grateful praise.

109

To THEE, my heart, eternal King,
Would now its thankful tribute bring;
To thee its humble homage raise
In songs of ardent, grateful praise.

2 All nature shows thy boundless love,
In worlds below and worlds above;
But in thy blessèd word I trace
The richer glories of thy grace.

3 Here what delightful truths are given;
Here Jesus shows the way to heaven;
His name salutes my listening ear,
Revives my heart and checks my fear.

4 For love like this, O may our song
Through endless years thy praise prolong;
And distant climes thy name adore,
Till time and nature are no more.
"EXETER COLL."

110

O SOURCE divine, and life of all,
    The fount of being's wondrous sea,
Thy depth would every heart appall,
    That saw not love supreme in thee.

2 We shrink before thy vast abyss,
    Where worlds on worlds eternal brood;
We know thee truly but in this,
    That thou bestowest all our good.

3 And so, 'mid boundless time and space,
    O grant us still in thee to dwell;
And through the ceaseless web to trace
    Thy presence working all things well.
JOHN STERLING.

111

How pleasant, how divinely fair,
O Lord of hosts, thy dwellings are!
With long desire my spirit faints
To meet th' assemblies of thy saints.

2 My soul would rest in thine abode,
My panting heart cries out for God;
My God, my King, why should I be
So far from all my joys and thee?

3 Blest are the souls who find a place
Within the temple of thy grace;
There they behold thy gentler rays,
And seek thy face, and learn thy praise.

4 Blest are the men whose hearts are set
To find the way to Zion's gate;
God is their strength, and through the road
They lean upon their helper, God.
ISAAC WATTS.

112

SOON may the last glad song arise
Through all the millions of the skies—
That song of triumph, which records
That all the earth is now the Lord's.

2 Let thrones and powers and kingdoms be
Obedient, mighty God, to thee;
And over land, and stream, and main,
Now wave the scepter of thy reign.

3 O let that glorious anthem swell;
Let host to host the triumph tell
That not one rebel heart remains,
But over all the Saviour reigns.
MRS. VOKE.

43

SESSIONS. L. M.

L. O. EMERSON.

King Jesus, reign for ev-er - more, Un-ri-valed in thy courts a-bove,

While we, with all thy saints, adore The wonders of re-deeming love.

113

KING Jesus, reign for evermore,
Unrivaled in thy courts above,
While we, with all thy saints, adore
The wonders of redeeming love.

2 No other Lord but thee we'll know,
No other power but thine confess;
We'll spread thine honors while below,
And heaven shall hear us shout thy grace.

3 We'll sing along the heavenly road
That leads us to thy blest abode;
Till, with the vast, unnumbered throng,
We join in heaven's triumphant song:

4 Till, with pure hands and voices sweet,
We cast our crowns at Jesus' feet,
And sing of everlasting love,
In everlasting strains above.
RALPH WARDLAW.

114

GREAT God, the followers of thy Son,
We bow before thy mercy-seat,
To worship thee, the holy One,
And pour our wishes at thy feet.

2 O grant thy blessing here to-day;
O give thy people joy and peace;
The tokens of thy love display,
And favors that shall never cease.

3 We seek the truth which Jesus brought,
His path of light we long to tread;
Here be his holy doctrine taught,
And here its purest influence shed.

4 May faith, and hope, and love abound,
Our sins and errors be forgiven;
And we, from day to day, be found
The sons of God and heirs of heaven.
H. WARE.

RUSSIAN HYMN. L. M.

THEODORE LWOFF.

In prayer to-geth-er let us fall, And cry for mer - cy, one and all;

And weep before the Judge, and say, O turn from us thy wrath a - way.

115

FATHER of mercies, bow thine ear,
Attentive to our earnest prayer.
We plead for those who plead for thee;
Successful pleaders may they be.

2 How great their work, how vast their charge!
Do thou their anxious souls enlarge;
Their best endowments are our gain;
We share the blessings they obtain.

3 O clothe with energy divine
Their words, and let those words be thine;
To them thy sacred truth reveal;
Suppress their fears, inflame their zeal.

4 Let thronging multitudes around
Hear from their lips the joyful sound;
In humble strains thy grace adore,
And feel thy new-creating power.
BENJ. BEDDOME.

116

LO! GOD is here—let us adore,
And own how dreadful is this place;
Let all within us feel his power,
And, silent, bow before his face.

2 Lo! God is here—him day and night
United choirs of angels sing;
To him, enthroned above all height,
Let saints their humble worship bring.

3 Lord God of hosts, O may our praise
Thy courts with grateful incense fill;
Still may we stand before thy face,
Still hear and do thy sovereign will.
J. WESLEY, tr.

117

IN PRAYER together let us fall,
And cry for mercy, one and all;
And weep before the Judge, and say,
O turn from us thy wrath away.

2 Thy grace have we offended sore
By sins, O God, which we deplore;
Pour down upon us from above
The riches of thy pardoning love.

3 Remember, Lord, though frail we be,
That yet thy handiwork are we;
Nor let the honor of thy name
Be by another put to shame.

4 Forgive the sin that we have wrought,
Increase the good that we have sought;
That we at length, our wanderings o'er,
May please thee here and evermore.
JOHN M. NEALE.

118

O BOW thine ear, Eternal One,
On thee our heart, adoring, calls;
To thee, the followers of thy Son
Have raised, and now devote these walls.

2 Here let thy holy days be kept;
And be this place to worship given,
Like that bright spot where Jacob slept,
The house of God, the gate of heaven.

3 Here may thine honor dwell; and here,
As incense, let thy children's prayer,
From contrite hearts and lips sincere,
Rise on the still and holy air.

4 Here be thy praise devoutly sung;
Here let thy truth beam forth to save,
As when, of old, thy Spirit hung,
On wings of light, o'er Jordan's wave.

5 And when the lips, that with thy name
Are vocal now, to dust shall turn,
On others may devotion's flame
Be kindled here, and purely burn.
JOHN PIERPONT.

119

WHILE o'er our guilty land, O Lord,
We view the terrors of thy sword,
O whither shall the helpless fly?
To whom but thee direct their cry?

2 The helpless sinner's cries and tears
Are grown familiar to thine ears;
Oft has thy mercy sent relief,
When all was fear and hopeless grief.

3 On thee, our guardian God, we call;
Before thy throne of grace we fall.
And is there no deliverance there?
And must we perish in despair?

4 See, we repent, we weep, we mourn,
To our forsaken God we turn;
O spare our guilty country; spare
The church which thou hast planted here.

5 We plead thy grace, indulgent God;
We plead thy Son's atoning blood;
We plead thy gracious promises—
And are they unavailing pleas?

6 These pleas, presented at thy throne,
Have brought ten thousand blessings down
On guilty lands in helpless woe;
Let them prevail to save us, too.
SAMUEL DAVIS.

45

ANVERN. L. M.   LOWELL MASON.

Triumphant Zi-on, lift thy head From dust, and darkness, and the dead; Tho' humbled

long, awake at length, And gird thee with thy Saviour's strength,
And gird thee with thy Saviour's strength.

120

TRIUMPHANT Zion, lift thy head
From dust, and darkness, and the dead;
Though humbled long, awake at length,
And gird thee with thy Saviour's strength.

2 Put all thy beauteous garments on,
And let thy excellence be known;
Decked in the robes of righteousness,
The world thy glories shall confess.

3 No more shall foes unclean invade,
And fill thy hallowed walls with dread;
No more shall hell's insulting host
Their victory and thy sorrows boast.

4 God, from on high, has heard thy prayer;
His hand thy ruins shall repair;
Nor will thy watchful monarch cease
To guard thee in eternal peace.
                        PHILIP DODDRIDGE.

ALL SAINTS. L. M.   WILLIAM KNAPP.

Now to the Lord, who makes us know The won-ders of his dy-ing love,

Be hum-ble hon-ors paid be-low, And strains of no-bler praise a-bove.

121

Now to the Lord, who makes us know
The wonders of his dying love,
Be humble honors paid below,
And strains of nobler praise above.

2 'Twas he who cleansed us from our sins,
And washed us in his precious blood;
'Tis he who makes us priests and kings,
And brings us, rebels, near to God.

3 Behold, on flying clouds he comes,
And every eye shall see him move;
Though with our sins we pierced him once,
Now he displays his pardoning love.

4 The unbelieving world shall wail,
While we rejoice to see the day.
Come, Lord, nor let thy promise fail,
Nor let thy chariot long delay.
                        ISAAC WATTS.

MISSIONARY CHANT. L. M.   H. C. ZEUNER.

Arm of the Lord, a-wake! a-wake! Put on thy strength, the nations shake;

And let the world, a-dor-ing, see Triumphs of mercy wrought by thee.

122

ARM of the Lord, awake! awake!
Put on thy strength, the nations shake;
And let the world, adoring, see
Triumphs of mercy wrought by thee.

2 Say to the heathen, from thy throne,
"I am Jehovah—God alone!"
Thy voice their idols shall confound,
And cast their altars to the ground.

3 No more let human blood be spilt—
Vain sacrifice for human guilt—
But to each conscience be applied
The blood that flowed from Jesus' side.

4 Almighty God, thy grace proclaim
In every land, of every name;
Let adverse powers before thee fall,
And crown the Saviour Lord of all.
WM. SHRUBSOLE.

123

YE Christian heralds, go, proclaim
Salvation in Immanuel's name;
To distant climes the tidings bear,
And plant the Rose of Sharon there.

2 He'll shield you with a wall of fire,
With holy zeal your hearts inspire,
Bid raging winds their fury cease,
And calm the savage breast to peace.

3 And when our labors are all o'er,
Then shall we meet to part no more—
Meet, with the blood-bought throng to fall,
And crown the Saviour Lord of all.
ANON.

124

HAIL! morning known among the blest,
Morning of hope, and joy, and love,
Of heavenly peace and holy rest,
Pledge of the endless rest above.

2 Blest be the Father of our Lord,
Who from the dead has brought his Son!
Hope to the lost was then restored,
And everlasting glory won.

3 Scarce morning twilight had begun
To chase the shades of night away,
When Christ arose—unsetting Sun—
The dawn of joy's eternal day.

4 Mercy looked down with smiling eye
When our Immanuel left the dead;
Faith marked his bright ascent on high,
And Hope with gladness raised her head.

5 God's goodness let us bear in mind,
Who to his saints this day has given,
For rest and serious joy designed,
To fit us for the bliss of heaven.
RALPH WARDLAW.

125

LORD, now we part in thy blest name,
In which we here together came;
Grant us our few remaining days,
To work thy will and spread thy praise.

2 Teach us, in life and death, to bless
Thee, Lord, our strength and righteousness,
And grant us all to meet above,
Where we shall better sing thy love.
REGINALD HEBER.

47

NEW CHRISTIAN

MIGDOL. L. M.　　　　　　　　　　　　　　LOWELL MASON.

Forgiveness! 'tis a joy-ful sound To mal-e-fac-tors doomed to die.

Publish the bliss the world around; You ser-aphs, shout it from the sky.

126

FORGIVENESS! 'tis a joyful sound
　To malefactors doomed to die.
Publish the bliss the world around;
　You seraphs, shout it from the sky.

2 'Tis the rich gift of love divine;
　'Tis full, outmeasuring every crime;
Unclouded shall its glories shine,
　And feel no change by changing time.

3 For this stupendous love of heaven
　What grateful honors shall we show?
Where much transgression is forgiven,
　Let love in equal ardor glow.

4 By this inspired, let all our days
　With gospel holiness be crowned;
Let truth and goodness, prayer and praise,
　In all abide, in all abound.

THOS. GIBBONS.

GRATITUDE. L. M.　　　　　　　　　　　　　AMI BOST.

127

My God, how endless is thy love!
　Thy gifts are every evening new;
And morning mercies, from above,
　Gently distill, like early dew.

2 Thou spreadst the curtains of the night,
　Great Guardian of my sleeping hours;
Thy sovereign word restores the light,
　And quickens all my drowsy powers.

3 I yield my powers to thy command;
　To thee I consecrate my days;
Perpetual blessings from thy hand
　Demand perpetual songs of praise.

ISAAC WATTS.

128

How sweetly flowed the gospel sound
　From lips of gentleness and grace,
When listening thousands gathered round,
　And joy and gladness filled the place.

2 From heaven he came, of heaven he spoke,
　To heaven he led his followers' way;
Dark clouds of gloomy night he broke,
　Unvailing an immortal day.

3 "Come, wanderers, to my Father's home;
　Come, all ye weary ones, and rest."
Yes, sacred Teacher, we will come,
　Obey thee, love thee, and be blest.

JOHN BOWRING.

48

ERNAN. L. M.

LOWELL MASON.

Happy the Church, thou sa-cred place, The seat of thy Cre - a - tor's grace!

Thy ho - ly courts are his a - bode, Thou earthly pal - ace of our God.

By permission.

129

HAPPY the Church, thou sacred place,
The seat of thy Creator's grace!
Thy holy courts are his abode,
Thou earthly palace of our God.

2 Thy walls are strength, and at thy gates
A guard of heavenly warriors waits;
Nor shall thy deep foundations move,
Fixed on his counsels and his love.

3 Thy foes in vain designs engage;
Against his throne in vain they rage,
Like rising waves, with angry roar,
That dash and die upon the shore.

4 God is our shield, and God our sun;
Swift as the fleeting moments run,
On us he sheds new beams of grace,
And we reflect his brightest praise.
ISAAC WATTS.

130

How sweet to leave the world awhile
And seek the presence of our Lord!
Dear Saviour, on thy people smile,
And come, according to thy word.

2 From busy scenes we now retreat,
That we may here converse with thee;
Ah! Lord, behold us at thy feet—
Let this the "gate of heaven" be.

3 "Chief of ten thousand," now appear,
That we, by faith, may see thy face;
O grant that we thy voice may hear,
And let thy presence fill this place.
THOS. KELLY.

131

JESUS, where'er thy people meet,
There they behold thy mercy-seat;
Where'er they seek thee, thou art found,
And every place is hallowed ground.

2 Dear Shepherd of thy chosen few,
Thy former mercies here renew;
Here to our waiting hearts proclaim
The sweetness of thy saving name.

3 Here may we prove the power of prayer,
To strengthen faith and banish care;
To teach our faint desires to rise,
And bring all heaven before our eyes.
WM. COWPER.

132

DEAR is the spot where Christians sleep,
And sweet the strains their spirits pour.
O why should we in anguish weep?
They are not lost, but gone before.

2 Secure from every mortal care,
By sin and sorrow vexed no more;
Eternal happiness they share,
Who are not lost, but gone before.

3 To Zion's peaceful courts above
In faith triumphant may we soar,
Embracing, in the arms of love,
The friends not lost, but gone before.

4 To Jordan's bank whene'er we come,
And hear the swelling waters roar,
Jesus, convey us safely home,
To friends not lost, but gone before.
UNKNOWN.

5

49

HAMBURG. L. M.   Arr. by LOWELL MASON.

When I survey the wondrous cross On which the Prince of glo - ry died,

My richest gain I count but loss, And pour contempt on all my pride.

133

WHEN I survey the wondrous cross
On which the Prince of glory died,
My richest gain I count but loss,
And pour contempt on all my pride.

2 Forbid it, Lord, that I should boast,
Save in the death of Christ, my Lord;
All the vain things that charm me most,
I sacrifice them to his blood.

3 See, from his head, his hands, his feet,
Sorrow and love flow mingled down;
Did e'er such love and sorrow meet,
Or thorns compose so rich a crown?

4 Were the whole realm of nature mine,
That were a present far too small:
Love so amazing, so divine,
Demands my soul, my life, my all.
ISAAC WATTS.

134

THEE we adore, O gracious Lord;
We praise thy name with one accord;
Thy saints, who here thy goodness see,
Through all the world do worship thee.

2 To thee aloud all angels cry,
And ceaseless raise their songs on high;
Both cherubim and seraphim,
The heavens and all the powers therein.

3 Th' apostles join the glorious throng;
The prophets swell th' immortal song;
The martyrs' noble army raise
Eternal anthems to thy praise.

4 Thee, holy, holy, holy King;
Thee, O Lord God of hosts, they sing;
Thus earth below, and heaven above,
Resound thy glory and thy love.
THOS. COTTERILL.

135

HE DIES, the Friend of sinners dies;
Lo! Salem's daughters weep around;
A solemn darkness vails the skies,
A sudden trembling shakes the ground.

2 Here's love and grief beyond degree—
The Lord of glory dies for men;
But, lo! what sudden joys we see—
Jesus, the dead, revives again.

3 The rising Lord forsakes the tomb
(The tomb in vain forbids his rise;)
Cherubic legions guard him home,
And shout him welcome to the skies.

4 Break off your tears, ye saints, and tell
How high our great Deliverer reigns;
Sing how he spoiled the hosts of hell,
And led the monster Death in chains.

5 Say, "Live forever, wondrous King,
Born to redeem, and strong to save;"
Then ask the monster, "Where's thy sting?
And where thy victory, boasting grave?"
ISAAC WATTS.

136

THE peace which God alone reveals,
And by his word of grace imparts,
Which only the believer feels,
Direct, and keep, and cheer our hearts.
JOHN NEWTON.

STONEFIELD. L. M.　　　　　　　　　　　　SAMUEL STANLEY.

Je-sus, and shall it ev-er be, A mor-tal man a-shamed of thee?

Ashamed of thee, whom angels praise, Whose glory shines thro' endless days?

137

JESUS, and shall it ever be,
A mortal man ashamed of thee?
Ashamed of thee, whom angels praise,
Whose glory shines through endless days?

2 Ashamed of Jesus! Sooner far
Let evening blush to own a star;
He sheds the beams of light divine
O'er this benighted soul of mine.

3 Ashamed of Jesus! Just as soon
Let midnight be ashamed of noon;
'Tis midnight with my soul till he,
Bright Morning Star, bid darkness flee.

4 Ashamed of Jesus, that dear Friend
On whom my hopes of heaven depend!
No; when I blush, be this my shame,
That I no more revere his name.

5 Ashamed of Jesus! Yes, I may,
When I've no guilt to wash away;
No tear to wipe, no good to crave,
No fears to quell, no soul to save.

6 Till then—nor is my boasting vain—
Till then I'll boast a Saviour slain;
And O may this my glory be,
That Christ is not ashamed of me!
JOSEPH GRIGG.

138

How beauteous were the marks divine,
That in thy meekness used to shine,
That lit thy lonely pathway, trod
In wondrous love, O Son of God!

2 O who like thee, so calm, so bright,
So pure, so made to live in light?
O who like thee did ever go
So patient, through a world of woe?

3 O who like thee so humbly bore
The scorn, the scoffs of men, before?
So meek, forgiving, godlike, high,
So glorious in humility?

4 E'en death, which sets the prisoner free,
Was pang, and scoff, and scorn to thee;
Yet love through all thy torture glowed,
And mercy with thy life-blood flowed.

5 O, in thy light be mine to go,
Illuming all my way of woe;
And give me ever on the road,
To trace thy footsteps, Son of God.
A. C. COXE.

139

O LOVE Divine, that stooped to share
Our sharpest pang, our bitterest tear,
On thee we cast each earth-born care;
We smile at pain while thou art near.

2 Though long the weary way we tread,
And sorrow crown each lingering year,
No path we shun, no darkness dread,
Our hearts still whispering, Thou art near.

3 On thee we fling our burdening woe,
O Love Divine, forever dear;
Content to suffer while we know,
Living or dying, thou art near.
O. W. HOLMES.

HEBRON. L. M.   LOWELL MASON.

Thou on-ly Sovereign of my heart, My Ref-uge, my al-might-y Friend!

And can my soul from thee de-part, On whom a-lone my hopes de-pend?

140

Thou only Sovereign of my heart,
  My Refuge, my almighty Friend!
And can my soul from thee depart,
  On whom alone my hopes depend?

2 Whither, ah! whither shall I go,
  A wretched wanderer, from my Lord?
Can this dark world of sin and woe
  One glimpse of happiness afford?

3 Thy name my inmost powers adore;
  Thou art my life, my joy, my care.
Depart from thee—'tis death—'tis more—
  'Tis endless ruin, deep despair!

4 Low at thy feet my soul would lie;
  Here safety dwells, and peace divine.
Still let me live beneath thine eye,
  For life, eternal life, is thine.
                              ANNE STEELE.

141

Thus far the Lord has led me on;
  Thus far his power prolongs my days;
And every evening shall make known
  Some fresh memorial of his grace.

2 Much of my time has run to waste,
  And I, perhaps, am near my home;
But he forgives my follies past,
  And gives me strength for days to come.

3 I lay my body down to sleep;
  Peace is the pillow for my head;
While well-appointed angels keep
  Their watchful stations round my bed.

4 Thus, when the night of death shall come,
  My flesh shall rest beneath the ground,
And wait thy voice to break my tomb,
  With sweet salvation in the sound.
                              ISAAC WATTS.

142

Jesus, thou Shepherd of the sheep,
  Thy little flock in safety keep;
These lambs within thine arms now take,
  Nor let them e'er thy fold forsake.

2 Secure them from the scorching beam,
  And lead them to the living stream;
In verdant pastures let them lie,
  And watch them with a shepherd's eye.

3 O teach them to discern thy voice,
  And in its sacred sound rejoice;
From strangers may they ever flee,
  And know no other guide but thee.

4 Lord, bring thy sheep that wander yet,
  And let their number be complete;
Then let the flock from earth remove,
  And reach the heavenly fold above.
                              W. B. COLLYER.

143

Welcome, ye hopeful heirs of heaven,
  To this rich feast of gospel love;
This pledge is but the prelude given
  To that immortal feast above.

2 How great the blessing, thus to meet,
  According to our Saviour's word,
And hold, by faith, communion sweet
  With our unseen, yet present, Lord!

3 And if so sweet this feast below,
  What will it be to meet above,
Where all we see, and feel, and know,
  Are fruits of everlasting love!

4 Soon shall we tune the heavenly lyre,
  While listening worlds the song approve;
Eternity itself expire,
  Ere we exhaust the theme of love.
                              UNKNOWN.

144

LET me but hear my Saviour say,
"Strength shall be equal to thy day;"
Then I rejoice in deep distress,
Leaning on all-sufficient grace.

2 I can do all things—or can bear
All suffering, if my Lord be there;
Sweet pleasures mingle with the pains,
While he my sinking head sustains.

3 I glory in infirmity,
That Christ's own power may rest on me;
When I am weak, then am I strong;
Grace is my shield, and Christ my song.
ISAAC WATTS.

145

KINDRED in Christ, for his dear sake
A hearty welcome here receive;
May we together now partake
The joys which only he can give.

2 May he, by whose kind care we meet,
Send his good Spirit from above,
Make our communications sweet,
And cause our hearts to burn with love.

3 Forgotten be each worldly theme,
When Christians meet together thus;
We only wish to speak of him
Who lived, and died, and reigns for us.

4 Thus, as the moments pass away,
We'll love, and wonder, and adore;
And hasten on the glorious day
When we shall meet to part no more.
JOHN NEWTON.

146

WHEN we the sacred grave survey,
In which the Saviour deigned to lie,
We see fulfilled what prophets say,
And all the power of death defy.

2 This empty tomb shall now proclaim
How weak the bands of conquered death;
Sure pledge that all who trust his name
Shall rise and draw immortal breath.

3 Jesus, once numbered with the dead,
Unseals his eyes to sleep no more;
And ever lives their cause to plead
For whom the pains of death he bore.

4 Then, though in dust we lay our head,
Yet, gracious God, thou wilt not leave
Our flesh forever with the dead,
Nor lose thy children in the grave.
UNKNOWN.

147

FOUNTAIN of grace, rich, full, and free,
What need I, that is not in thee—
Full pardon, strength to meet the day,
And peace which none can take away?

2 Doth sickness fill my heart with fear?
'Tis sweet to know that thou art near.
Am I with dread of justice tried?
'Tis sweet to know that Christ hath died.

3 In life, thy promises of aid
Forbid my heart to be afraid;
In death, peace gently vails the eyes—
Christ rose, and I shall surely rise.
J. EDMESTON.

148

TO-DAY, if you will hear his voice,
Now is the time to make your choice;
Say, will you to Mount Zion go?
Say, will you come to Christ or no?

2 Say, will you be forever blest,
And with this glorious Jesus rest?
Will you be saved from guilt and pain?
Will you with Christ forever reign?

3 Make now your choice, and halt no more,
He now is waiting for the poor;
Say, now, poor souls, what will you do?
Say, will you come to Christ or no?

4 Fathers and sons, for ruin bound,
Amidst the gospel's joyful sound,
Come, go with us, and seek to prove
The joys of Christ's redeeming love.

5 Matrons and maids, we look to you—
Are you resolved to perish, too?
To rush in carnal pleasures on,
And sink in flaming ruin down?

6 Once more we ask you in his name,
(We know his love remains the same),
Say, will you to Mount Zion go?
Say, will you come to Christ or no?
MILLER.

149

DISMISS us with thy blessing, Lord;
Help us to feed upon thy word;
All that has been amiss, forgive,
And let thy truth within us live.

2 Though we are guilty, thou art good;
Cleanse all our sins in Jesus' blood,
Give every burdened soul release,
And bid us all depart in peace.
JOS. HART.

ROLLAND. L. M.

WM. B. BRADBURY.

Jesus, the Spring of joys divine, Whence all our hopes and comforts flow; Je-sus, no oth-er name but thine Can save us from e-ter-nal woe, Can save us from e-ter-nal woe.

By permission of Biglow & Main.

150

JESUS, the Spring of joys divine,
  Whence all our hopes and comforts flow;
Jesus, no other name but thine
  Can save us from eternal woe.

2 In vain would boasting reason find
  The way to happiness and God;
Her weak directions leave the mind
  Bewildered in a dubious road.

3 No other name will heaven approve;
  Thou art the true, the living Way,
Ordained by everlasting love,
  To the bright realms of endless day.

4 Here let our constant feet abide,
  Nor from the heavenly path depart;
O let thy Spirit, gracious Guide,
  Direct our steps, and cheer our heart.
            ANNE STEELE.

151

MY GOD, my heart with love inflame,
That I may, in thy holy name,
Aloud in songs of praise rejoice,
While I have breath to raise my voice.

2 No more let my ungrateful heart
One moment from thy praise depart;
But live and sing, in sweet accord,
The glories of my sovereign Lord.

3 Jesus, thou hope of glory, come
And make my heart thy constant home;
Through all the remnant of my days,
O let me speak and live thy praise.
            UNKNOWN.

152

BEHOLD the Christian warrior stand
  In all the armor of his God:
The Spirit's sword is in his hand,
  His feet are with the gospel shod;

2 In panoply of truth complete,
  Salvation's helmet on his head;
With righteousness a breastplate meet,
  And faith's broad shield before him spread,

3 Undaunted to the field he goes;
  Yet vain were skill and valor there,
Unless, to foil his legion foes,
  He takes the trustiest weapon, prayer.

4 Thus, strong in his Redeemer's strength,
  Sin, death, and hell he tramples down;
Fights the good fight, and wins at length,
  Through mercy, an immortal crown.
            JAMES MONTGOMERY.

153

EXALTED Prince of Life, we own
The royal honors of thy throne;
'Tis fixed by God's almighty hand,
And seraphs bow at thy command.

2 Exalted Saviour, we confess
The mighty triumphs of thy grace,
Where beams of gentle radiance shine,
And temper majesty divine.

3 Wide thy resistless scepter sway,
Till all thine enemies obey;
Wide let thy cross its virtues prove,
And conquer millions by its love.
            PHILIP DODDRIDGE.

BLESSING. L. M.

I. B. WOODBURY.

O peace of God, sweet peace of God, Where broods on earth this gen-tle dove?

Where spread those pure and downy wings To shel-ter him whom God doth love?

By permission.

154

O PEACE of God, sweet peace of God,
  Where broods on earth this gentle dove?
Where spread those pure and downy wings
  To shelter him whom God doth love?

2 Whence comes this blessing of the soul,
  This silent joy that can not fade;
This glory, tranquil, holy, bright,
  Pervading sorrow's deepest shade?

3 The peace of God, the peace of God,
  It shines as clear 'mid cloud and storm
As in the calmest summer day;
  'Mid chill as in the sunlight warm.

4 O peace of God, earth hath no power
  To shed thine unction o'er the heart;
Its smile can never bring it here—
  Its frown ne'er bid its light depart.

5 Sweet peace! O let thy heavenly ray
  Shed its calm radiance o'er my road;
Its kindly light shall cheer me on—
  Guide to the endless peace of God.
      UNKNOWN.

155

How vain is all beneath the skies!
  How transient every earthly bliss!
How slender all the fondest ties
  That bind us to a world like this!

2 The evening cloud, the morning dew,
  The withering grass, the fading flower,
Of earthly hopes are emblems true—
  The glory of a passing hour.

3 But though earth's fairest blossoms die,
  And all beneath the skies is vain,
There is a brighter world on high,
  Beyond the reach of care and pain.

4 Then let the hope of joys to come
  Dispel our cares and chase our fears;
If God be ours, we're traveling home,
  Though passing through a vale of tears.
      D. E. FORD.

156

How blest are they whose transient years
  Pass like an evening meteor's flight;
Not dark with guilt, nor dim with tears,
  Whose course is short, unclouded, bright!

2 O cheerless were our lengthened way;
  But heaven's own light dispels the gloom,
Streams downward from eternal day,
  And casts a glory round the tomb.

3 O stay thy tears: the blest above
  Have hailed a spirit's heavenly birth,
And sung a song of joy and love—
  Then why should anguish reign on earth?
      NORTON.

157

O FOR a strong, a lasting faith,
To credit what th' Almighty saith,
T' embrace the message of his Son,
And call the joys of heaven our own!

2 Then, should the earth's old pillars shake,
And all the wheels of nature break,
Our steady souls should fear no more
Than solid rocks when billows roar.
      ISAAC WATTS.

WELTON. L. M.   C. H. A. MALAN.

By faith in Christ I walk with God, With heaven, my journey's end, in view;

Sup-port-ed by his staff and rod, My road is safe, and pleas-ant too.

158

By faith in Christ I walk with God,
  With heaven, my journey's end, in view;
Supported by his staff and rod,
  My road is safe, and pleasant too.

2 I travel through a desert wide,
  Where many round me blindly stray;
But he vouchsafes to be my Guide,
  And keep me in the narrow way.

3 With him sweet converse I maintain;
  Great as he is, I dare be free;
I tell him all my grief and pain,
  And he reveals his love to me.

4 I pity all that worldlings talk
  Of pleasures that will quickly end;
Be this my choice, O Lord! to walk
  With thee, my Guide, my Guard, my Friend.
                  JOHN NEWTON.

159

LET thoughtless thousands choose the road
That leads the soul away from God;
This happiness, blest Lord, be mine,
To live and die entirely thine.

2 On Christ, by faith, my soul would live,
From him my life, my all, receive;
To him devote my fleeting hours,
Serve him alone with all my powers.

3 Christ is my everlasting all;
To him I look, on him I call;
He will my every want supply
In time, and through eternity.

4 Soon will the Lord, my life, appear;
Soon shall I end my trials here;
Leave sin and sorrow, death and pain;
To live is Christ, to die is gain.
                  JOSIAH HOPKINS.

160

BLEST are the humble souls that see
Their emptiness and poverty;
Treasures of grace to them are given,
And crowns of joy laid up in heaven.

2 Blest are the men of broken heart,
Who mourn for sin with inward smart;
The blood of Christ divinely flows,
A healing balm for all their woes.

3 Blest are the souls who thirst for grace,
Hunger and thirst for righteousness;
They shall be well supplied and fed
With living streams and living bread.

4 Blest are the men of peaceful life,
Who quench the glowing coals of strife;
They shall be called the heirs of bliss,
The sons of God, the God of peace.
                  ISAAC WATTS.

161

THE tempter to my soul hath said,
  "There is no help in God for thee;"
Lord, lift thou up thy servant's head;
  My glory, shield, and solace be.

2 Thus to the Lord I raised my cry;
  He heard me from his holy hill;
At his command the waves rolled by;
  He beckoned—and the winds were still.

3 I laid me down and slept—I woke—
  Thou, Lord, my spirit didst sustain;
Bright from the east the morning broke—
  Thy comforts rose on me again.

4 I will not fear, though arméd throngs
  Surround my steps in all their wrath;
Salvation to the Lord belongs:
  His presence guards his people's path.
                  J. MONTGOMERY.

MALVERN. L. M.

LOWELL MASON.

How pleasing to be-hold and see The friends of Je-sus all a-gree—

To sit a-round the sa-cred board As members of one com-mon Lord.

162

How pleasing to behold and see
The friends of Jesus all agree—
To sit around the sacred board
As members of one common Lord.

2 Here we behold the dawn of bliss;
Here we behold the Saviour's grace;
Here we behold his precious blood,
Which sweetly pleads for us with God.

3 While here we sit we would implore,
That love may spread from shore to shore,
Till all the saints, like us, combine
To praise the Lord in songs divine.

4 To all we freely give our hand,
Who love the Lord in every land;
For all are one in Christ our head,
To whom be endless honors paid.
JOHN DOBELL.

163

No change of time shall ever shock
   My firm affection, Lord, to thee;
For thou hast always been my rock,
   A fortress and defense to me.

2 Thou my deliverer art, my God!
   My trust is in thy mighty power;
Thou art my shield from foes abroad,
   At home my safeguard and my tower.

3 To thee will I address my prayer,
   To whom all praise I justly owe;
So shall I, by thy watchful care,
   Be guarded from my treacherous foe.
TATE AND BRADY.

164

GLORY to thee, my God, this night,
For all the blessings of the light;
Keep me, O keep me, King of kings,
Beneath thine own almighty wings.

2 Forgive me, Lord, for thy dear Son,
The ill which I this day have done;
That with the world, myself, and thee,
I, ere I sleep, at peace may be.

3 Be thou my Guardian while I sleep;
Thy watchful station near me keep;
My heart with love celestial fill,
And guard me from th' approach of ill.

4 Lord, let my soul forever share
The bliss of thy paternal care;
'Tis heaven on earth, 'tis heaven above,
To see thy face, and sing thy love!
THOS. KEN.

165

A BROKEN heart, my God, my King,
Is all the sacrifice I bring;
The God of grace will ne'er despise
A broken heart for sacrifice.

2 My soul lies humbled in the dust,
And owns thy dreadful sentence just;
Look down, O Lord, with pitying eye,
And save the soul condemned to die.

3 Then will I teach the world thy ways;
Sinners shall learn thy sovereign grace;
I'll lead them to my Saviour's blood,
And they shall praise a pardoning God.
ISAAC WATTS.

TAPPAN. L. M. Geo. Kingsley.

Tho' all the world my choice deride, Yet Je-sus shall my portion be; For I am pleased with none beside; The fairest of the fair is he, The fairest of the fair is he.

166

Though all the world my choice deride,
  Yet Jesus shall my portion be;
For I am pleased with none beside;
  The fairest of the fair is he.

2 Sweet is the vision of thy face,
  And kindness o'er thy lips is shed;
Lovely art thou, and full of grace,
  And glory beams around thy head.

3 Thy sufferings I embrace with thee,
  Thy poverty and shameful cross;
The pleasures of the world I flee,
  And deem its treasures only dross.

4 Be daily dearer to my heart,
  And ever let me feel thee near;
Then willingly with all I'd part,
  Nor count it worthy of a tear.
                          G. Tersteegen.

OVERBERG. L. M. J. C. H. Rink.

My gracious Lord, I own thy right To ev-ery serv-ice I can pay, And call it my supreme de-light To hear thy dic-tates, and o-bey.

167

My gracious Lord, I own thy right
  To every service I can pay,
And call it my supreme delight
  To hear thy dictates, and obey.

2 What is my being but for thee,
  Its sure support, its noblest end?
'Tis my delight thy face to see,
  And serve the cause of such a Friend.

3 I would not sigh for worldly joy,
  Or to increase my worldly good;

Nor future days nor powers employ
  To spread a sounding name abroad.

4 'Tis to my Saviour I would live,
  To him who for my ransom died;
Nor could all worldly honor give
  Such bliss as crowns me at his side.

5 His work my hoary age shall bless,
  When youthful vigor is no more;
And my last hour of life confess
  His dying love, his saving power.
                          Philip Doddridge.

58

HURSLEY. L. M.   Arr. by W. H. Monk.

Sun of my soul, thou Saviour dear, It is not night if thou be near;

O may no earth-born cloud a-rise To hide thee from thy servant's eyes.

168

Sun of my soul, thou Saviour dear,
It is not night if thou be near;
O may no earth-born cloud arise
To hide thee from thy servant's eyes.

2 When soft the dews of kindly sleep
My wearied eyelids gently steep,
Be my last thought—how sweet to rest
Forever on my Saviour's breast!

3 Abide with me from morn till eve,
For without thee I can not live;
Abide with me when night is nigh,
For without thee I dare not die.

4 Be near to bless me when I wake,
Ere through the world my way I take;
Abide with me till, in thy love,
I lose myself in heaven above.
                                        J. Keble.

169

My dear Redeemer, and my Lord,
I read my duty in thy word;
But in thy life the law appears
Drawn out in living characters.

2 Such was thy truth, and such thy zeal,
Such deference to thy Father's will,
Such love, and meekness so divine,
I would transcribe and make them mine.

3 Be thou my pattern; make me bear
More of thy gracious image here;
Then God, the Judge, shall own my name
Among the followers of the Lamb.
                                        Isaac Watts.

170

Father of spirits, nature's God,
Our inmost thoughts are known to thee;
Thou, Lord, canst hear each idle word,
And every private action see.

2 Could we on morning's swiftest wings,
Pursue our flight through trackless air,
Or dive beneath deep ocean's springs,
Thy presence still would meet us there.

3 In vain may guilt attempt to fly,
Concealed beneath the pall of night;
One glance from thy all-piercing eye
Can kindle darkness into light.

4 Search thou our hearts, and there destroy
Each evil thought, each secret sin,
And fit us for those realms of joy,
Where naught impure shall enter in.
                                        John Bowring.

171

Now let our souls, on wings sublime,
Rise from the vanities of time;
Draw back the parting vail, and see
The glories of eternity.

2 Born by a new, celestial birth,
Why should we grovel here on earth?
Why grasp at vain and fleeting toys,
So near to heaven's eternal joys?

3 Shall aught beguile us on the road,
While we are walking back to God?
For strangers into life we come,
And dying is but going home.
                                        Thos. Gibbons.

WARD. L. M.   Arr. by LOWELL MASON.

Earth has a joy unknown In heaven—The new-born joy of sins for-given!

Tears of such pure and deep de - light, O an-gels, nev-er dimmed your sight.

172

EARTH has a joy unknown in heaven—
The new-born joy of sins forgiven!
Tears of such pure and deep delight,
O angels, never dimmed your sight.

2 You saw of old on chaos rise
The beauteous pillars of the skies;
You know where morn exulting springs,
And evening folds her drooping wings.

3 Bright heralds of th' Eternal Will,
Abroad his errands you fulfill;
Or, throned in floods of beamy day,
Symphonious in his presence play.

4 But I amid your choirs shall shine,
And all your knowledge shall be mine;
You on your harps must lean to hear
A secret chord that mine shall bear.
A. L. HILLHOUSE.

173

GREAT was the day, the joy was great,
When the beloved disciples met;
And on their heads the Spirit came,
And sat like tongues of cloven flame.

2 What gifts, what miracles he gave—
The power to kill, the power to save!
Furnished their tongues with wondrous words
Instead of shields, and spears, and swords!

3 Thus armed, he sent the champions forth,
From east to west, from south to north;
Go, and assert your Saviour's cause—
Go, spread the mystery of the cross.

4 These weapons of the holy war,
Of what almighty force they are,
To make our stubborn passions bow,
And lay the proudest rebel low!
ISAAC WATTS.

174

THOU, Saviour, from thy throne on high,
Enrobed with light, and girt with power,
Dost note the thought, the prayer, the sigh,
Of hearts that love the tranquil hour.

2 Oft thou thyself didst steal away,
At eventide from labor done,
In some still, peaceful shade to pray,
Till morning watches were begun.

3 Thou hast not, dearest Lord, forgot
Thy wrestlings on Judea's hills;
And still thou lov'st the quiet spot
Where praise the lowly spirit fills.

4 Now to our souls, withdrawn awhile
From earth's rude noise, thy face reveal,
And, as we worship, kindly smile,
And for thine own our spirits seal.
RAY PALMER.

175

How blest the sacred tie that binds,
In sweet communion, kindred minds!
How swift the heavenly course they run,
Whose hearts and faith and hopes are one.

2 To each the soul of each how dear!
What tender love, what holy fear!
How doth the generous flame within
Refine from earth, and cleanse from sin!

3 Their streaming eyes together flow
For human guilt and mortal woe;
Their ardent prayers together rise
Like mingling flames in sacrifice.

4 Nor shall the glowing flame expire,
When dimly burns frail nature's fire;
Soon shall they meet in realms above,
A heaven of joy, a heaven of love.
A. L. BARBAULD.

176

Not all the nobles of the earth,
Who boast the honors of their birth,
So high a dignity can claim,
As those who bear the Christian name.

2 To them the privilege is given
To be the sons and heirs of heaven—
Sons of the God who reigns on high,
And heirs of joy beyond the sky.

3 His will he makes them early know,
And teaches their young feet to go;
Imparts instruction to their minds,
And on their hearts his precepts binds.

4 Their daily wants his hands supply,
Their steps he guards with watchful eye;
Leads them from earth to heaven above,
And crowns them with eternal love.
S. STENNETT.

177

When Jesus dwelt in mortal clay,
What were his works, from day to day,
But miracles of power and grace,
That spread salvation through our race.

2 Teach us, O Lord, to keep in view
Thy pattern, and thy steps pursue;
Let alms bestowed, let kindness done,
Be witnessed by each rolling sun.

3 That man may last, but never lives,
Who much receives, but nothing gives,
Whom none can love, whom none can thank,
Creation's blot, creation's blank.

4 But he who marks from day to day
In generous acts his radiant way,
Treads the same path the Saviour trod,
The path to glory and to God.
THOS. GIBBONS.

178

Blest hour, when mortal man retires
To hold communion with the Lord;
To send to heaven his warm desires,
And listen to the sacred word!

2 Blest hour, when earthly cares resign
Their empire o'er his anxious breast,
While, all around, the calm divine
Proclaims the holy day of rest!

3 Blest hour, when God himself draws nigh,
Well pleased his people's voice to hear,
To hush the penitential sigh,
And wipe away the mourner's tear!
T. RAFFLES.

179

Behold, the blind their sight receive!
Behold, the dead awake and live!
The dumb speak wonders, and the lame
Leap like the hart, and bless his name!

2 Thus doth the Holy Spirit own
And seal the mission of the Son;
The Father vindicates his cause,
While he hangs bleeding on the cross.

3 He dies—the heavens in mourning stood;
He rises by the power of God!
Behold, the Lord ascending high,
No more to bleed, no more to die.

4 Hence and forever from my heart
I bid my doubts and fears depart;
And to those hands my soul resign,
Which bear credentials so divine.
ISAAC WATTS.

180

Our Saviour bowed beneath the wave,
And meekly sought a watery grave;
Come, see the sacred place he trod,
A path well-pleasing to our God.

2 His voice we hear, his footsteps trace,
And hither come to seek his face,
To do his will, to feel his love,
And join our songs with songs above.

3 Hosanna to the Lamb divine!
Let endless glories round him shine!
High o'er the heavens forever reign,
O Lamb of God, for sinners slain.
UNKNOWN.

181

While life prolongs its precious light,
Mercy is found, and peace is given;
But soon, ah! soon, approaching night
Shall blot out every hope of heaven.

2 While God invites, how blest the day!
How sweet the gospel's charming sound!
Come, sinners, haste, O haste away,
While yet a pardoning God is found.

3 Soon, borne on time's most rapid wing,
Shall death command you to the grave,
Before his bar your spirits bring,
And none be found to hear or save.

4 Now God invites: how blest the day!
How sweet the gospel's charming sound!
Come, sinners, haste, O haste away,
While yet a pardoning God is found.
TIMOTHY DWIGHT.

NEW CHRISTIAN

OLIVE'S BROW. L. M. WM. B. BRADBURY.

'Tis midnight, and on Olive's brow The star is dimmed that lately shone;

'Tis midnight—in the garden now The suffering Saviour prays alone.

By permission of Biglow & Main.

182

'Tis midnight, and on Olive's brow
The star is dimmed that lately shone;
'Tis midnight—in the garden now
The suffering Saviour prays alone.

2 'Tis midnight, and from all removed
The Saviour wrestles lone with fears—
E'en that disciple whom he loved
Heeds not his Master's grief and tears.

3 Tis midnight, and for others' guilt
The Man of Sorrows weeps in blood;
Yet he that hath in anguish knelt
Is not forsaken by his God.

4 'Tis midnight, and from ether-plains
Is borne the song that angels know—
Unheard by mortals are the strains
That sweetly soothe the Saviour's woe.

W. B. TAPPAN.

FEDERAL STREET. L. M. H. K. OLIVER.

From Calvary a cry was heard—A bitter and heart-rending cry;

My Saviour, every mournful word Bespeaks thy soul's deep agony.

183

From Calvary a cry was heard—
A bitter and heart-rending cry;
My Saviour, every mournful word
Bespeaks thy soul's deep agony.

2 A horror of great darkness fell
On thee, thou spotless, holy One,
And all the swarming hosts of hell
Conspired to tempt God's only Son.

3 The scourge, the thorns, the deep disgrace,
These thou couldst bear, nor once repine;
But when Jehovah vailed his face,
Unutterable pangs were thine.

4 Lord, on thy cross I fix mine eye;
If e'er I lose its strong control,
O let that dying, piercing cry
Melt and reclaim my wandering soul.

J. W. CUNNINGHAM.

62

ZEPHYR. L. M.

Wm. B. Bradbury.

My on-ly Sav-iour, when I feel O'er-whelmed in spir-it, faint, oppressed,

'Tis sweet to tell thee, while I kneel Low at thy feet, thou art my rest.

By permission of Biglow & Main.

184

My only Saviour, when I feel
O'erwhelmed in spirit, faint, oppressed,
'Tis sweet to tell thee, while I kneel
Low at thy feet, thou art my rest.

2 I'm weary of the strife within;
Strong powers against my soul contest;
O let me turn from self and sin
To thy dear cross, for there is rest.

3 O sweet will be the welcome day
When, from her toils and woes released,
My parting soul in death shall say,
"Now, Lord, I come to thee for rest."
UNKNOWN.

185

Away from earth my spirit turns—
Away from every transient good;
With strong desire my bosom burns
To feast on heaven's diviner food.

2 Thou, Saviour, art the living bread;
Thou wilt my every want supply;
By thee sustained, and cheered, and led,
I'll press through dangers to the sky.

3 What though temptations oft distress,
And sin assails and breaks my peace,
Thou wilt uphold, and save, and bless,
And bid the storms of passion cease.

4 Then let me take thy gracious hand,
And walk beside thee onward still,
Till my glad feet shall safely stand,
Forever firm, on Zion's hill.
RAY PALMER.

186

O SUFFERING Friend of human kind,
How, as the fatal hour drew near,
Came thronging on thy holy mind
The images of grief and fear!

2 Gethsemane's sad midnight scene,
The faithless friends, th' exulting foes,
The thorny crown, the insult keen,
The scourge, the cross, before thee rose.

3 Did not thy spirit shrink dismayed,
As the dark vision o'er it came,
And, though in sinless strength arrayed,
Turn, shuddering, from the death of shame?

4 Onward, like thee, thro' scorn and dread
May we our Father's call obey,
Steadfast the path of duty tread,
And rise, through death, to endless day.
S. G. BULFINCH.

187

COME, weary souls, with sin distressed;
The Saviour offers heavenly rest;
The kind, the gracious call obey,
And cast your gloomy fears away.

2 Oppressed with guilt, a heavy load,
O come, and bow before your God.
Divine compassion, mighty love,
Will all the painful load remove.

3 Here mercy's boundless ocean flows,
To cleanse your guilt and heal your woes;
Pardon, and life, and endless peace—
How rich the gift, how free the grace!
ANNE STEELE.

REST. L. M.   WM. B. BRADBURY.

A-sleep in Je - sus! Blessed sleep, From which none ev - er wakes to weep;

A calm and un - disturbed re - pose, Unbrok - en by the last of foes!

By permission of Biglow & Main.

188

ASLEEP in Jesus! blessèd sleep,
From which none ever wakes to weep;
A calm and undisturbed repose,
Unbroken by the last of foes!

2 Asleep in Jesus! O how sweet
To be for such a slumber meet;
With holy confidence to sing,
That death has lost its venomed sting!

3 Asleep in Jesus! Peaceful rest,
Whose waking is supremely blest!
No fear, no woe, shall dim that hour
That manifests the Saviour's power.

4 Asleep in Jesus! O for me
May such a blissful refuge be!
Securely shall my ashes lie,
And wait the summons from on high.

5 Asleep in Jesus! Time nor space
Affects this precious hiding-place;
On Indian plains, on Lapland snows,
Believers find the same repose.

6 Asleep in Jesus! Far from thee
Thy kindred and their graves may be;
But thine is still a blessèd sleep,
From which none ever wakes to weep.

MRS. M. MACKAY.

PALESTINE. L. M. 6 l.   JOSEPH MEZZINGHI.

Peace, troubled soul, whose plaintive moan Hath taught each scene the notes of woe;
Cease thy complaint, sup-

press thy groan, And let thy tears for-get to flow. Be-hold! the precious balm is found
D. S. To lull thy pain, to heal thy wound.

Fine.   D. S.

189

PEACE, troubled soul, whose plaintive moan
Hath taught each scene the notes of woe;
Cease thy complaint, suppress thy groan,
And let thy tears forget to flow.
Behold the precious balm is found
To lull thy pain, to heal thy wound.

2 Come, freely come, by sin oppressed,
On Jesus cast thy weighty load;
In him thy refuge find, thy rest,
Safe in the mercy of thy God.
Thy God's thy Saviour—glorious word!
O hear, believe and bless the Lord.

WALTER SHIRLEY.

64

ST. LOUIS. L. M., with Sanctus.

ANON.

On Zion's glorious summit stood A numerous host, redeemed by blood; They hymned their King in

strains di - vine; I heard the song, and strove to join, I heard the song, and strove to join.

190

On Zion's glorious summit stood
A numerous host, redeemed by blood;
They hymned their King in strains divine;
I heard the song, and strove to join.

2 Here all who suffered sword or flame
For truth, or Jesus' lovely name,
Shout victory now, and hail the Lamb,
And bow before the great I AM.

3 While everlasting ages roll,
Eternal love shall feast their soul,
And scenes of bliss, forever new,
Rise in succession to their view.

KENT.

191

O sweet employ, to sing and trace
Th' amazing heights and depths of grace;
And spend, from sin and sorrow free,
A blissful, vast eternity!

2 O what a sweet, exalted song,
When every tribe, and every tongue,
Redeemed by blood, with Christ appear,
And join in one full chorus there!

3 My soul anticipates the day—
Would stretch her wings and soar away,
To aid the song, the palm to bear,
And praise my great Redeemer there.

KENT.

SANCTUS. To be sung at the close of the hymn.

"MANHATTAN COLL."

Ho - ly, ho - ly, ho - ly, Lord God of hosts, on high a - dored!

1st time. 2nd time. Dim.

Who like me thy praise should sing, O Al-might-y King! (Omit.) Ho-ly, ho-ly, ho - ly.

6

ARIEL. C. P. M.   LOWELL MASON.

O could I speak the matchless worth, O could I sound the glories forth, Which in my Saviour shine,

{ I'd soar and touch the heavenly strings, }
{ And vie with Gabriel, while he sings, } In notes almost divine, In notes almost divine.

192

O COULD I speak the matchless worth,
O could I sound the glories forth,
  Which in my Saviour shine,
I'd soar and touch the heavenly strings,
And vie with Gabriel while he sings,
  In notes almost divine.

2 I'd sing the precious blood he spilt,
My ransom from the dreadful guilt
  Of sin, and wrath divine;
I'd sing his glorious righteousness,
In which all-perfect, heavenly dress
  My soul shall ever shine.

3 I'd sing the characters he bears,
And all the forms of love he wears,
  Exalted on his throne;
In loftiest songs of sweetest praise,
I would to everlasting days
  Make all his glories known.

4 Well—the delightful day will come,
When my dear Lord will bring me home,
  And I shall see his face;
Then, with my Saviour, Brother, Friend,
A blest eternity I'll spend,
  Triumphant in his grace.

S. MEDLEY.

193

HAD I ten thousand gifts beside,
I'd cleave to Jesus crucified,
  And build on him alone;

For no foundation is there given
On which to place my hopes of heaven,
  But Christ, the corner-stone.

2 Possessing Christ, I all possess—
Wisdom, and strength, and righteousness,
  And holiness complete;
Bold in his name, I dare draw nigh
Before the Ruler of the sky,
  And all his justice meet.

3 There is no path to heavenly bliss,
To solid joy or lasting peace,
  But Christ, th' appointed road;
O may we tread the sacred way,
By faith rejoice, and praise, and pray,
  Till we sit down with God.

CHATHAM.

194

O LORD, how happy should we be,
If we could cast our care on thee;
  If we from self could rest,
And feel, at heart, that One above,
In perfect wisdom, perfect love,
  Is working for the best!

2 Help us, O Lord, to trust in thee,
And in our trials still to see
  The tokens of thy love;
Let no temptation overcome,
To lure us from the pathway home,
  To live with thee above.

J. ANSTICE.

BREMEN. C. P. M.   THOS. HASTINGS.

O love di-vine, how sweet thou art! When shall I find my wan-dering heart All

taken up in thee? {O may I dai-ly live to prove } The love of Christ to me!
{The sweetness of redeeming love, }

195

O LOVE divine, how sweet thou art!
When shall I find my wandering heart
　All taken up in thee?
O may I daily live to prove
The sweetness of redeeming love,
　The love of Christ to me!

2 God only knows the love of God;
O may it now be shed abroad
　To cheer my fainting heart!
I want to feel that love divine;
This heavenly portion, Lord, be mine—
　Be mine this better part.

3 O that I could forever sit
With Mary at the Master's feet!
　Be this my happy choice:
My only care, delight, and bliss,
My joy, my heaven on earth, be this,
　To hear the Bridegroom's voice.

4 O that I might with happy John,
Recline my weary head upon
　The blest Redeemer's breast!
From care, and fear, and sorrow free,
Give me, O Lord, to find in thee
　My everlasting rest.
                          CHARLES WESLEY.

196

COME join, ye saints, with heart and voice,
Alone in Jesus to rejoice,
　And worship at his feet;

Come, take his praises on your tongues,
And raise to him your thankful songs—
　"In him ye are complete."

2 In him, who all our praise excels,
The fullness of the Godhead dwells,
　And all perfections meet;
The head of all celestial powers,
Divinely theirs, divinely ours—
　"In him ye are complete."

3 Still onward urge your heavenly way;
Dependent on him day by day,
　His presence still entreat;
His precious name forever bless,
Your glory, strength, and righteousness—
　"In him ye are complete."
                                    ANON.

197

BE it my only wisdom here,
To serve the Lord with filial fear,
　With loving gratitude;
Superior sense may I display,
By shunning every evil way,
　And walking in the good.

2 O may I still from sin depart;
A wise and understanding heart,
　Jesus, to me be given;
And let me through thy Spirit know
To glorify my God below,
　And find my way to heaven.
                          CHARLES WESLEY.

CORONATION. C. M.   OLIVER HOLDEN.

All hail the power of Jesus' name! Let angels prostrate fall; Bring forth the royal di - a - dem,

And crown him Lord of all, Bring forth the royal di - a - dem, And crown him Lord of all.

198

ALL hail the power of Jesus' name!
  Let angels prostrate fall;
Bring forth the royal diadem,
  And crown him Lord of all.

2 Crown him, you martyrs of our God,
  Who from his altar call;
Extol the stem of Jesse's rod,
  And crown him Lord of all.

3 You chosen seed of Israel's race,
  A remnant weak and small,
Hail him who saves you by his grace,
  And crown him Lord of all.

4 You Gentile sinners, ne'er forget
  The wormwood and the gall;
Go, spread your trophies at his feet,
  And crown him Lord of all.

5 Let every kindred, every tribe,
  On this terrestrial ball,
To him all majesty ascribe,
  And crown him Lord of all.

6 O that with yonder sacred throng
  We at his feet may fall!
We'll join the everlasting song,
  And crown him Lord of all.
          EDWARD PERRONET.

MILES LANE. C. M.   WM. SHRUBSOLE.

All hail the power of Je - sus' name! Let an-gels prostrate fall; Bring forth the roy-al

di - a - dem, And crown him, crown him, crown him, crown him Lord of all.

ST. MARTIN'S. C. M.   WILLIAM TANSUR.

O for a thou - sand tongues, to sing My dear Re-deem-er's praise,

The glo-ries of my God and King, The tri - umphs of his grace!

199

O FOR a thousand tongues, to sing
My dear Redeemer's praise,
The glories of my God and King,
The triumphs of his grace!

2 My gracious Master and my God,
Assist me to proclaim,
To spread, through all the earth abroad,
The honors of thy name.

3 Jesus! the name that calms our fears,
That bids our sorrows cease—
'Tis music to my ravished ears,
'Tis life, and health, and peace.

4 He breaks the power of reigning sin;
He sets the prisoner free;
His blood can make the foulest clean:
His blood availed for me.
C. WESLEY.

200

GIVE me the wings of faith, to rise
Within the vail, and see
The saints above, how great their joys,
How bright their glories be.

2 Once they were mourning here below,
And poured out cries and tears;
They wrestled hard, as we do now,
With sins, and doubts, and fears.

3 I ask them whence their victory came;
They, with united breath,
Ascribe their conquest to the Lamb,
Their triumph to his death.

4 They marked the footsteps that he trod;
His zeal inspired their breast;
And, following their incarnate God,
Possess the promised rest.
ISAAC WATTS.

201

To HIM that loved the sons of men,
And washed us in his blood,
To royal honors raised our heads,
And made us priests to God—

2 To him let every tongue be praise,
And every heart be love,
All grateful honors paid on earth,
And nobler songs above.

3 Behold! on flying clouds he comes;
His saints shall bless the day,
While they that pierced him sadly mourn
In anguish and dismay.

4 Thou art the First, and thou the Last;
Time centers all in thee,
Almighty Lord, who wast, and art,
And evermore shalt be!
UNKNOWN.

202

O THOU, my light, my life, my joy,
My glory and my all!
Unsent by thee, no good can come,
Nor evil can befall.

2 Such are thy schemes of providence,
And methods of thy grace,
That I may safely trust in thee
Through all this wilderness.

3 'Tis thine outstretched and powerful arm
Upholds me in the way;
And thy rich bounty well supplies
The wants of every day.

4 For such compassion, O my God,
Ten thousand thanks are due;
For such compassion I esteem
Ten thousand thanks too few.
J. MONTGOMERY.

DEVIZES. C. M.   ISAAC TUCKER.

This is the day the first ripe sheaf Be-fore the Lord was waved, And Christ, first

fruits of them that slept, Was from the dead received, Was from the dead received.

203

This is the day the first ripe sheaf
Before the Lord was waved,
And Christ, first-fruits of them that slept,
Was from the dead received.

2 He rose for them for whom he died,
That, like to him, they may
Rise when he comes, in glory great,
That ne'er shall fade away.

3 This is the day the Spirit came,
With us on earth to stay—

A Comforter, to fill our hearts
With joys that ne'er decay.

4 His comforts are the earnest sure
Of that same heavenly rest
Which Jesus entered on, when he
Was made forever blest.

5 This day the Church of Christ began,
Formed by his wondrous grace;
This day the saints in concord meet,
To join in prayer and praise.
UNKNOWN.

CHOPIN. C. M.   I. B. WOODBURY.

Within thy house, O Lord, our God, In glo-ry now ap-pear; Make this a

place of thine a-bode, And shed thy blessings here, And shed thy bless-ings here.

By permission.

204

Within thy house, O Lord, our God,
In glory now appear;
Make this a place of thine abode,
And shed thy blessings here.

2 When we thy mercy-seat surround,
Thy Spirit, Lord, impart;
And let thy gospel's joyful sound,
With power, reach every heart.

3 Here let the blind their sight obtain;
Here give the mourners rest;
Let Jesus here triumphant reign,
Enthroned in every breast.

4 Here let the voice of sacred joy
And humble prayer arise,
Till higher strains our tongues employ
In realms beyond the skies.
UNKNOWN.

HYMN AND TUNE-BOOK.

PETERBORO. C. M. — RALPH HARRISON.

Once more, my soul, the ris-ing day Sa-lutes thy wak-ing eyes;

Once more, my voice, thy trib-ute pay To him that rules the skies.

205

Once more, my soul, the rising day
Salutes thy waking eyes;
Once more, my voice, thy tribute pay
To him that rules the skies.

2 Night unto night his name repeats,
The day renews the sound,
Wide as the heavens on which he sits
To turn the seasons round.

3 'Tis he supports my mortal frame;
My tongue shall speak his praise;
My sins might rouse his wrath to flame,
But yet his wrath delays.

4 Great God, let all my hours be thine,
Whilst I enjoy the light;
Then shall my sun in smiles decline,
And bring a peaceful night.
ISAAC WATTS.

206

Arise, ye people, and adore,
Exulting strike the chord;
Let all the earth, from shore to shore,
Confess th' almighty Lord.

2 Glad shouts aloud, wide echoing round,
Th' ascending Lord proclaim;
Th' angelic choir respond the sound,
And shake creation's frame.

3 They sing of death and hell o'erthrown
In that triumphant hour;
And God exalts his conquering Son
To his right hand of power.
H. F. LYTE.

207

This is the day the Lord hath made,
He calls the hours his own;
Let heaven rejoice, let earth be glad,
And praise surround the throne.

2 To-day he rose and left the dead,
And Satan's empire fell;
To-day the saints his triumphs spread,
And all his wonders tell.

3 Hosanna to th' anointed King,
To David's holy Son;
Help us, O Lord—descend and bring
Salvation from thy throne.

4 Hosanna in the highest strains
The Church on earth can raise!
The highest heavens, in which he reigns,
Shall give him nobler praise.
ISAAC WATTS.

208

How rich thy favors, God of grace,
How various and divine!
Full as the ocean they are poured,
And bright as heaven they shine.

2 He to eternal glory calls,
And leads the wondrous way
To his own palace, where he reigns
In uncreated day.

3 The songs of everlasting years
That mercy shall attend,
Which leads, through sufferings of an hour,
To joys that never end.
PHILIP DODDRIDGE.

71

NEW CHRISTIAN

ARLINGTON. C. M.   THOMAS A. ARNE.

A - gain the Lord of light and life A - wakes the kin - dling ray,

Un - seals the eye - lids of the morn, And pours in - creas - ing day.

209

AGAIN the Lord of light and life
  Awakes the kindling ray,
Unseals the eyelids of the morn,
  And pours increasing day.

2 O what a night was that which wrapt
  The heathen world in gloom!
O what a Sun which rose this day
  Triumphant from the tomb!

3 This day be grateful homage paid,
  And loud hosannas sung;
Let gladness dwell in every heart,
  And praise on every tongue.

4 Ten thousand different lips shall join
  To hail this welcome morn,
Which scatters blessings from its wings
  To nations yet unborn.
                        ANNA L. BARBAULD.

210

WE sing the Saviour's wondrous death;
  He conquered when he fell;
'Tis finished, said his dying breath,
  And shook the gates of hell.

2 'Tis finished, our Immanuel cries;
  The dreadful work is done;
Hence shall his sovereign throne arise;
  His kingdom is begun.

3 His cross a sure foundation laid
  For glory and renown,
When through the regions of the dead
  He passed to reach the crown.
                        UNKNOWN.

211

HOSANNA to the Prince of light,
  That clothed himself in clay,
Entered the iron gates of death,
  And tore the bars away!

2 Death is no more the king of dread,
  Since our Immanuel rose;
He took the tyrant's sting away,
  And spoiled our hellish foes.

3 Raise your devotion, mortal tongues,
  To reach his blest abode;
Sweet be the accents of your songs
  To our incarnate God.

4 Bright angels, strike your loudest strings,
  Your sweetest voices raise:
Let heaven, and all created things,
  Sound our Immanuel's praise.
                        ISAAC WATTS.

212

SALVATION! O the joyful sound!
  'Tis pleasure to our ears;
A sovereign balm for every wound,
  A cordial for our fears.

2 Buried in sorrow and in sin,
  At hell's dark door we lay;
But we arise, by grace divine,
  To see a heavenly day.

3 Salvation! let the echo fly
  The spacious earth around;
While all the armies of the sky
  Conspire to raise the sound.
                        ISAAC WATTS.

72

MARLOW. C. M.   JOHN CHETHAM.

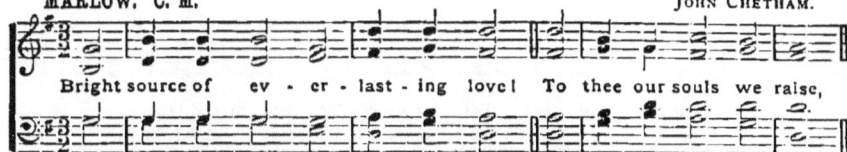

Bright source of ev - er - last - ing love! To thee our souls we raise,

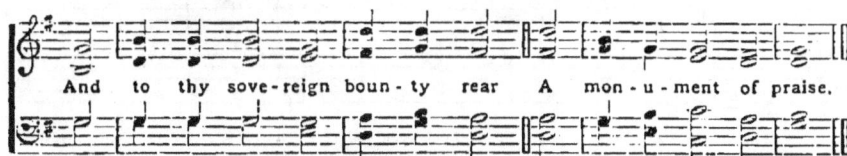

And to thy sove-reign boun - ty rear A mon-u-ment of praise.

213

BRIGHT source of everlasting love!
  To thee our souls we raise,
And to thy sovereign bounty rear
  A monument of praise.

2 Thy mercy gilds the path of life
  With every cheering ray,
Kindly restrains the rising tear,
  Or wipes that tear away.

3 To tents of woe, to beds of pain,
  We cheerfully repair,
And with the gifts thy hand bestows,
  Relieve the mourners there.

4 The widow's heart shall sing for joy;
  The orphan shall be fed;
The hungering soul we'll gladly point
  To Christ, the living Bread.
                                        JAMES BODEN.

214

THE Saviour risen to-day we praise,
  In concert with the blest;
For now we see his work complete,
  And enter into rest.

2 On this first day a brighter scene
  Of glory was displayed,
By the Creating Word, than when
  The universe was made.

3 He rises who mankind has bought
  With grief and pain extreme:
'Twas great to speak the world from naught;
  'Twas greater to redeem.

4 How vain the stone, the watch, the seal!
  Naught can forbid his rise;
'Tis he who shuts the gates of hell,
  And opens paradise.
                                        UNKNOWN.

215

BLEST morning, whose young, dawning rays
  Beheld our rising Lord;
That saw him triumph o'er the dust,
  And leave his dark abode!

2 In the cold prison of a tomb
  The great Redeemer lay,
Till the revolving skies had brought
  The third, th' appointed day.

3 Death and the grave unite their force,
  To hold our Lord, in vain;
The sleeping Captive soon awakes,
  And bursts their feeble chain.

4 To thy great name, almighty Lord,
  These sacred hours we pay;
And loud hosannas shall proclaim
  The triumph of the day.
                                        ISAAC WATTS.

216

HOW free and boundless is the grace
  Of our redeeming God,
Extending to the Greek and Jew,
  And men of every blood!

2 Come, all you wretched sinners, come:
  He'll form your souls anew;
His gospel and his heart have room
  For rebels such as you.

3 His doctrine is almighty love;
  There's virtue in his name
To turn a raven to a dove,
  A lion to a lamb.

4 Come, then, accept the offered grace,
  And make no more delay:
His love will all your guilt efface,
  And soothe your fears away.
                                        BENJ. BEDDOME.

NEW CHRISTIAN

HEBER. C. M.   GEO. KINGSLEY.

With sacred joy we lift our eyes To those bright realms a - bove,

That glo-rious tem - ple in the skies, Where dwells e - ter - nal love.

217

WITH sacred joy we lift our eyes
   To those bright realms above,
That glorious temple in the skies,
   Where dwells eternal love.

2 Before the gracious throne we bow
   Of heaven's almighty King;
Here we present the solemn vow,
   And hymns of praise we sing.

3 O Lord, while in thy house we kneel,
   With trust and holy fear,
Thy mercy and thy truth reveal,
   And lend a gracious ear.

4 With fervor teach our hearts to pray,
   And tune our lips to sing;
Nor from thy presence cast away
   The sacrifice we bring.
                     ISAAC WATTS.

BRADFORD. C. M.   HANDEL.

I know that my Re - deem - er lives, And ev - er prays for me;

A to - ken of his love he gives, A pledge of lib - er - ty.

218

I KNOW that my Redeemer lives,
   And ever prays for me;
A token of his love he gives,
   A pledge of liberty.

2 I find him lifting up my head;
   He brings salvation near:
His presence makes me free indeed,
   And he will soon appear.

3 He wills that I should holy be—
   Shall I withstand his will?
The counsel of his grace in me
   He surely shall fulfill.

4 Jesus, I hang upon thy word;
   I steadfastly believe
Thou wilt return, and claim me, Lord,
   And to thyself receive.
                    CHARLES WESLEY.

WARWICK. C. M. SAMUEL STANLEY.

To our Re - deem-er's glo-rious name A - wake the sa - cred song;

O may his love (im - mor - tal flame!) Tune ev - ery heart and tongue.

219

To our Redeemer's glorious name
Awake the sacred song;
O may his love (immortal flame!)
Tune every heart and tongue.

2 His love, what mortal thought can reach,
What mortal tongue display!
Imagination's utmost stretch
In wonder dies away.

3 He left his radiant throne on high,
Left the bright realms of bliss,
And came to earth to bleed and die!
Was ever love like this?

4 Blest Lord, while we adoring pay
Our humble thanks to thee,
May every heart with rapture say,
"The Saviour died for me."

5 O may the sweet, the blissful theme
Fill every heart and tongue,
Till strangers love thy charming name,
And join the sacred song.
HARRIET B. STEELE.

220

O God, my heart is fully bent
To magnify thy name;
My tongue, with cheerful songs of praise,
Shall celebrate thy fame.

2 To all the listening tribes, O Lord,
Thy wonders I will tell;
And to those nations sing thy praise
That round about us dwell;

3 Because thy mercy's boundless height
The highest heaven transcends;
And far beyond th' aspiring clouds
Thy faithful truth extends.

4 Be thou, O God, exalted high
Above the starry frame;
And let the world, with one consent,
Confess thy glorious name.
TATE AND BRADY.

221

BEHOLD, the mountain of the Lord
In latter days shall rise
On mountain tops, above the hills,
And draw the wondering eyes.

2 To this the joyful nations round,
All tribes and tongues, shall flow;
"Up to the hill of God," they'll say,
"And to his house we'll go."

3 The beam that shines from Zion's hill
Shall lighten every land;
The King who reigns in Salem's towers
Shall all the world command.

4 No strife shall vex Messiah's reign,
Or mar the peaceful years;
To plowshares men shall beat their swords,
To pruning-hooks their spears.

5 No longer hosts, encountering hosts,
Their millions slain deplore;
They hang the trumpet in the hall,
And study war no more.
M. BRUCE.

NEW CHRISTIAN

HENRY. C. M.   SYLVANUS B. POND.

Be-hold the glo - ries of the Lamb A-midst his Fa - ther's throne!

Pre-pare new hon - ors for his name, And songs be-fore un-known.

222

BEHOLD the glories of the Lamb
  Amidst his Father's throne!
Prepare new honors for his name,
  And songs before unknown.

2 Let elders worship at his feet,
  The Church adore around,
With vials full of odors sweet,
  And harps of sweeter sound.

3 Now to the Lamb that once was slain
  Be endless blessings paid!
Salvation, glory, joy remain
  Forever on thy head!

4 Thou hast redeemed our souls with blood,
  Hast set the prisoners free;
Hast made us kings and priests to God,
  And we shall reign with thee.
ISAAC WATTS.

223

ALMIGHTY Father, gracious Lord,
  Kind Guardian of my days,
Thy mercies let my heart record,
  In songs of grateful praise.

2 In life's first dawn, my tender frame
  Was thine indulgent care,
Long ere I could pronounce thy name,
  Or breathe the infant prayer.

3 Each rolling year new favors brought
  From thine exhaustless store—
But, ah! in vain my laboring thought
  Would count thy mercies o'er.

4 Still I adore thee, gracious Lord,
  For favors more divine:
That I have known thy sacred word
  Where all thy glories shine.
ANNE STEELE.

CHESTERFIELD. C. M.   THOMAS HAWEIS.

Sing, all ye ransomed of the Lord, Your great De - liv - erer sing;

Ye pil-grims, now for Zi - on bound, Be joy - ful in your King.

DEDHAM. C. M.

WILLIAM GARDINER.

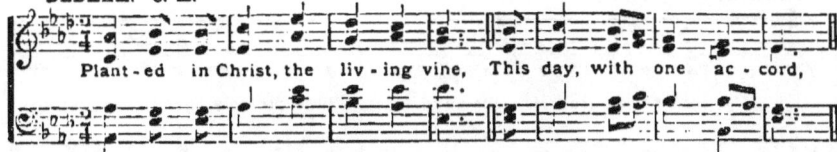

Plant-ed in Christ, the liv-ing vine, This day, with one ac-cord,

Ourselves, with hum-ble faith and joy, We yield to thee, O Lord.

224

PLANTED in Christ, the living vine,
This day, with one accord,
Ourselves, with humble faith and joy,
We yield to thee, O Lord.

2 Joined in one body may we be;
One inward life partake;
One be our heart; one heavenly hope
In every bosom wake.

3 In prayer, in effort, tears, and toils,
One wisdom be our guide;
Taught by one Spirit from above,
In thee may we abide.

4 Then, when among the saints in light
Our joyful spirits shine,
Shall anthems of immortal praise,
O Lamb of God, be thine.
                              S. F. SMITH.

225

SING, all ye ransomed of the Lord,
Your great Deliverer sing;
Ye pilgrims, now for Zion bound,
Be joyful in your King.

2 His hand divine shall lead you on,
Through all the blissful road,
Till to the sacred mount you rise,
And see your gracious God.

3 Bright garlands of immortal joy
Shall bloom on every head;
While sorrow, sighing, and distress,
Like shadows, all are fled.

4 March on in your Redeemer's strength,
Pursue his footsteps still;
And let the prospect cheer your eye
While laboring up the hill.
                          PHILIP DODDRIDGE.

226

COME, let us join in songs of praise
To our ascended Priest;
He entered heaven with all our names
Engraven on his breast.

2 On earth he washed our guilt away
By his atoning blood;
Now he appears before the throne,
And pleads our cause with God.

3 Clothed with our nature still, he knows
The weakness of our frame,
And how to shield us from the foes
Which he himself o'ercame.

4 O may we ne'er forget his grace,
Nor blush to wear his name!
Still may our hearts hold fast his faith,
Our lips his praise proclaim!
                          ALEXANDER PIRIE.

227

AGAIN our earthly cares we leave,
And to thy courts repair;
Again with joyful feet we come
To meet our Saviour here.

2 Within these walls let holy peace,
And love and concord dwell;
Here give the troubled conscience ease,
The wounded spirit heal.

3 The feeling heart, the melting eye,
The humble mind, bestow;
And shine upon us from on high,
To make our graces grow.

4 In faith may we receive thy word,
In faith present our prayers,
And in the presence of our Lord
Unbosom all our cares.
                              J. NEWTON.

NEW CHRISTIAN

CHELMSFORD. C. M. AARON CHAPIN.

E - ter - nal Source of life and light, Su - premely good and wise,

To thee we bring our grateful vows, To thee lift up our eyes.

228

ETERNAL Source of life and light,
  Supremely good and wise,
To thee we bring our grateful vows,
  To thee lift up our eyes.

2 Our dark and erring minds illume
  With truth's celestial rays;
Inspire our hearts with sacred love,
  And tune our lips to praise.

3 Safely conduct us, by thy grace,
  Through life's perplexing road;
And place us, when that journey's o'er,
  At thy right hand, O God.
                         PHILIP DODDRIDGE.

229

How happy is the Christian's state!
  His sins are all forgiven;
A cheering ray confirms the grace,
  And lifts his hopes to heaven.

2 Though in the rugged path of life
  He heaves the pensive sigh,
Yet, trusting in his God, he finds
  Delivering grace is nigh.

3 If, to prevent his wandering steps,
  He feels the chastening rod,
The gentle stroke shall bring him back
  To his forgiving God.

4 And when the welcome message comes
  To call his soul away,
His soul in raptures shall ascend
  To everlasting day.
                         UNKNOWN.

230

WHAT shall I render to my God
  For all his kindness shown?
My feet shall visit thine abode,
  My songs address thy throne.

2 Among the saints who fill thy house,
  My offering shall be paid;
There shall my zeal perform the vows
  My soul, in anguish, made.

3 How happy all thy servants are!
  How great thy grace to me!
My life, which thou hast made thy care,
  Lord, I devote to thee.

4 Now I am thine, forever thine;
  Nor shall my purpose move;
Thy hand hath loosed my bonds of pain,
  And bound me with thy love.

5 Here, in thy courts, I leave my vow,
  And thy rich grace record;
Witness, ye saints, who hear me now,
  If I forsake the Lord.
                         I. WATTS.

231

O HOW divine, how sweet the joy,
  When but one sinner turns,
And, with a humble, broken heart,
  His sins and errors mourns!

2 Pleased with the news, the saints below
  In songs their tongues employ;
Beyond the skies the tidings go,
  And heaven is filled with joy.

78

3 Well pleased the Father sees, and hears
  The contrite sinner's moan;
Jesus receives him in his arms,
  And claims him for his own;

4 Nor angels can their joy contain,
  But kindle with new fire;
"The sinner lost is found," they sing,
  And strike the sounding lyre.
                    JOHN NEEDHAM.

232

My soul, how lovely is the place
  To which thy God resorts!
'Tis heaven to see his smiling face,
  Though in his earthly courts.

2 There the great Monarch of the skies
  His saving power displays,
And light breaks in upon our eyes
  With kind and quickening rays.

3 There, mighty God, thy words declare
  The secrets of thy will;
And still we seek thy mercy there,
  And sing thy praises still.
                    ISAAC WATTS.

233

Blest be the dear, uniting love,
  That will not let us part;
Our bodies may far off remove,
  We still are one in heart.

2 Joined in one Spirit to our Head,
  Where he appoints, we go;
And still in Jesus' footsteps tread,
  And show his praise below.

3 Partakers of the Saviour's grace,
  The same in mind and heart,
Nor joy, nor grief, nor time, nor place,
  Nor life, nor death, can part.
                    CHARLES WESLEY.

234

"Proclaim," saith Christ, "my wondrous
  To all the sons of men;   [grace
He that believes, and is baptized,
  Salvation shall obtain."

2 Let plenteous grace descend on those
  Who, hoping in thy word,
This day have publicly declared
  That Jesus is their Lord.

3 With cheerful feet may they advance,
  And run the Christian race,
And, through the troubles of the way,
  Find all-sufficient grace.
                    JAS. NEWTON.

235

Let every mortal ear attend,
  And every heart rejoice;
The trumpet of the gospel sounds
  With an inviting voice.

2 Ho! all you hungry, starving souls,
  Who feed upon the wind,
And vainly strive with earthly toys
  To fill an empty mind,

3 Eternal wisdom has prepared
  A soul-reviving feast,
And bids your longing appetites
  The rich provision taste.

4 Ho! you that pant for living streams,
  And pine away and die,
Here may you quench your raging thirst
  From springs that never dry.

5 Rivers of love and mercy here
  In a rich ocean join;
Salvation in abundance flows,
  Like floods of milk and wine.

6 Great God, the treasures of thy love
  Are everlasting mines;
Deep as our helpless miseries are,
  And boundless as our sins.
                    ISAAC WATTS.

236

And now, my soul, another year
  Of thy short life is past;
I can not long continue here,
  And this may be my last.

2 Much of my hasty life is gone,
  Nor will return again;
And swift my passing moments run
  The few that yet remain.

3 Awake, my soul; with utmost care
  Thy true condition learn:
What are thy hopes? how sure? how fair?
  What is thy great concern?

4 Behold, another year begins:
  Set out afresh for heaven;
Seek pardon for thy former sins,
  In Christ so freely given;

5 Devoutly yield thyself to God,
  And on his grace depend;
With zeal pursue the heavenly road,
  Nor doubt a happy end.
                    UNKNOWN.

79

MEAR. C. M.   AARON WILLIAMS.

O God of Beth-el, by whose hand Thy peo - ple still are fed,

Who through this wea - ry pil - grim - age Hast all our fa - thers led!

237

O GOD of Bethel, by whose hand
  Thy people still are fed,
Who through this weary pilgrimage
  Hast all our fathers led!

2 Our vows, our prayers, we now present
  Before thy throne of grace:
God of our fathers, be the God
  Of their succeeding race.

3 Through each succeeding path of life
  Our wandering footsteps guide;
Give us each day our daily bread,
  And raiment fit provide.

4 O spread thy covering wings around,
  Till all our wanderings cease,
And at our Father's loved abode
  We all arrive in peace.

5 Such blessings from thy gracious hand
  Our humble prayers implore;
And thou shalt be our chosen God,
  Our portion evermore.
                          PHILIP DODDRIDGE.

238

IN memory of the Saviour's love
  We keep the sacred feast,
Where every humble, contrite heart
  Is made a welcome guest.

2 Under his banner thus we sing
  The wonders of his love,
And thus anticipate by faith
  The heavenly feast above.
                          UNKNOWN.

239

FAITH adds new charms to earthly bliss,
  And saves us from its snares;
It yields support in all our toils,
  And softens all our cares.

2 The wounded conscience knows its power
  The healing balm to give;
That balm the saddest heart can cheer,
  And make the dying live.

3 Unvailing wide the heavenly world,
  Where endless pleasures reign,
It bids us seek our portion there,
  Nor bids us seek in vain.

4 There still unshaken would we rest
  Till this frail body dies;
And then, on faith's triumphant wing,
  To endless glory rise.
                          D. TURNER.

240

AND did the Holy and the Just,
  The Sovereign of the skies,
Stoop down to wretchedness and dust,
  That guilty man might rise?

2 Yes, the Redeemer left his throne,
  His radiant throne on high—
Surpassing mercy! love unknown!—
  To suffer, bleed, and die.

3 He took the dying rebel's place,
  And suffered in our stead;
For sinful man—O wondrous grace!—
  For sinful man he bled!
                          ANNE STEELE.

CHRISTMAS. C. M.   HANDEL.

A - wake, my soul, stretch ev-er-y nerve, And press with vig - or on; A

heavenly race demands thy zeal, And an im-mor-tal crown, And an im - mor - tal crown.

241

AWAKE, my soul, stretch every nerve,
  And press with vigor on;
A heavenly race demands thy zeal,
  And an immortal crown.

2 A cloud of witnesses around
  Hold thee in full survey;
Forget the steps already trod,
  And onward urge thy way.

3 'Tis God's all-animating voice
  That calls thee from on high;
'Tis his own hand presents the prize
  To thine aspiring eye.

4 Blest Saviour, introduced by thee,
  Have I my race begun;
And, crowned with victory, at thy feet
  I'll lay my honors down.
                          PHILIP DODDRIDGE.

242

BRIGHT was the guiding star that led,
  With mild, benignant ray,
The Gentiles to the lowly shed
  Where the Redeemer lay.

2 But, lo! a brighter, clearer light
  Now points to his abode;
It shines through sin and sorrow's night
  To guide us to our God.

3 O gladly tread the narrow path
  While light and grace are given:
Who meekly follow Christ on earth
  Shall reign with him in heaven.
                          HARRIET AUBER.

243

RISE, O my soul, pursue the path
  By ancient heroes trod;
Ambitious view those holy men
  Who lived and walked with God.

2 Though dead, they speak in reason's ear,
  And in example live;
Their faith and hope and mighty deeds
  Still fresh instruction give.

3 'Twas through the Lamb's most precious blood
  They conquered every foe;
And to his power and matchless grace
  Their crowns and honors owe.

4 Lord, may we ever keep in view
  The patterns thou hast given,
And ne'er forsake the blessèd road
  Which led them safe to heaven.
                          JOHN NEEDHAM.

244

COME, let us join, with one accord,
  In hymns around the throne;
This is the day our risen Lord
  Hath made and called his own.

2 This is the day which God hath blest,
  The brightest of the seven,
Type of the everlasting rest
  The saints enjoy in heaven.

3 Then let us in his name sing on,
  And hasten on that day
When our Redeemer shall come down,
  And shadows pass away.
                          CHARLES WESLEY.

81

AVON. C. M.

HUGH WILSON.

Great God! thy pen - e - trat - ing eye Per-vades my in-most powers;

With awe pro-found my wondering soul Falls pros - trate and a - dores.

245

GREAT God! thy penetrating eye
Pervades my inmost powers;
With awe profound my wondering soul
Falls prostrate and adores.

2 To be encompassed round with God,
The Holy and the Just,
Armed with omnipotence to save,
Or crush me to the dust—

3 O how tremendous is the thought!
Deep may it be impressed;
And may thy Spirit firmly grave
This truth within my breast.

4 Begirt with thee, my fearless soul
The gloomy vale shall tread;
And thou wilt bind th' immortal crown
Of glory on my head.
E. SCOTT.

246

LORD, lead the way the Saviour went,
By lane and cell obscure,
And let love's treasures still be spent,
Like his, upon the poor.

2 Like him, through scenes of deep distress,
Who bore the world's sad weight,
We, in their crowded loneliness,
Would seek the desolate.

3 For thou hast placed us side by side
In this wide world of ill;
And that thy followers may be tried,
The poor are with us still.

4 Mean are all offerings we can make;
Yet thou hast taught us, Lord,
If given for the Saviour's sake,
They lose not their reward.
W. CROSWELL.

CADDO. C. M.

WM. B. BRADBURY.

Now let our cheer-ful eyes sur - vey Our great High Priest a - bove,

And cel - e - brate his con - stant care And sym - pa - thet - ic love.

COOLING. C. M.

A. J. ABBEY.

O could I find, from day to day, A near-ness to my God,

Then would my hours glide sweet a-way While lean-ing on his word.

By permission.

247

O could I find, from day to day,
  A nearness to my God,
Then would my hours glide sweet away
  While leaning on his word.

2 Lord, I desire with thee to live
  Anew from day to day,
In joys the world can never give,
  Nor ever take away.

3 Blest Jesus, come and rule my heart,
  And make me wholly thine,
That I may never more depart,
  Nor grieve thy love divine.

4 Thus, till my last, expiring breath,
  Thy goodness I'll adore;
And when my frame dissolves in death,
  My soul shall love thee more.

B. CLEVELAND.

248

Now let our cheerful eyes survey
  Our great High Priest above,
And celebrate his constant care
  And sympathetic love.

2 Though raised to heaven's exalted throne,
  Where angels bow around,
And high o'er all the hosts of light,
  With matchless honors crowned—

3 The names of all his saints he bears
  Deep graven on his heart;
Nor shall the weakest Christian say
  That he has lost his part.

4 So, gracious Saviour! on my breast
  May thy dear name be worn,
A sacred ornament and guard,
  To endless ages borne.

PHILIP DODDRIDGE.

249

And can my heart aspire so high,
  To say, "My Father God!"
Lord, at thy feet I long to lie,
  And learn to kiss the rod.

2 I would submit to all thy will,
  For thou art good and wise;
Let every anxious thought be still,
  Nor one faint murmur rise.

3 Thy love can cheer the darkest gloom,
  And bid me wait serene,
Till hopes and joys immortal bloom,
  And brighten all the scene.

4 My Father! O permit my heart
  To plead her humble claim,
And ask the bliss those words impart,
  In my Redeemer's name.

ANNE STEELE.

250

O happy they who know the Lord,
  With whom he deigns to dwell!
He feeds and cheers them by his word,
  His arm supports them well.

2 To them, in each distressing hour,
  His throne of grace is near;
And when they plead his love and power,
  He stands engaged to hear.

3 His presence sweetens all our cares,
  And makes our burdens light;
A word from him dispels our fears,
  And gilds the gloom of night.

4 May we enjoy and highly prize
  These tokens of thy love,
Till thou shalt bid our spirits rise
  To worship thee above.

UNKNOWN.

NEW CHRISTIAN

WHITNEY. C. M.

Arr. by Lowell Mason.

How sweet the name of Je-sus sounds In a be-liev-er's ear! It soothes his sorrows, heals his wounds, And drives away his fear, And drives away his fear.

By permission.

251

How sweet the name of Jesus sounds
In a believer's ear!
It soothes his sorrows, heals his wounds,
And drives away his fear.

2 It makes the wounded spirit whole,
And calms the troubled breast;
'Tis manna to the hungry soul,
And to the weary, rest.

3 Jesus, my Shepherd, Guardian, Friend,
My Prophet, Priest, and King,
My Lord, my Life, my Way, my End,
Accept the praise I bring.

4 Weak is the effort of my heart,
And cold my warmest thought;
But when I see thee as thou art,
I'll praise thee as I ought.
JOHN NEWTON.

252

Our souls are in the Saviour's hand,
And he will keep them still;
And you and I shall surely stand
With him on Zion's hill.

2 Him eye to eye we there shall see,
Our face like his shall shine;
O what a glorious company,
When saints and angels join!

3 O what a joyful meeting there,
In robes of white array!
Palms in our hands we all shall bear,
And crowns that ne'er decay.

4 When we've been there ten thousand years,
Bright shining as the sun,
We've no less days to sing God's praise
Than when we first begun!
UNKNOWN.

SERENITY. C. M.

WM. V. WALLACE.

Lord, all I am is known to thee; In vain my soul would try To shun thy pres-ence, or to flee The no-tice of thine eye.

SILOAM. C. M.　　　　　　　　　　　　　　I. B. WOODBURY.

The Sav-iour bids thee watch and pray Through life's mo-ment-ous hour;

And grants the Spir-it's quickening ray To those who seek his power.

By permission.

253

THE Saviour bids thee watch and pray
　Through life's momentous hour;
And grants the Spirit's quickening ray
　To those who seek his power.

2 The Saviour bids thee watch and pray,
　Maintain a warrior's strife;
O Christian, hear his voice to-day:
　Obedience is thy life.

3 The Saviour bids thee watch and pray;
　For soon the hour will come
That calls thee from the earth away
　To thine eternal home.

4 The Saviour bids thee watch and pray;
　O hearken to his voice,
And follow where he leads the way,
　To heaven's eternal joys!
　　　　　　　　　　　　T. HASTINGS.

254

LORD, all I am is known to thee;
　In vain my soul would try
To shun thy presence, or to flee
　The notice of thine eye.

2 Thy all-observing eye surveys
　My rising and my rest,
My public walks, my private ways,
　The secrets of my breast.

3 My thoughts lie open to thee, Lord,
　Before they're formed within;
And ere my lips pronounce the word,
　Thou knowest all I mean.

4 O let thy grace surround me still,
　And like a bulwark prove,
To guard my soul from every ill,
　Secured by sovereign love.
　　　　　　　　　　　　ISAAC WATTS.

255

How shall the young secure their hearts,
　And guard their lives from sin?
Thy word the choicest rules imparts
　To keep the conscience clean.

2 'Tis like the sun, a heavenly light,
　That guides us all the day;
And, through the dangers of the night,
　A lamp to lead our way.

3 Thy precepts make us truly wise:
　We hate the sinner's road;
We hate our own vain thoughts that rise,
　But love thy law, O God!

4 Thy word is everlasting truth;
　How pure is every page!
That holy book shall guide our youth,
　And well support our age.
　　　　　　　　　　　　ISAAC WATTS.

256

IF HUMAN kindness meets return,
　And owns the grateful tie;
If tender thoughts within us burn
　To feel a friend is nigh—

2 O shall not warmer accents tell
　The gratitude we owe
To him who died our fears to quell,
　Who bore our guilt and woe?

3 While yet his anguished soul surveyed
　Those pangs he would not flee,
What love his latest words displayed—
　"Meet, and remember me!"

4 Remember thee! thy death, thy shame,
　The pangs which thou didst bear!
O memory, leave no other name
　But his recorded there!
　　　　　　　　　　　　G. T. NOEL.

NEW CHRISTIAN

BALERMA. C. M.
R. SIMPSON.

A - las! what hour - ly dan-gers rise, What snares be - set my way!

To heaven, O let me lift mine eyes, And hour - ly watch and pray.

257

ALAS! what hourly dangers rise!
 What snares beset my way!
To heaven, O let me lift mine eyes,
 And hourly watch and pray.

2 O gracious God, in whom I live,
 My feeble efforts aid ;
Help me to watch and pray and strive,
 Though trembling and afraid.

3 Increase my faith, increase my hope,
 When foes and fears prevail;
And bear my fainting spirit up,
 Or soon my strength will fail.

4 O keep me in thy heavenly way,
 And bid the tempter flee ;
And let me never, never stray
 From happiness and thee.
ANNE STEELE.

258

How oft, alas ! this wretched heart
 Has wandered from the Lord !
How oft my roving thoughts depart,
 Forgetful of his word !

2 Yet sovereign mercy calls, "Return!"
 Dear Lord, and may I come?
My vile ingratitude I mourn—
 O take the wanderer home !

3 And canst thou, wilt thou yet forgive,
 And bid my crimes remove?
And shall a pardoned rebel live
 To speak thy wondrous love?

4 Almighty grace ! thy healing power
 How glorious—how divine,
That can to life and bliss restore
 A heart so vile as mine.

5 Thy pardoning love—so free, so sweet—
 Dear Saviour, I adore ;
O keep me at thy sacred feet,
 And let me rove no more.
ANNE STEELE.

259

THOU art my hiding-place, O Lord !
 In thee I put my trust,
Encouraged by thy holy word,
 A feeble child of dust.

2 I have no argument beside,
 I urge no other plea—
And 'tis enough—the Saviour died,
 The Saviour died for me.

3 When storms of fierce temptation beat,
 And furious foes assail,
My refuge is the mercy-seat,
 My hope within the vail.

4 And when thy awful voice commands
 This body to decay,
And life, in its last lingering sands,
 Is ebbing fast away—

5 Then, though it be in accents weak,
 My voice shall call on thee,
And ask for strength in death to speak,
 "My Saviour died for me."
THOS. RAFFLES.

260

ASHAMED of Christ! Our souls disdain
The mean, ungenerous thought:
Shall we disown that Friend whose blood
To man salvation brought?

2 With the glad news of love and peace,
From heaven to earth he came;
For us endured the painful cross,
For us despised the shame.

3 To his command let us submit
Ourselves without delay;
Our lives—yea, thousand lives of ours—
His love can ne'er repay.

4 To bear his name—his cross to bear—
Our highest honor this!
Who nobly suffers for him now,
Shall reign with him in bliss.
UNKNOWN.

261

COME, humble sinner, in whose breast
A thousand thoughts revolve;
Come, with your guilt and fear oppressed,
And make this last resolve:

2 I'll go to Jesus, though my sin
Has like a mountain rose;
His kingdom now I'll enter in,
Whatever may oppose.

3 Humbly I'll bow at his command,
And there my guilt confess;
I'll own I am a wretch undone,
Without his sovereign grace.

4 Surely he will accept my plea,
For he has bid me come;
Forthwith I'll rise, and to him flee,
For yet, he says, there's room.

5 I can not perish if I go;
I am resolved to try;
For if I stay away, I know
I must forever die.
E. JONES.

262

FATHER, I wait before thy throne;
Call me a child of thine,
And let the Spirit of thy Son
Fill this poor heart of mine.

2 There shed thy promised love abroad,
And make my comfort strong;
Then shall I say, my Father, God!
With an unwavering tongue.
ISAAC WATTS.

263

LORD, at thy table we behold
The wonders of thy grace;
But, most of all, admire that we
Should find a welcome place.

2 What strange, surprising grace is this,
That we, so lost, have room?
Jesus our weary souls invites,
And freely bids us come!

3 Ye saints below, and hosts of heaven,
Join all your sacred powers:
No theme is like redeeming love;
No Saviour is like ours.
JOSEPH STENNETT.

264

BURIED beneath the yielding wave,
The great Redeemer lies;
Faith views him in the watery grave,
And thence beholds him rise.

2 And thus do willing souls, to-day,
Their ardent zeal express,
And, in the Lord's appointed way,
Fulfill all righteousness.

3 With joy we in his footsteps tread,
And would his cause maintain;
Like him be numbered with the dead,
And with him rise and reign.

4 Now we, blest Saviour, would to thee
Our grateful voices raise;
Washed in the fountain of thy blood,
Our lives shall be thy praise.
BENJ. BEDDOME.

265

WHEN languor and disease invade
This trembling house of clay,
'Tis sweet to look beyond my pains,
And long to fly away;

2 Sweet to look inward, and attend
The whispers of his love;
Sweet to look upward to the place
Where Jesus pleads above;

3 Sweet to look back and see my name
In life's fair book set down;
Sweet to look forward, and behold
Eternal joys my own;

4 Sweet to rejoice in lively hope
That when my change shall come,
Angels shall hover round my bed,
And waft my spirit home.
A. M. TOPLADY.

CLARENDON. C. M.   ISAAC TUCKER.

There is an hour of hallowed peace For those with care op-pressed,

When sighs and sor-rowing tears shall cease, And all be hushed to rest.

266

THERE is an hour of hallowed peace
  For those with care oppressed,
When sighs and sorrowing tears shall cease,
  And all be hushed to rest.

2 'Tis then the soul is freed from fears
  And doubts which here annoy;
Then they that oft had sown in tears
  Shall reap again in joy.

3 There is a home of sweet repose,
  Where storms assail no more;
The stream of endless pleasure flows
  On that celestial shore.

4 There purity with love appears,
  And bliss without alloy;
There they that oft had sown in tears
  Shall reap again in joy.
                              W. B. TAPPAN.

267

How happy every child of grace,
  Who knows his sins forgiven!
This earth, he cries, is not my place—
  I seek my home in heaven.

2 A country far from mortal sight,
  Yet O, by faith, I see
The land of rest, the saints' delight,
  The heaven prepared for me.

3 O what a blessèd hope is ours!
  While here on earth we stay,
We more than taste the heavenly powers,
  And antedate that day.

4 We feel the resurrection near,
  Our life in Christ concealed,
And with his glorious presence here,
  Our earthen vessels filled.
                              CHARLES WESLEY.

PENIEL. C. M.   THOS. HASTINGS.

My God, the spring of all my joys, The life of my de-lights,

The glo-ry of my bright-est days, And com-fort of my nights!

PRAYER. C. M.

T. J. COOK.

O for a heart to praise my God, A heart from sin set free;

A heart that al-ways feels the blood So free-ly shed for me;

268

O FOR a heart to praise my God,
A heart from sin set free;
A heart that always feels the blood
So freely shed for me;

2 A heart resigned, submissive, meek,
My great Redeemer's throne—
Where only Christ is heard to speak,
Where Jesus reigns alone!

3 O for a lowly, contrite heart,
Confiding, true, and clean,
Which neither life nor death can part
From him that dwells within;

4 A heart in every thought renewed,
And full of love divine,
Perfect and right, and pure and good,
A copy, Lord, of thine!

5 Thy Spirit, gracious Lord, impart;
Direct me from above;
May thy dear name be near my heart—
That dear, best name is Love.
WM. COWPER.

269

My GOD, the spring of all my joys,
The life of my delights,
The glory of my brightest days,
The comfort of my nights!

2 In darkest shades, if thou appear,
My dawning is begun;
Thou art my soul's bright morning star,
And thou my rising sun.

3 The opening heavens around me shine
With beams of sacred bliss,
While Jesus shows his mercy mine,
And whispers, "I am his."

4 My soul would leave this heavy clay
At that transporting word,
And run with joy the shining way,
To meet my dearest Lord.
ISAAC WATTS.

270

WITH joy we meditate the grace
Of our High Priest above;
His heart is full of tenderness,
His bosom glows with love.

2 Touched with a sympathy within,
He knows our feeble frame;
He knows what sore temptations mean,
For he has felt the same.

3 He, in the days of feeble flesh,
Poured out his cries and tears;
And in his measure feels afresh
What every member bears.

4 Then let our humble faith address
His mercy and his power;
We shall obtain delivering grace
In each distressing hour.
ISAAC WATTS.

271

O FATHER, though the anxious fear
May cloud to-morrow's way,
No fear nor doubt shall enter here;
All shall be thine to-day.

2 We will not bring divided hearts
To worship at thy shrine;
But each unworthy thought departs,
And leaves this temple thine.

3 Sleep, sleep to-day, tormenting cares,
Of earth and folly born;
Ye shall not dim the light that streams
From this celestial morn.
MRS. A. L. BARBAULD.

8

NEW CHRISTIAN

WOODSTOCK. C. M.   D. DUTTON.

I love to steal a-while a-way From ev-ery cum-bering care,

And spend the hours of set-ting day In hum-ble, grate-ful prayer.

272

I LOVE to steal awhile away
  From every cumbering care,
And spend the hours of setting day
  In humble, grateful prayer.

2 I love in solitude to shed
  The penitential tear;
And all his promises to plead,
  Where none but God can hear.

3 I love to think on mercies past,
  And future good implore,
And all my cares and sorrows cast
  On him whom I adore.

4 I love, by faith, to take a view
  Of brighter scenes in heaven;
The prospect doth my strength renew,
  While here by tempests driven.
MRS. P. H. BROWN.

OAKSVILLE. C. M.   H. C. ZEUNER.

O for a faith that will not shrink, Tho' pressed by ev - ery foe;

That will not trem-ble on the brink Of a - ny earth-ly woe;

273

O FOR a faith that will not shrink,
  Though pressed by every foe;
That will not tremble on the brink
  Of any earthly woe;

2 That will not murmur or complain
  Beneath the chastening rod,
But, in the hour of grief or pain,
  Will lean upon its God;

3 A faith that shines more bright and clear
  When tempests rage without;
That, when in danger, knows no fear,
  In darkness, feels no doubt!

4 Lord, give us such a faith as this;
  And then, whate'er may come,
We'll taste, e'en here, the hallowed bliss
  Of an eternal home.
W. H. BALHURST.

MANOAH. C. M.   HAYDN.

Help us, O Lord, thy yoke to wear, De-light-ing in thy will;

Each oth-er's bur-dens learn to bear; The law of love ful-fill.

274

HELP us, O Lord, thy yoke to wear,
  Delighting in thy will;
Each other's burdens learn to bear;
  The law of love fulfill.

2 He that hath pity on the poor
  Doth lend unto the Lord;
And, lo! his recompense is sure,
  For more shall be restored.

3 To thee our all devoted be,
  In whom we move and live;
Freely we have received from thee,
  And freely may we give.

4 And while we thus obey thy word,
  And every want relieve,
O may we find it, gracious Lord,
  More blest than to receive.
                        T. COTTERILL.

275

O FOR a closer walk with God,
  A calm and heavenly frame,
A light to shine upon the road
  That leads me to the Lamb!

2 Where is the blessedness I knew
  When first I saw the Lord?
Where is the soul-refreshing view
  Of Jesus and his word?

3 What peaceful hours I once enjoyed!
  How sweet their memory still!
But they have left an aching void
  The world can never fill.

4 Return, O holy Dove, return,
  Sweet messenger of rest!
I hate the sins that made thee mourn,
  And drove thee from my breast.
                        WM. COWPER.

276

O THOU who driest the mourner's tear,
  How dark this world would be,
If, when deceived and wounded here,
  We could not fly to thee!

2 But thou wilt heal the broken heart
  Which, like the plants that throw
Their fragrance from the wounded part,
  Breathes sweetness out of woe.

3 When joy no longer soothes or cheers,
  And e'en the hope that threw
A moment's sparkle o'er our tears
  Is dimmed and vanished too—

4 Then sorrow, touched by thee, grows bright
  With more than rapture's ray;
The darkness shows us worlds of light
  We never saw by day.
                        THOS. MOORE.

277

HOSANNA to our conquering King!
  All hail, incarnate Love!
Ten thousand songs and glories wait
  To crown thy head above.

2 Thy victories and thy deathless fame
  Through all the world shall run,
And everlasting ages sing
  The triumphs thou hast won.
                        ISAAC WATTS.

NEW CHRISTIAN

ARCADIA. C. M.   THOS. HASTINGS.

Fa-ther of mer-cies, God of love, My Fa-ther and my God, I'll sing the
hon-ors of thy name, And spread thy praise abroad, And spread thy praise a-broad.

278

FATHER of mercies, God of love,
  My Father and my God,
I'll sing the honors of thy name,
  And spread thy praise abroad.

2 In every period of my life
  Thy thoughts of love appear;
Thy mercies gild each transient scene,
  And crown each passing year.

3 In all thy mercies, may my soul
  A Father's bounty see;
Nor let the gifts thy grace bestows
  Estrange my heart from thee.
                           O. HEGINBOTHAM.

279

IN EVERY trouble, sharp and strong,
  My soul to Jesus flies;
My anchor-hold is firm in him
  When swelling billows rise.

2 His comforts bear my spirit up:
  I trust a faithful God;
The sure foundation of my hope
  Is in a Saviour's blood.

3 Loud hallelujahs sing, my soul,
  To thy Redeemer's name;
In joy and sorrow, life and death,
  His love is still the same.
                             UNKNOWN.

ADULLAM. C. M.   P. H. DAVHOFF.

Dark was the night, and cold the ground On which the Lord was laid;
His sweat, like drops of blood, ran down; In ag-o-ny he prayed:

280

DARK was the night, and cold the ground
  On which the Lord was laid;
His sweat, like drops of blood, ran down;
  In agony he prayed:

2 "Father, remove this bitter cup,
  If such thy sacred will;
If not, content to drink it up,
  Thy pleasure I fulfill."

3 Go to the garden, sinner; see
  Those precious drops that flow,
The heavy load he bore for thee—
  For thee he lies so low.

4 Then learn of him the cross to bear;
  Thy Father's will obey;
And when temptations press thee near,
  Awake to watch and pray.
                             UNKNOWN.

CHIMES. C. M.   LOWELL MASON.

What grace, O Lord, and beau-ty shone A-round thy steps be-low!

What pa-tient love was seen in all Thy life and death of woe!

281

WHAT grace, O Lord, and beauty shone
  Around thy steps below!
What patient love was seen in all
  Thy life and death of woe!

2 For, ever on thy burdened heart
  A weight of sorrow hung;
Yet no ungentle, murmuring word
  Escaped thy silent tongue.

3 Thy foes might hate, despise, revile,
  Thy friends unfaithful prove;
Unwearied in forgiveness still,
  Thy heart could only love.

4 O give us hearts to love like thee;
  Like thee, O Lord, to grieve
Far more for others' sins than all
  The wrongs that we receive.

5 One with thyself, may every eye,
  In us, thy brethren, see
The gentleness and grace that spring
  From union, Lord, with thee.
        EDWARD DENNY.

282

THE Saviour! O what endless charms
  Dwell in the blissful sound!
Its influence every fear disarms,
  And spreads sweet peace around.

2 Here pardon, life, and joys divine
  In rich profusion flow,
For guilty rebels, lost in sin,
  And doomed to endless woe.

3 Th' almighty Former of the skies
  Stooped to our vile abode,
While angels viewed with wondering eyes,
  And hailed th' incarnate God.

4 O the rich depths of love divine;
  Of bliss, a boundless store!
Blest Saviour, let me call thee mine;
  I can not wish for more.
        ANNE STEELE.

283

Do NOT I love thee, O my Lord?
  Behold my heart, and see;
And turn the dearest idol out
  That dares to rival thee.

2 Is not thy name melodious still
  To mine attentive ear?
Doth not each pulse with pleasure bound,
  My Saviour's voice to hear?

3 Hast thou a lamb in all thy flock
  I would disdain to feed?
Hast thou a foe, before whose face
  I fear thy cause to plead?

4 Would not my heart pour forth its blood
  In honor of thy name,
And challenge the cold hand of death
  To damp th' immortal flame?

5 Thou knowest that I love thee, Lord;
  But, O, I long to soar
Far from the sphere of mortal joys,
  And learn to love thee more.
        P. DODDRIDGE.

GOULD. C. M.

J. E. GOULD.

Come, let us join our cheerful songs With an-gels round the throne;

Ten thousand thousand are their tongues, But all their joys are one.

284

COME, let us join our cheerful songs
  With angels round the throne;
Ten thousand thousand are their tongues,
  But all their joys are one.

2 "Worthy the Lamb that died," they cry,
  "To be exalted thus!"
"Worthy the Lamb," our lips reply,
  "For he was slain for us!"

3 Jesus is worthy to receive
  Honor and power divine;
And blessings more than we can give,
  Be, Lord, forever thine.

4 The whole creation join in one
  To bless the sacred name
Of him that sits upon the throne,
  And to adore the Lamb.

ISAAC WATTS.

285

THOU art the Way: to thee alone
  From sin and death we flee;
And he who would the Father seek,
  Must seek him, Lord, by thee.

2 Thou art the Truth: thy word alone
  True wisdom can impart;
Thou, only, canst inform the mind,
  And purify the heart.

3 Thou art the Life: the rending tomb
  Proclaims thy conquering arm;
And those who put their trust in thee,
  Nor death nor hell shall harm.

4 Thou art the Way, the Truth, the Life:
  Grant us that way to know,
That truth to keep, that life to win,
  Whose joys eternal flow.

GEORGE W. DOANE.

ALLHALLOWS. C. M.

SAMUEL WEBBE.

Thou art the Way: to thee a - lone From sin and death we flee;

And he who would the Fa-ther seek, Must seek him, Lord, by thee.

EVAN. C. M.　　　　　　　　　　　　　Arr. by H. W. HAVERGAL.

Ap-proach, my soul, the mer-cy-seat, Where Je-sus an-swers prayer;

There humbly fall be-fore his feet, For none can per-ish there.

286

APPROACH, my soul, the mercy-seat,
　Where Jesus answers prayer;
There humbly fall before his feet,
　For none can perish there.

2 Thy promise is my only plea,
　With this I venture nigh;
Thou callest burdened souls to thee,
　And such, O Lord, am I.

3 Bowed down beneath a load of sin,
　By Satan sorely pressed—
By war without, and fear within—
　I come to thee for rest.

4 Be thou my shield and hiding-place,
　That, sheltered near thy side,
I may my fierce accuser face,
　And tell him thou hast died.

5 O wondrous love, to bleed and die,
　To bear the cross and shame,
That guilty sinners, such as I,
　Might plead thy gracious name!
　　　　　　　　　　　　JOHN NEWTON.

287

GLORY to God, who deigns to bless
　This consecrated day,
Unfolds his wondrous promises,
　And makes it sweet to pray!

2 Glory to God, who deigns to hear
　The humblest sigh we raise,
And answers every heartfelt prayer,
　And hears our hymn of praise.
　　　　　　　　　　　　UNKNOWN.

288

FATHER of mercies, in thy word
　What endless glory shines!
Forever be thy name adored
　For these celestial lines.

2 Here may the wretched sons of want
　Exhaustless riches find—
Riches above what earth can grant,
　And lasting as the mind.

3 Here springs of consolation rise
　To cheer the fainting mind,
And thirsty souls receive supplies,
　And sweet refreshment find.

4 O may these heavenly pages be
　My ever dear delight;
And still new beauties may I see,
　And still increasing light.
　　　　　　　　　　　　ANNE STEELE.

289

MERCY alone can meet my case:
　For mercy, Lord, I cry;
Jesus, Redeemer, show thy face
　In mercy, or I die.

2 I perish, and my doom were just;
　But wilt thou leave me? No.
I hold thee fast, my hope, my trust;
　I will not let thee go.

3 To thee, thee only will I cleave;
　Thy word is all my plea—
That word is truth, and I believe;
　Have mercy, Lord, on me.
　　　　　　　　　　　　J. MONTGOMERY.

95

EDGEWORTH. C. M.　　　　　　　　　　　　　　　Thos. Hastings.

My Fa-ther, to thy mer-cy-seat My soul for shel-ter flies; 'Tis

here I find a safe retreat When storms and tempests rise, When storms and tempests rise.

290

My Father, to thy mercy-seat,
　My soul for shelter flies;
'Tis here I find a safe retreat
　When storms and tempests rise.

2 My cheerful hope can never die,
　If thou, my God, art near;
Thy grace can raise my comforts high,
　And banish every fear.

3 My great Protector and my Lord,
　Thy constant aid impart;
O let thy kind, thy gracious word
　Sustain my trembling heart.

4 O never let my soul remove
　From this divine retreat;
Still let me trust thy power and love,
　And dwell beneath thy feet.
　　　　　　　　　　ANNE STEELE.

291

My God, my Father—blissful name!—
　O may I call thee mine?
May I with sweet assurance claim
　A portion so divine?

2 This only can my fears control,
　And bid my sorrows fly:
What harm can ever reach my soul
　Beneath my Father's eye?

3 Whate'er thy providence denies,
　I calmly would resign;
For thou art good and just and wise;
　O bend my will to thine.

4 Whate'er thy sacred will ordains,
　O give me strength to bear;
And let me know my Father reigns,
　And trust his tender care.
　　　　　　　　　　ANNE STEELE.

GROTON. C. M.　　　　　　　　　　　　　　　H. C. Zeuner.

Plunged in a gulf of dark de-spair, We wretched sin-ners lay,

With-out one cheer-ful beam of hope, Or spark of glimmering day.

AZMON. C. M.

C. G. GLASER.

Come, you that love the Saviour's name, And joy to make it known,

The Sovereign of your hearts proclaim, And bow be-fore his throne.

292

COME, you that love the Saviour's name,
And joy to make it known,
The Sovereign of your hearts proclaim,
And bow before his throne.

2 Behold your King, your Saviour, crowned
With glories all divine;
And tell the wondering nations round
How bright these glories shine.

3 Infinite power and boundless grace
In him unite their rays;
You that have seen his lovely face,
Can you forbear his praise?

4 When in the earthly courts we view
The beauties of our King,
We long to love as angels do,
And wish like them to sing.

5 And shall we long and wish in vain?
Lord, teach our songs to rise!
Thy love can animate our strain,
And bid it reach the skies.
ANNE STEELE.

293

PLUNGED in a gulf of dark despair,
We wretched sinners lay,
Without one cheerful beam of hope,
Or spark of glimmering day.

2 With pitying eyes, the Prince of grace
Beheld our helpless grief;
He saw, and—O, amazing love!—
He ran to our relief.

3 Down from the shining seats above,
With joyful haste he fled;
Entered the grave in mortal flesh,
And dwelt among the dead.

4 O for this love let rocks and hills
Their lasting silence break,
And all harmonious human tongues
The Saviour's praises speak.

5 Angels, assist our mighty joys;
Strike all your harps of gold;
But, when you raise your highest notes,
His love can ne'er be told.
ISAAC WATTS.

294

YE wretched, hungry, starving poor,
Behold a royal feast;
Where mercy spreads her bounteous store
For every humble guest.

2 See, Jesus stands with open arms;
He calls, he bids you come.
Guilt holds you back, and fear alarms;
But see, there yet is room—

3 Room in the Saviour's bleeding heart:
There love and pity meet,
Nor will he bid the soul depart
That trembles at his feet.

4 And yet ten thousand thousand more
Are welcome still to come.
Ye longing souls, the grace adore;
Approach—there yet is room.
ANNE STEELE.

9

BURLINGTON. C. M.   J. F. BURROWES.

Since I can read my ti - tle clear To mansions in the skies,

I bid fare-well to ev-ery fear, And wipe my weep-ing eyes.

295

SINCE I can read my title clear
    To mansions in the skies,
I bid farewell to every fear,
    And wipe my weeping eyes.

2 Should earth against my soul engage,
    And fiery darts be hurled,
Then I would smile at Satan's rage,
    And face a frowning world.

3 Let cares, like a wild deluge, come,
    And storms of sorrow fall,
May I but safely reach my home,
    My God, my heaven, my all.

4 There shall I bathe my weary soul
    In seas of heavenly rest;
And not a wave of trouble roll
    Across my peaceful breast.
                              ISAAC WATTS.

296

O LAND of rest, for thee I sigh;
    When will the moment come
When I shall lay my armor by,
    And dwell in peace at home?

2 No tranquil joy on earth I know,
    No peaceful, sheltering dome;
This world's a wilderness of woe,
    This world is not my home.

3 When, by affliction sharply tried,
    I view the opening tomb,
Although I dread death's chilling tide,
    Yet still I sigh for home.

4 Weary of wandering round and round
    This vale of sin and gloom,
I long to quit th' unhallowed ground,
    And dwell with Christ at home.
                              UNKNOWN.
                              ANON.

ASPIRATION. C. M.

Since I can read my ti - tle clear To mansions in the skies, I bid farewell to

ev-ery fear, I bid farewell to ev - ery fear, And wipe my weeping eyes.

ELIZABETHTOWN. C. M. GEORGE KINGSLEY.

Thy goodness, Lord, our souls con-fess; Thy good-ness we a-dore—

A spring whose waters nev-er fail, A sea with-out a shore.

297

THY goodness, Lord, our souls confess;
  Thy goodness we adore—
A spring whose waters never fail,
  A sea without a shore.

2 Sun, moon and stars thy love attest
  In every golden ray;
Love draws the curtains of the night,
  And love brings back the day.

3 Thy bounty every season crowns
  With all the bliss it yields,
With joyful clusters loads the vines,
  With strengthening grain the fields.

4 But chiefly thy compassion, Lord,
  Is in the gospel seen;
There, like a sun, thy mercy shines,
  Without a cloud between.
                    THOS. GIBBONS.

298

O GOD, unseen, yet ever near,
  Reveal thy presence now,
While we, in love that hath no fear,
  Before thy glory bow.

2 Here may obedient spirits find
  The blessings of thy love—
The streams that through the desert wind,
  The manna from above.

3 Awhile beside the fount we stay
  And eat this bread of thine;
Then go, rejoicing, on our way,
  Renewed with strength divine.
                    UNKNOWN.

299

AS PANTS the hart for cooling streams,
  When heated in the chase,
So pants my soul, O Lord, for thee,
  And thy refreshing grace.

2 For thee, my God, the living God,
  My thirsty soul doth pine;
O when shall I behold thy face,
  Thou Majesty Divine?

3 I sigh to think of happier days,
  When thou, O Lord, wast nigh;
When every heart was tuned to praise,
  And none more blest than I.

4 Why restless, why cast down, my soul?
  Trust God, who will employ
His aid for thee, and change those sighs
  To thankful hymns of joy.
                    TATE AND BRADY.

300

ALMIGHTY Father of mankind,
  On thee my hopes remain;
And when the day of trouble comes,
  I shall not trust in vain.

2 In early years thou wast my guide,
  And of my youth the friend;
And, as my days began with thee,
  With thee my days shall end.

3 I know the Power in whom I trust,
  The arm on which I lean;
He will my Saviour ever be,
  Who hath my Saviour been.
                    MICHAEL BRUCE.

BYEFIELD. C. M.　　　　　　　　　　　　　　　　　THOS. HASTINGS.

Scorn not the slightest word or deed, Nor deem it void of power;

There's fruit in each wind-waft-ed seed, That waits its na - tal hour.

301

Scorn not the slightest word or deed,
　Nor deem it void of power;
There's fruit in each wind-wafted seed,
　That waits its natal hour.

2 A whispered word may touch the heart,
　And call it back to life;
A look of love bid sin depart,
　And still unholy strife.

3 No act falls fruitless; none can tell
　How vast its powers may be,
Nor what results infolded dwell
　Within it silently.

4 Work on, despair not; bring thy mite,
　Nor care how small it be;
God is with all that serve the right,
　The holy, true, and free.
　　　　　　　　　　　　　　UNKNOWN.
　　　　　　　　　　　　　　ANON.

PEORIA. C. M.

There's not a tint that paints the rose, Or decks the lil - y fair,

Or streaks the hum-blest flower that blows, But God has placed it there.

302

There's not a tint that paints the rose,
　Or decks the lily fair,
Or streaks the humblest flower that blows,
　But God has placed it there.

2 There's not a star whose twinkling light
　Illumes the distant earth,
And cheers the solemn gloom of night,
　But goodness gave it birth.

3 There's not a cloud whose dews distill
　Upon the parching clod,
And clothe with verdure vale and hill,
　That is not sent of God.

4 Around, beneath, below, above,
　Wherever space extends,
There heaven displays its boundless love,
　And power with goodness blends.
　　　　　　　　　　　　　　J. A. WALLACE.

BROWN. C. M.　　　　　　　　　　　　Wm. B. Bradbury.

Lord, as to thy dear cross we flee, And pray to be for-given,

So let thy life our pat-tern be, And form our souls for heaven.

By permission of Biglow & Main.

303

LORD, as to thy dear cross we flee,
　And pray to be forgiven,
So let thy life our pattern be,
　And form our souls for heaven.

2 Help us, through good report and ill,
　Our daily cross to bear;
Like thee, to do our Father's will,
　Our brother's griefs to share.

3 Let grace our selfishness expel,
　Our earthliness refine;
And kindness in our bosoms dwell,
　As free and true as thine.

4 If joy shall at thy bidding fly,
　And grief's dark day come on,
We, in our turn, would meekly cry,
　"Father, thy will be done!"

5 Kept peaceful in the midst of strife,
　Forgiving and forgiven,
O may we lead the pilgrim's life,
　And follow thee to heaven!
　　　　　　　　　　　J. H. GURNEY.

304

LORD, when my raptured thought surveys
　Creation's beauties o'er,
All nature joins to teach thy praise,
　And bid my soul adore.

2 Where'er I turn my gazing eyes,
　Thy radiant footsteps shine;
Ten thousand pleasing wonders rise,
　And speak their source divine.

3 On me thy providence hath shone
　With gentle, smiling rays;
O let my lips and life make known
　Thy goodness and thy praise.

4 All-bounteous Lord, thy grace impart;
　O teach me to improve
Thy gifts, with ever-grateful heart,
　And crown them with thy love!
　　　　　　　　　　　ANNE STEELE.

305

How sweet, how heavenly is the sight,
　When those that love the Lord
In one another's peace delight,
　And so fulfill the word;

2 When each can feel his brother's sigh,
　And with him bear a part;
When sorrow flows from eye to eye,
　And joy from heart to heart;

3 When, free from envy, scorn, and pride,
　Our wishes all above,
Each can his brother's failings hide,
　And show a brother's love;

4 When love in one delightful stream
　Through every bosom flows;
When union sweet and dear esteem
　In every action glows!

5 Love is the golden chain that binds
　The happy souls above;
And he's an heir of heaven who finds
　His bosom glow with love.
　　　　　　　　　　　J. SWAIN.

CHESTER. C. M.

Thos. Hastings.

Thou art our Shepherd, glo-rious God! Thy lit-tle flock be - hold, And guide us

by thy staff and rod, The chil-dren of thy fold, The children of thy fold.

306

Thou art our Shepherd, glorious God!
Thy little flock behold,
And guide us by thy staff and rod,
The children of thy fold.

2 We praise thy name that we were brought
To this delightful place,
Where we are watched and warned and taught,
The children of thy grace.

3 May all our friends, thy servants here,
Meet with us all above,
And we and they in heaven appear,
The children of thy love.

UNKNOWN.

307

Unshaken as the sacred hill,
And fixed as mountains be,
Firm as a rock the soul shall rest,
That leans, O Lord, on thee.

2 Not walls nor hills could guard so well
Old Salem's happy ground,
As those eternal arms of love
That every saint surround.

3 Deal gently, Lord, with souls sincere,
And lead them safely on
To the bright gates of Paradise,
Where Christ, their Lord, is gone.

ISAAC WATTS.

HAYDN. C. M.

HAYDN.

Un - shak-en as the sa-cred hill, And fixed as mountains be,

Firm as a rock the soul shall rest, That leans, O Lord, on thee.

EDMESTON. C. M.   ANON.

Je - sus, in thy trans-port-ing name, What bliss-ful glo - ries rise—

Je - sus, the an - gels' sweetest theme, The won - der of the skies!

308

Jesus, in thy transporting name,
  What blissful glories rise—
Jesus, the angels' sweetest theme,
  The wonder of the skies!

2 Well might the skies with wonder view
  A love so strange as thine;
No thought of angels ever knew
  Compassion so divine.

3 Jesus, and didst thou leave the sky
  To bear our sins and woes?
And didst thou bleed and groan and die,
  For vile, rebellious foes?

4 Victorious love! can language tell
  The wonders of thy power,
Which conquered all the force of hell
  In that tremendous hour!

5 What glad return can I impart
  For favors so divine?
O take this heart, this worthless heart,
  And make it only thine!
      ANNE STEELE.

309

Thou art my portion, O my God;
  Soon as I know thy way,
My heart makes haste t' obey thy word,
  And suffers no delay.

2 I choose the path of heavenly truth,
  And glory in my choice;
Not all the riches of the earth
  Could make me so rejoice.

3 The testimonies of thy grace
  I set before mine eyes;
Thence I derive my daily strength,
  And there my comfort lies.

4 If once I wander from thy path,
  I think upon my ways,
Then turn my feet to thy command,
  And trust thy pardoning grace.

5 Now I am thine, forever thine;
  O save thy servant, Lord!
Thou art my shield, my hiding-place;
  My hope is in thy word.
      ISAAC WATTS.

310

Our blest Redeemer, ere he breathed
  His tender, last farewell,
A Guide, a Comforter bequeathed,
  With us on earth to dwell.

2 He came in tongues of living flame,
  To teach, convince, subdue;
All powerful as the wind he came,
  And all as viewless, too.

3 He came, sweet influence to impart,
  A gracious, willing Guest,
While he can find one humble heart
  Wherein to fix his rest.

4 Spirit of purity and grace,
  Our weakness, pitying, see;
O make our hearts thy dwelling-place,
  Purer and worthier thee!
      HARRIET AUBER.

NEW CHRISTIAN

ORTONVILLE. C. M.   Thos. Hastings.

Ma-jes-tic sweetness sits enthroned Up-on the Saviour's brow; His head with radiant

glories crowned, His lips with grace o'er - flow, His lips with grace o'er-flow.

311
MAJESTIC sweetness sits enthroned
  Upon the Saviour's brow;
His head with radiant glories crowned,
  His lips with grace o'erflow.

2 No mortal can with him compare
  Among the sons of men;
Fairer is he than all the fair
  Who fill the heavenly train.

3 He saw me plunged in deep distress,
  And flew to my relief;
For me he bore the shameful cross,
  And carried all my grief.

4 To him I owe my life and breath,
  And all the joys I have;
He makes me triumph over death,
  And saves me from the grave.

5 To heaven, the place of his abode,
  He brings my weary feet;
Shows me the glories of my God,
  And makes my joys complete.

6 Since from thy bounty I receive
  Such proofs of love divine,
Had I a thousand hearts to give,
  Lord, they should all be thine.
                              S. STENNETT.

312
WITH joy we own thy servant, Lord,
  Thy minister below,
Ordained to spread thy truth abroad,
  That all thy name may know.

2 O may he now, and ever, keep
  His eye intent on thee;
Do thou, great Shepherd of the sheep,
  His bright example be.

3 With plenteous grace his heart prepare
  To execute thy will;
And give him patience, love, and care,
  And faithfulness and skill.

4 As showers refresh the thirsty plain,
  So let his labors prove;
By him extend thy righteous reign—
  The reign of truth and love.
                              J. MONTGOMERY.

313
O FOR an overcoming faith,
  To cheer my dying hours;
To triumph o'er approaching death,
  And all his frightful powers!

2 Joyful, with all the strength I have,
  My quivering lip should sing,—
"Where is thy boasted victory, grave?
  And where, O death, thy sting?"

3 If sin be pardoned, I'm secure—
  Death has no sting beside:
The law gives sin its fatal power;
  But Christ, my ransom, died.

4 Now to the God of vic-to-ry
  Immortal thanks be paid,
Who makes us conquerors while we die,
  Through Christ, our living Head.
                              ISAAC WATTS.

104

314

BEHOLD the Saviour of mankind
  Nailed to the shameful tree !
How vast the love that him inclined
  To bleed and die for me !

2 Hark ! how he groans, while nature shakes,
    And earth's strong pillars bend !
  The temple's vail asunder breaks,
    The solid marbles rend.

3 "'Tis finished !" now the ransom's paid,
    "Receive my soul !" he cries ;
  See how he bows his sacred head ;
    He bows his head and dies !

4 But soon from death he'll rise again,
    And in full glory shine ;
  O Lamb of God, was ever pain,
    Was ever love like thine?
                              S. WESLEY.

315

ALL as God wills, who wisely heeds
  To give or to withhold,
And knoweth more of all my needs
  Than all my prayers have told.

2 Enough that blessings undeserved
    Have marked my erring track ;
  That, whereso'er my feet have swerved,
    His chastening turned me back ;

3 That more and more a Providence
    Of love is understood,
  Making the springs of time and sense
    Sweet with eternal good ;

4 That death seems but a covered way
    Which opens into light,
  Wherein no blinded child can stray
    Beyond the Father's sight.
                              J. G. WHITTIER.

316

BLEST is the man whose softening heart
  Feels all another's pain,
To whom the supplicating eye
  Was never raised in vain ;

2 Whose breast expands with generous warmth,
    A stranger's woes to feel ;
  And bleeds in pity o'er the wound
    He wants the power to heal.

3 He spreads his kind supporting arms
    To every child of grief ;
  His sacred bounty largely flows,
    And brings unasked relief.

4 To gentle offices of love
    His feet are never slow ;
  He views, through mercy's melting eye,
    A brother in a foe.

5 Peace from the bosom of his God
    The Saviour's grace shall give ;
  And when he kneels before the throne,
    His trembling soul shall live.
                          MRS. A. L. BARBAULD.

317

FATHER, I know thy ways are just,
  Although to me unknown ;
O grant me grace thy love to trust,
  And cry, "Thy will be done !"

2 If thou shouldst hedge with thorns my path,
    Should wealth and friends be gone,
  Still, with a firm and lively faith,
    I'll cry, "Thy will be done !"

3 Although thy steps I can not trace,
    Thy sovereign right I'll own ;
  And, as instructed by thy grace,
    I'll cry, " Thy will be done ! "
                          PERCY CHAPEL COLL.

MERTON. C. M.   JAS. P. JEWSON.

Fa - ther, I know thy ways are just, Al-though to me unknown;

O grant me grace thy love to trust, And cry, "Thy will be done!"

DOWNS. C. M.   LOWELL MASON.

There is a name I love to hear, I love to speak its worth;

It sounds like mu - sic in mine ear— The sweetest name on earth.

318

THERE is a name I love to hear,
  I love to speak its worth;
It sounds like music in mine ear—
  The sweetest name on earth.

2 It tells me of a Saviour's love,
  Who died to set me free;
It tells me of his precious blood,
  The sinner's perfect plea.

3 Jesus! the name I love so well,
  The name I love to hear!
No saint on earth its worth can tell,
  No heart conceive how dear.

4 This name shall shed its fragrance still
  Along this thorny road;
Shall sweetly smooth the rugged hill
  That leads me up to God.
               FREDERICK WHITFIELD.

319

How sweet to be allowed to pray
  To God, the Holy One,
With filial love and trust to say,
  O God, thy will be done!

2 We in these sacred words can find
  A cure for every ill;
They calm and soothe the troubled mind,
  And bid all care be still.

3 O could my heart thus ever pray,
  Thus imitate thy Son!
Teach me, O God, with truth to say,
  Thy will, not mine, be done.
               UNKNOWN.

320

THINK gently of the erring one:
  O let us not forget,
However darkly stained by sin,
  He is our brother yet;

2 Heir of the same inheritance,
  Child of the self-same God,
He hath but stumbled in the path
  We have in weakness trod.

3 Speak gently to the erring ones:
  We yet may lead them back,
With holy words and tones of love,
  From misery's thorny track.

4 Forget not, brother, thou hast sinned,
  And sinful yet may be;
Deal gently with the erring heart,
  As God hath dealt with thee.
              MISS E. FLETCHER.

321

MAKE channels for the streams of love,
  Where they may broadly run;
And love has overflowing streams,
  To fill them every one.

2 But if at any time we cease
  Such channels to provide,
The very founts of love for us
  Will soon be parched and dried.

3 For we must share, if we would keep
  That blessing from above;
Ceasing to give, we cease to have:
  Such is the law of love.
              FRENCH.

NAOMI. C. M.   H. G. NAGELI.

Fa - ther, what-e'er of earth-ly bliss Thy sovereign will de - nies,

Ac - cept- ed at thy throne of grace, Let this pe - ti - tion rise:

322

Father, whate'er of earthly bliss
 Thy sovereign will denies,
Accepted at thy throne of grace,
 Let this petition rise:

2 Give me a calm, a thankful heart,
 From every murmur free;
The blessings of thy grace impart,
 And make me live to thee;

3 Let the sweet hope that thou art mine
 My life and death attend;
Thy presence through my journey shine,
 And crown my journey's end.
                            ANNE STEELE.

323

Jesus, I love thy charming name;
 'Tis music to my ear;
Fain would I sound it out so loud
 That all the earth might hear.

2 Yes, thou art precious to my soul,
 My transport and my trust;
Jewels to thee are gaudy toys,
 And gold is sordid dust.

3 All that my ardent soul can wish,
 In thee doth richly meet;
Nor to my eyes is light so dear,
 Nor friendship half so sweet.

4 Thy grace shall dwell upon my heart,
 And shed its fragrance there—
The noblest balm of all its wounds,
 The cordial of its care.
                        PHILIP DODDRIDGE.

324

Lord, in whose might the Saviour trod
 The dark and stormy wave,
And trusted in his Father's arm,
 Omnipotent to save,

2 When thickly round our footsteps rise
 The floods and storms of life,
Grant us thy Spirit, Lord, to still
 The dark and fearful strife.

3 Strong in our trust, on thee reposed,
 The ocean path we'll dare,
Though waves around us rage and foam,
 Since thou art present there.
                        L. S. BULFINCH.

325

She loved her Saviour, and to him
 Her costliest present brought;
To crown his head, or grace his name,
 No gift too rare, she thought.

2 So let the Saviour be adored,
 And not the poor despised;
Give to the hungry from your hoard,
 But all, give all to Christ.

3 Go, clothe the naked, lead the blind,
 Give to the weary rest;
For sorrow's children comfort find,
 And help for all distressed.

4 But give to Christ alone thy heart,
 Thy faith, thy love supreme;
Then for his sake thine alms impart,
 And so give all to him.
                        W. CUTTER.

CORINTH. C. M. LOWELL MASON.

A - maz-ing grace! how sweet the sound That saved a wretch like me!

I once was lost, but now am found; Was blind, but now I see.

By permission.

326

AMAZING grace! how sweet the sound
That saved a wretch like me!
I once was lost, but now am found;
Was blind, but now I see.

2 Through many dangers, toils, and snares
I have already come;
'Tis grace has brought me safe thus far,
And grace will lead me home.

3 The Lord has promised good to me,
His word my hope secures;
He will my shield and portion be
As long as life endures.

4 Yes, when this heart and flesh shall fail,
And mortal life shall cease,
I shall possess, within the vail,
A life of joy and peace.
JOHN NEWTON.

327

HAPPY the home, when God is there,
And love fills every breast;
Where one their wish, and one their prayer,
And one their heavenly rest.

2 Happy the home, where Jesus' name
Is sweet to every ear;
Where children early lisp his fame,
And parents hold him dear.

3 Happy the home where prayer is heard,
And praise is wont to rise;
Where parents love the sacred word,
And live but for the skies.

4 Lord, let us in our homes agree
This blessèd peace to gain;
Unite our hearts in love to thee,
And love to all will reign.
UNKNOWN.

328

WHEN blooming youth is snatched away
By death's resistless hand,
Our hearts the mournful tribute pay
Which pity must demand.

2 While pity prompts the rising sigh,
O may this truth, impressed
With awful power, "I, too, must die,"
Sink deep in every breast.

3 Let this vain world engage no more;
Behold the opening tomb:
It bids us seize the present hour,
To-morrow death may come.

4 O let us fly, to Jesus fly,
Whose powerful arm can save;
Then shall our hopes ascend on high,
And triumph o'er the grave.
ANNE STEELE.

329

VOUCHSAFE, O Lord, thy presence now;
Direct us in thy fear;
Before thy throne we humbly bow,
And offer fervent prayer.

2 Give us the men whom thou shalt choose
Thy house on earth to guide;
Those who shall ne'er their power abuse,
Or rule with haughty pride.

3 Inspired with wisdom from above,
And with discretion blest,
Displaying meekness, temperance, love,
Of every grace possessed—

4 These are the men we seek of thee,
O God of righteousness!
Such may thy servants ever be;
With such thy people bless.
G. B. IDE.

108

WOODLAND. C. M. 5 l. N. D. GOULD.

There is an hour of peaceful rest To mourning wanderers given; There is a tear for

souls distressed, A balm for ev-ery wounded breast; 'Tis found above—in heaven.

330

THERE is an hour of peaceful rest
  To mourning wanderers given;
There is a tear for souls distressed,
A balm for every wounded breast;
  'Tis found above—in heaven.

2 There is a home for weary souls,
  By sins and sorrows driven,
When tossed on life's tempestuous shoals,
Where storms arise and ocean rolls,
  And all is drear—but heaven.

3 There faith lifts up the tearless eye,
  The heart with anguish riven;
It views the tempest passing by,
Sees evening shadows quickly fly,
  And all serene in heaven.

4 There fragrant flowers immortal bloom,
  And joys supreme are given;
There rays divine disperse the gloom;
Beyond the dark and narrow tomb
  Appears the dawn of heaven.

W. B. TAPPAN.

GOING HOME. C. M., with Chorus. A. D. FILLMORE.

Jerusa-lem, my happy home, O how I long for thee! When will my sorrows have an end?

Chorus.

Thy joys, when shall I see? We're going home, we're going home, We're going home, to live forever.

331

JERUSALEM, my happy home,
  O how I long for thee!
When will my sorrows have an end?
  Thy joys, when shall I see?—CHO.

2 Thy walls are all of precious stones,
  Most glorious to behold;
Thy gates are richly set with pearl,
  Thy streets are paved with gold.—CHO.

3 Thy gardens and thy pleasant greens
  My study long have been—

Such sparkling gems by human sight
  Have never yet been seen.—CHO.

4 If heaven be thus glorious, Lord,
  Why should I stay from thence?
What folly 'tis that I should dread
  To die and go from hence!—CHO.

5 Reach down, reach down thine arms of grace,
  And cause me to ascend
Where congregations ne'er break up,
  And praises never end.—CHO.

UNKNOWN.

VARINA. C. M. D.   Arr. by G. F. ROOT.

{ There is a land of pure delight, Where saints immortal reign; } There everlasting spring abides,
{ In-finite day excludes the night, And pleasures banish pain. }

And never-withering flowers; Death, like a narrow sea, divides This heavenly land from ours.

332

THERE is a land of pure delight,
  Where saints immortal reign;
Infinite day excludes the night,
  And pleasures banish pain.
There everlasting spring abides,
  And never-withering flowers;
Death, like a narrow sea, divides
  This heavenly land from ours.

2 Sweet fields, beyond the swelling flood
  Stand dressed in living green;
So to the Jews old Canaan stood,
  While Jordan rolled between.
But timorous mortals start and shrink
  To cross this narrow sea,
And linger, shivering, on the brink,
  And fear to launch away.

3 O could we make our doubts remove,
  Those gloomy doubts that rise,
And see the Canaan that we love,
  With unbeclouded eyes—
Could we but climb where Moses stood,
  And view the landscape o'er,
Not Jordan's stream, nor death's cold flood,
  Should fright us from the shore.
                                ISAAC WATTS.

333

HAIL, sweetest, dearest tie, that binds
  Our glowing hearts in one!
Hail, sacred hope, that tunes our minds,
  To harmony divine!
REF.—It is the hope, the blissful hope,
  Which Jesus' grace has given;
The hope, when days and years are past,
  We all shall meet in heaven.

2 What though the northern wintry blast
  Shall howl around our cot!
What though beneath an eastern sun
  Be cast our distant lot!
REF.—Yet still we share the blissful hope, etc.

3 From eastern shores, from northern lands,
  From western hill and plain;
From southern climes, the brother-bands
  May hope to meet again.
REF.—It is the hope, the blissful hope, etc.

4 No lingering look, nor parting sigh,
  Our future meeting knows;
There friendship beams from every eye,
  And love immortal glows.
REF.—O sacred hope! O blissful hope! etc.
                                SUTTON.

334

O GOD, unchanging fount of good,
  Thy mercy faileth not;
And yet, by man's unthankful mood,
  Thy mercy is forgot.
Thy bounty as unceasing falls,
  As falls the plenteous light;
And every blessing on us calls,
  Thy goodness to requite.

2 If mercy, too, comes as the rain,
  'Mid clouds of seeming wrath,
Yet still the ministry of pain
  A kindly mission hath.
Yea, whatsoe'er thy dealings here,
  They are in mercy given;
To fit us for a nobler sphere
  Of life, with thee, in heaven.
                                C. W. PEARSON.

BRATTLE STREET. C. M. D. I. PLEYEL.

While thee I seek, protecting Power, Be my vain wishes stilled; And may this consecrated hour
D. S. Thy mercy o'er my life has flowed:

With better hopes be filled. Thy love the power of thought bestowed:
That mer-cy I a-dore.
To thee my thoughts would soar:

335

WHILE thee I seek, protecting Power,
  Be my vain wishes stilled;
And may this consecrated hour
  With better hopes be filled.
Thy love the power of thought bestowed:
  To thee my thoughts would soar;
Thy mercy o'er my life has flowed:
  That mercy I adore.

2 In each event of life, how clear
  Thy ruling hand I see—
Each blessing to my soul more dear,
  Because conferred by thee!
In every joy that crowns my days,
  In every pain I bear,
My heart shall find delight in praise,
  Or seek relief in prayer.

3 When gladness wings my favored hour,
  Thy love my thoughts shall fill;
Resigned, when storms of sorrow lower,
  My soul shall meet thy will.
My lifted eye, without a tear,
  The gathering storm shall see;
My steadfast heart shall know no fear;
  That heart shall rest on thee.
            Miss H. M. WILLIAMS.

336

ALMIGHTY God! thy word is cast,
  Like seed, into the ground;
Now let the dew of heaven descend,
  And righteous fruits abound.
Let not the foe of Christ and man
  This holy seed remove;
But give it root in every heart,
  To bring forth fruits of love.
            J. CAWOOD.

337

FALLEN, on Zion's battle-field,
  A soldier of renown,
Armed in the panoply of God,
  In conflict cloven down!
His helmet on, his armor bright,
  His cheek unblanched with fear,
While round his head there gleamed a light,
  His dying hour to cheer.

2 Fallen, while cheering with his voice
  The sacramental host!
With banners floating on the air,
  Death found him at his post.
In life's high prime the warfare closed,
  But not ingloriously,
He fell beyond the outer wall,
  And shouted vic-to-ry!

3 Fallen, a holy man of God,
  An Israelite indeed,
A standard-bearer of the cross,
  Mighty in word and deed;
A master spirit of the age,
  A bright and burning light,
Whose beams across the firmament
  Scattered the clouds of night!

4 Fallen, as sets the sun at eve,
  To rise in splendor where
His kindred luminaries shine,
  Their heaven of bliss to share!
Beyond the stormy battle-field
  He reigns in triumph now,
Sweeping a harp of wondrous song,
  With glory on his brow.
            J. N. MAFFITT.

METROPOLIS. C. M. D.   'FROM "MODERN HARP."

Je - ru - sa - lem, my glorious home, Name ev - er dear to me!

When shall my la - bors have an end, In joy and peace and thee?
D. S. *Thy bulwarks with sal - va - tion strong, And streets of shin - ing gold?*

When shall these eyes thy heaven-built wall And pearl - ly gates be - hold;

338

JERUSALEM, my glorious home,
  Name ever dear to me!
When shall my labors have an end,
  In joy and peace and thee?
When shall these eyes thy heaven-built wall
  And pearly gates behold;
Thy bulwarks with salvation strong,
  And streets of shining gold?

2 There happier bowers than Eden's bloom,
    Nor sin nor sorrow know:
  Blest seats, thro' rude and stormy scenes
    I onward press to you.
  Why should I shrink at pain and woe,
    Or feel, at death, dismay?
  I've Canaan's goodly land in view,
    And realms of endless day.

3 Apostles, martyrs, prophets there,
    Around my Saviour stand;
  And soon my friends in Christ below
    Will join the glorious band.
  Jerusalem, my glorious home!
    My soul still pants for thee;
  Then shall my labors have an end,
    When I thy joys shall see.

UNKNOWN.

339

COME, let us join our friends above
  Who have obtained the prize,
And, on the eagle wings of love,
  To joys celestial rise.
Let saints below in concert sing
  With those to glory gone;
For all the servants of our King
  In heaven and earth are one:

2 One family—we dwell in him;
    One church—above, beneath—
  Though now divided by the stream,
    The narrow stream of death;
  One army of the living God,
    To his command we bow—
  Part of the host have crossed the flood,
    And part are crossing now.

3 E'en now to their eternal home
    Some happy spirits fly;
  And we are to the margin come,
    Expecting soon to die.
  Dear Saviour, be our constant guide;
    Then, when the word is given,
  Bid Jordan's narrow stream divide,
    And land us safe in heaven.

CHARLES WESLEY.

MERIBAH. C. P. M.   LOWELL MASON.

When thou, my righteous Judge, shalt come, To take thy ransomed people home, Shall

I among them stand? { Shall such a worthless worm as I,
{ Who sometimes am afraid to die, } Be found at thy right hand?

340

WHEN thou, my righteous Judge, shalt come,
To take thy ransomed people home,
 Shall I among them stand?
Shall such a worthless worm as I,
Who sometimes am afraid to die,
 Be found at thy right hand?

2 I love to meet thy people now,
Before thy feet with them to bow,
 Though vilest of them all;
But—can I bear the piercing thought?—
What if my name should be left out
 When thou for them shalt call?

3 O Lord, prevent it by thy grace;
Be thou my only hiding-place
 In this, th' accepted day;
Thy pardoning voice, O let me hear,
To still my unbelieving fear;
 Nor let me fall, I pray.

4 And when the final trump shall sound,
Among thy saints let me be found,
 To bow before thy face;
Then in triumphant strains I'll sing,
While heaven's resounding mansions ring
 With praise of sovereign grace.
COUNTESS OF HUNTINGTON.

341

To HIM who did salvation bring
Wake every tuneful power, and sing
 A song of sweetest praise;

His grace diffuses, as the rains
Crown nature's flowery hills and plains,
 And spreads a thousand ways.

2 Salvation is the noblest song;
O may it dwell on every tongue,
 And all repeat, Amen!
The Lord will come from heaven to earth,
To give his people second birth,
 And make them one again.

3 By faith we view him coming down,
With angels hovering all around;
 He smiles upon his saints;
He cries aloud in melting strains,
"I come to save you from your pains,
 And end your sore complaints."
UNKNOWN.

342

LORD thou hast won—at length I yield;
My heart, by mighty grace compelled,
 Surrenders all to thee:
Against thy terrors long I strove,
But who can stand against thy love?—
 Love conquers even me.

2 Now, Lord, I would be thine alone—
Come, take possession of thine own,
 For thou hast set me free;
Released from Satan's hard command,
See all my powers in waiting stand,
 To be employed by thee.
JOHN NEWTON.

10   113

CALM. C. L. M.

THOS. HASTINGS.

How calm and beautiful the morn That gilds the sacred tomb Where once the Crucified was borne,

And vailed in midnight gloom! O weep no more the Saviour slain; The Lord is risen, he lives again.

343

How calm and beautiful the morn
  That gilds the sacred tomb
Where once the Crucified was borne,
  And vailed in midnight gloom!
O weep no more the Saviour slain;
The Lord is risen, he lives again.

2 Ye mourning saints, dry every tear
  For your departed Lord;
"Behold the place—he is not here;"
  The tomb is all unbarred:
The gates of death were closed in vain;
The Lord is risen, he lives again.

3. How tranquil now the rising day!
  'Tis Jesus still appears,
A risen Lord, to chase away
  Your unbelieving fears;
O weep no more your comforts slain;
The Lord is risen, he lives again.

4 And when the shades of evening fall,
  When life's last hour draws nigh,
If Jesus shine upon the soul,
  How blissful then to die!
Since he has risen who once was slain,
Ye die in Christ to live again.

THOS. HASTINGS.

NORTHFIELD. C. M.

JEREMIAH INGALLS.

The

Lo! what a glorious sight appears To our be-liev-ing eyes!

earth and seas are passed away, And the old rolling skies,

The earth and seas are

The earth and seas are passed a-way, And the old roll-ing skies.
The earth and seas are passed away,

passed away, The earth and seas are passed away,

CAMBRIDGE. C. M. JOHN RANDALL.

With songs and hon-ors sounding loud, Ad-dress the Lord on high; O - ver the heavens he

spreads his cloud, And waters vail the sky, And waters vail the sky, And waters vail the sky.

344

WITH songs and honors sounding loud,
Address the Lord on high;
Over the heavens he spreads his cloud,
And waters vail the sky.

2 He sends his showers of blessings down,
To cheer the plains below;
He makes the grass the mountains crown,
And corn in valleys grow.

3 His steady counsels change the face
Of the declining year;
He bids the sun cut short his race,
And wintry days appear.

4 His hoary frost, his fleecy snow,
Descend and clothe the ground;
The liquid streams forbear to flow,
In icy fetters bound.

5 He sends his word, and melts the snow,
The fields no longer mourn;
He calls the warmer gales to blow,
And bids the spring return.

6 The changing wind, the flying cloud,
Obey his mighty word;
With songs and honors sounding loud,
Praise ye the sovereign Lord.
ISAAC WATTS.

345

Lo! WHAT a glorious sight appears
To our believing eyes!
The earth and seas are passed away,
And the old rolling skies.

2 From the third heaven, where God resides,
That holy, happy place,
The New Jerusalem comes down,
Adorned with shining grace.

3 Attending angels shout for joy,
And the bright armies sing:
"Mortals! behold the sacred seat
Of your descending King.

4 "The God of glory down to men
Removes his blest abode—
Men, the dear objects of his grace,
And he, the loving God.

5 "His own soft hand shall wipe the tears
From every weeping eye;
And pains and groans, and griefs and fears,
And death itself, shall die."

6 How long, dear Saviour, O how long
Shall this bright hour delay?
Fly swifter round, ye wheels of time,
And bring the welcome day!
ISAAC WATTS.

NEW CHRISTIAN

DALSTON. S. P. M.   A. WILLIAMS.

How pleased and blest was I   To hear the people cry, "Come, let us seek our God to-day!"

Yes, with a cheerful zeal,   We haste to Zion's hill, And there our vows and honors pay.

346

How pleased and blest was I,
 To hear the people cry,
"Come, let us seek our God to-day!"
 Yes, with a cheerful zeal,
 We haste to Zion's hill,
And there our vows and honors pay.

2 Zion, thrice happy place,
 Adorned with wondrous grace,
And walls of strength embrace thee round;
 In thee our tribes appear,
 To pray, and praise, and hear
The sacred gospel's joyful sound.

3 May peace attend thy gate,
 And joy within thee wait,
To bless the soul of every guest;
 The man who seeks thy peace,
 And wishes thine increase—
A thousand blessings on him rest!
                        ISAAC WATTS.

347

'Tis heaven begun below
 To hear Christ's praises flow
In Zion, where his name is known.
 What will it be above
 To sing redeeming love,
And cast our crowns before his throne!

2 O what sweet company
 We then shall hear and see!
What harmony will there abound,
 When souls unnumbered sing
 The praise of Zion's King,
Nor one dissenting voice be found!

3 Till that blest period come,
 Zion shall be our home;
And may we never thence remove,
 Till from the Church below
 To that on high we go,
And there commune in perfect love.
                        JOSEPH SWAIN.

PETERS. S. P. M.   ANON.

How pleased and blest was I   To hear the people cry, "Come, let us seek   our God to-day!"

Yes, with a cheerful zeal,   We haste to Zi-on's hill, And there our vows and hon-ors pay.

116

DIADEMATA. S. M. D.　　　　　　　　　GEORGE J. ELVEY.

Crown him with ma-ny crowns, The Lamb up-on his throne; Hark! how the heavenly

an-them drowns All mu-sic but its own! A-wake, my soul, and sing

Of him who died for thee; And hail him as thy matchless King Thro' all e-ter-ni-ty.

348

CROWN him with many crowns,
　The Lamb upon his throne;
Hark! how the heavenly anthem drowns
　All music but its own!
Awake, my soul, and sing
　Of him who died for thee;
And hail him as thy matchless King
　Through all eternity.

2 Crown him the Lord of love;
　Behold his hands and side—
Those wounds, yet visible above,
　In beauty glorified!
No angel in the sky
　Can fully bear that sight,
But downward bends his wondering eye
　At mysteries so bright.

3 Crown him the Lord of heaven,
　One with the Father known,—
And the blest Spirit through him given
　From yonder glorious throne!
All hail, Redeemer, hail!
　For thou hast died for me;
Thy praise and glory shall not fail
　Throughout eternity.
　　　　　　　M. BRIDGES.

349

BEYOND the starry skies,
　Far as th' eternal hills,
There, in the boundless world of light,
　Our great Redeemer dwells.
Around him angels fair
　In countless armies shine;
And ever, in exalted lays,
　They offer songs divine.

2 "Hail, Prince of life!" they cry,
　"Whose unexampled love
Moved thee to quit these glorious realms
　And royalties above."
And when he stooped to earth,
　And suffered rude disdain,
They cast their honors at his feet,
　And waited in his train.

3 They saw him on the cross,
　While darkness vailed the skies,
And when he burst the gates of death,
　They saw the Conqueror rise.
They thronged his chariot wheels,
　And bore him to his throne;
Then swept their golden harps and sung,
　"The glorious work is done."
　　　　　　　J. FANCH.

117

NEW CHRISTIAN

LISBON. S. M. — DANIEL READ.

Wel-come, sweet day of rest, That saw the Lord a-rise;

Welcome to this re-viv-ing breast, And these re-joic-ing eyes!

350

WELCOME, sweet day of rest,
That saw the Lord arise;
Welcome to this reviving breast,
And these rejoicing eyes!

2 The King himself comes near,
And feasts his saints to-day;
Here may we sit and see him here,
And love, and praise, and pray.

3 One day, amid the place
Where my dear Lord hath been,
Is sweeter than ten thousand days
Within the tents of sin.

4 My willing soul would stay
In such a frame as this,
And sit and sing herself away
To everlasting bliss.

ISAAC WATTS.

351

LET party names no more
The Christian world o'erspread;
Gentile and Jew, and bond and free,
Are one in Christ, their Head.

2 Among the saints on earth
Let mutual love be found;
Heirs of the same inheritance,
With mutual blessings crowned.

3 Thus will the Church below
Resemble that above,
Where streams of pleasure ever flow,
And every heart is love.

BENJ. BEDDOME.

352

COME, we who love the Lord,
And let our joys be known;
Join in a song of sweet accord,
And thus surround the throne.

2 Let those refuse to sing
Who never knew our God;
But children of the heavenly King
May speak their joys abroad.

3 The men of grace have found
Glory begun below;
Celestial fruits on earthly ground
From faith and hope may grow.

4 The hill of Zion yields
A thousand sacred sweets,
Before we reach the heavenly fields,
Or walk the golden streets.

5 Then let our songs abound,
And every tear be dry;
We're marching through Immanuel's ground
To fairer worlds on high.

ISAAC WATTS.

353

TO BLESS thy chosen race,
In mercy, Lord, incline;
And cause the brightness of thy face
On all thy saints to shine,

2 That so thy wondrous way
May through the world be known,
While distant lands their homage pay,
And thy salvation own.

TATE AND BRADY.

118

THATCHER. S. M.   HANDEL.

How hon-ored is the place Where we a-dor-ing stand—
Zi-on, the glo-ry of the earth, And beau-ty of the land!

354

How honored is the place
  Where we adoring stand—
Zion, the glory of the earth,
  And beauty of the land!

2 Bulwarks of grace defend
  The city where we dwell;
While walls, of strong salvation made,
  Defy th' assaults of hell.

3 Lift up th' eternal gates,
  The doors wide open fling;
Enter, ye nations, that obey
  The statutes of our King.

4 Here taste unmingled joys,
  And live in perfect peace,
You that have known Jehovah's name,
  And ventured on his grace.
             ISAAC WATTS.

355

BEHOLD, what wondrous grace
  The Father hath bestowed
On sinners of a mortal race,
  To call them sons of God!

2 Nor doth it yet appear
  How great we must be made;
But when we see our Saviour here,
  We shall be like our Head.

3 If in my Father's love
  I share a filial part,
His Holy Spirit, like a dove,
  Will rest within my heart!

4 We would no longer lie
  Like slaves beneath the throne;
Our faith shall Abba, Father! cry,
  And thou the kindred own.
             ISAAC WATTS.

356

MY SPIRIT on thy care,
  Blest Saviour, I recline;
Thou wilt not leave me to despair,
  For thou art love divine.

2 In thee I place my trust;
  On thee I calmly rest;
I know thee good, I know thee just,
  And count thy choice the best.

3 Whate'er events betide,
  Thy will they all perform;
Safe in thy breast my head I hide,
  Nor fear the coming storm.

4 Let good or ill befall,
  It must be good for me—
Secure of having thee in all,
  Of having all in thee.
             H. F. LYTE.

357

FOREVER here my rest,
  Close to thy bleeding side;
This all my hope, and all my plea—
  For me the Saviour died.

2 My Saviour and my God,
  Fountain for guilt and sin,
Sprinkle me ever with thy blood,
  And cleanse and keep me clean.
             CHARLES WESLEY.

NEW CHRISTIAN

SHIRLAND. S. M.

SAMUEL STANLEY.

This is the glo - rious day That our Re - deem - er made; Let

us re - joice, and sing, and pray; Let all the Church be glad.

358

THIS is the glorious day
  That our Redeemer made;
Let us rejoice, and sing, and pray,
  Let all the Church be glad.

2 The work, O Lord, is thine,
  And wondrous in our eyes;
This day declares it all divine,
  This day did Jesus rise.

3 Hosanna to the King,
  Of David's royal blood!
Bless him, you saints; he comes to bring
  Salvation from your God.

4 We bless thy Holy Word,
  Which all this grace displays,
And offer on thine altar, Lord,
  Our sacrifice of praise.
                    ISAAC WATTS.

359

SOLDIERS of Christ, arise,
  And put your armor on;
Strong in the strength which God supplies
  Through his belovéd Son.

2 Strong in the Lord of hosts,
  And in his mighty power;
Who in the strength of Jesus trusts
  Is more than con-quer-or.

3 Stand, then, in his great might,
  With all his strength endued;
But take, to arm you for the fight,
  The panoply of God.

4 Leave no unguarded place,
  No weakness of the soul,
Take every virtue, every grace,
  And fortify the whole;

5 That, having all things done,
  And all your conflicts past,
You may o'ercome, through Christ alone,
  And stand entire at last.
                    CHARLES WESLEY.

360

OUR heavenly Father calls,
  And Christ invites us near;
With both our friendship shall be sweet,
  And our communion dear.

2 God pities all our griefs;
  He pardons every day,
Almighty to protect our souls,
  And wise to guide our way.

3 How large his bounties are!
  What various stores of good,
Diffused from our Redeemer's hand,
  And purchased with his blood!

4 Jesus, our living Head,
  We bless thy faithful care;
Our Advocate before the throne,
  And our Forerunner there.

5 Here fix, my roving heart,
  Here wait, my warmest love,
Till the communion be complete,
  In nobler scenes above.
                    PHILIP DODDRIDGE.

FERGUSON. S. M.   GEO. KINGSLEY.

How charm-ing is the place Where my Re-deem-er, God,

Un-vails the beau-ties of his face, And sheds his love a-broad!

361

How charming is the place
Where my Redeemer, God,
Unvails the beauties of his face,
And sheds his love abroad!

2 Not the fair palaces
To which the great resort
Are once to be compared with this,
Where Jesus holds his court.

3 Here, on the mercy-seat,
With radiant glory crowned,
Our joyful eyes behold him sit,
And smile on all around.

4 To him their prayers and cries
Each humble soul presents;
He listens to their broken sighs,
And grants them all their wants.

5 Give me, O Lord, a place
Within thy blest abode,
Among the children of thy grace,
The servants of my God.
SAMUEL STENNETT.

362

HAD I the gift of tongues,
Great God, without thy grace,
My loudest words, my loftiest songs,
Would be but sounding brass.

2 Though thou shouldst give me skill
Each mystery to explain,
Without a heart to do thy will,
My knowledge would be vain.

3 Had I such faith in God
As mountains to remove,
No faith could work effectual good,
That did not work by love.

4 Grant, then, this one request,
Whatever be denied—
That love divine may rule my breast,
And all my actions guide.
SAMUEL STENNETT.

363

WE GIVE thee but thine own,
Whate'er the gift may be:
All that we have is thine alone,
A trust, O Lord, from thee.

2 May we thy bounties thus
As stewards true receive,
And gladly, as thou blessest us,
To thee our first-fruits give.

3 To comfort and to bless,
To find a balm for woe,
To tend the lone and fatherless,
Is angels' work below.

4 The captive to release,
To God the lost to bring,
To teach the way of life and peace—
It is a Christ-like thing.

5 And we believe thy word,
Though dim our faith may be,
Whate'er for thine we do, O Lord,
We do it unto thee.
W. W. HOW.

11   121

NEW CHRISTIAN

J. G. NAGELI.

Blest be the tie that binds Our hearts in Christian love;

The fel-low-ship of kin-dred minds Is like to that a-bove.

364

BLEST be the tie that binds
  Our hearts in Christian love;
The fellowship of kindred minds
  Is like to that above.

2 Before our Father's throne
    We pour our ardent prayers;
Our fears, our hopes, our aims are one,
    Our comforts and our cares.

3 We share our mutual woes,
    Our mutual burdens bear;
And often for each other flows
    The sympathizing tear.

4 Here we must often part,
    In sorrow and in pain;
But we shall still be joined in heart,
    And hope to meet again.

5 This glorious hope revives
    Our courage by the way;
While each in expectation lives,
    And longs to see the day.

6 From sorrow, toil, and pain,
    And sin we shall be free;
And perfect love and friendship reign
    Through all eternity.
                          JOHN FAWCETT.

365

LET men their songs employ,
  Angels their music raise,
And earth and heaven unite their joy
  To sound our Father's praise.
                          C. Q. WRIGHT.

366

How gentle God's commands!
  How kind his precepts are!
Come, cast your burdens on the Lord,
  And trust his constant care.

2 Beneath his watchful eye
    His saints securely dwell;
That hand which bears creation up,
    Shall guard his children well.

3 Why should this anxious load
    Press down your weary mind?
O seek your heavenly Father's throne,
    And peace and comfort find.

4 His goodness stands approved,
    Unchanged from day to day;
I'll drop my burden at his feet,
    And bear a song away.
                          PHILIP DODDRIDGE.

367

To GOD the only wise,
  Who keeps us by his word,
Be glory now and evermore,
  Through Jesus Christ, our Lord.

2 Hosanna to the Word,
    Who from the Father came!
Ascribe salvation to the Lord,
    And ever bless his name.

3 The grace of Christ our Lord,
    The Father's boundless love,
The Spirit's blest communion, too,
    Be with us from above.
                          ISAAC WATTS.

122

ST. THOMAS. S. M.   A. WILLIAMS.

The Lord my Shep-herd is; I shall be well sup-plied.

Since he is mine, and I am his, What can I want be-side?

368

THE Lord my Shepherd is;
  I shall be well supplied.
Since he is mine, and I am his,
  What can I want beside?

2 He leads me to the place
  Where heavenly pasture grows,
Where living waters gently pass,
  And full salvation flows.

3 If e'er I go astray,
  He doth my soul reclaim,
And guides me in his own right way,
  For his most holy name.

4 While he affords his aid,
  I can not yield to fear;
Though I should walk through death's dark shade,
  My Shepherd's with me there.
                                    ISAAC WATTS.

369

IN EVERY trying hour
  My soul to Jesus flies;
I trust in his almighty power,
  When swelling billows rise.

2 His comforts bear me up;
  I trust a faithful God;
The sure foundation of my hope
  Is in my Saviour's blood.

3 Loud hallelujahs sing
  To our Redeemer's name;
In joy or sorrow—life or death—
  His love is still the same.
                                    UNKNOWN.

370

THOU source of life and light,
  When in thy word we read
The wondrous love to mortals given,
  To save us in our need,

2 Our hearts to thee we turn,
  In gratitude and love,
That when no other power could save,
  Thy Son came from above.

3 O gracious gift of God—
  His love to manifest
To sinful man, that he may turn
  And be forever blest!

4 Our Father and our God,
  Accept our grateful praise;
Help us, that we may always live
  And walk in wisdom's ways.
                                    J. C. TULLY.

371

IN ALL my ways, O God,
  I would acknowledge thee;
And seek to keep my heart and house
  From all pollution free.

2 Where'er I have a tent,
  An altar will I raise;
And thither my oblations bring
  Of humble prayer and praise.

3 Could I my wish obtain,
  My household, Lord, should be
Devoted to thyself alone,
  A nursery for thee.
                                    UNKNOWN.

BOYLSTON. S. M.   LOWELL MASON.

Not all the blood of beasts, On Jew-ish al-tars slain,

Could give the guilt-y conscience peace, Or wash a-way its stain.

372
Not all the blood of beasts,
  On Jewish altars slain,
Could give the guilty conscience peace,
  Or wash away its stain.

2 But Christ, the heavenly Lamb,
  Bears all our sins away;
A sacrifice of nobler name
  And richer blood than they.

3 My faith would lay her hand
  On that dear head of thine,
While, like a penitent, I stand,
  And there confess my sin.

4 Believing, we rejoice
  To see the curse remove;
We bless the Lamb with cheerful voice,
  And sing his dying love.
            ISAAC WATTS.

373
Hungry, and faint, and poor,
  Behold us, Lord, again
Assembled at thy mercy's door,
  Thy bounty to obtain.

2 Thy word invites us nigh,
  Or we would starve indeed;
For we no money have to buy,
  Nor righteousness to plead.

3 The food our spirits want,
  Thy hand alone can give;
O hear the prayer of faith, and grant
  That we may eat and live!
            UNKNOWN.

374
Did Christ o'er sinners weep,
  And shall our cheeks be dry?
Let tears of penitential grief
  Flow forth from every eye.

2 The Son of God in tears
  The wondering angels see;
Be thou astonished, O my soul:
  He shed those tears for thee.

3 He wept that we might weep—
  Each sin demands a tear;
In heaven alone no sin is found,
  And there's no weeping there.
            BENJ. BEDDOME.

375
And can I yet delay
  My little all to give;
To tear my soul from earth away,
  My Saviour to receive?

2 Nay, but I yield, I yield;
  I can hold out no more;
I sink, by dying love compelled,
  And own thee Con-quer-or.

3 Though late, I all forsake;
  My friends, my all, resign;
Gracious Redeemer, take, O take,
  And seal me ever thine!

4 Come, and possess me whole,
  Nor hence again remove;
Settle and fix my wavering soul
  With all thy weight of love.
            CHARLES WESLEY.

376

I BLESS the Christ of God,
I rest on love divine,
And with unfaltering lip and heart,
I call this Saviour mine.

2 His cross dispels each doubt;
I bury in his tomb
Each thought of unbelief and fear,
Each lingering shade of gloom.

3 I praise the God of peace;
I trust his truth and might;
He calls me his, I call him mine
My God, my joy, my light.

4 'Tis he who saveth me,
And freely pardon gives:
I love because he loveth me;
I live because he lives.
H. BONAR.

377

YE SERVANTS of the Lord,
Each in his office wait;
With joy obey his heavenly word,
And watch before his gate.

2 Let all your lamps be bright,
And trim the golden flame;
Gird up your loins, as in the might
Of his most holy name.

3 Watch! 'Tis the Lord's command,
And while we speak he's near;
Mark the first signal of his hand,
And ready all appear.

4 O happy servant he,
In such a posture found!
He shall his Lord with rapture see,
And be with honor crowned.
PHILIP DODDRIDGE.

378

SEE how the rising sun
Pursues his shining way,
And wide proclaims his Maker's praise
With every brightening ray.

2 Thus would my rising soul
Its heavenly parent sing;
And to its great Original
A humble tribute bring.

3 O may I grateful use
The blessings I receive,
And ne'er in thought, or word, or deed,
His Holy Spirit grieve.
ELIZABETH SCOTT.

379

JESUS invites his saints
To meet around his board;
Here pardoned rebels sit, and hold
Communion with their Lord.

2 This holy bread and wine
Maintain our fainting breath,
By union with our living Lord,
And interest in his death.

3 Let all our powers be joined
His glorious name to raise;
Let holy love fill every mind,
And every voice be praise.
ISAAC WATTS.

380

YE MESSENGERS of Christ,
His sovereign voice obey;
Arise and follow where he leads,
And peace attend your way.

2 The Master whom you serve
Will needful strength bestow:
Depending on his promised aid,
With sacred courage go.

3 Mountains shall sink to plains,
And hell in vain oppose;
The cause is God's, and will prevail,
In spite of all his foes.

4 Go, spread a Saviour's fame,
And tell his matchless grace
To the most guilty and depraved
Of Adam's fallen race.
MRS. VOKE.

381

LORD, at this closing hour,
Establish every heart
Upon thy word of truth and power,
To keep us when we part.

2 Peace to our brethren give;
Fill all our hearts with love;
In faith and patience may we live,
And seek our rest above.

3 Through changes, bright or drear,
We would thy will pursue;
And toil to spread thy kingdom here,
Till we its glory view.

4 To God, the only wise,
In every age adored,
Let glory from the Church arise,
Through Jesus Christ our Lord!
E. T. FITCH.

LABAN. S. M. — LOWELL MASON.

A charge to keep I have, A God to glo-ri-fy,

A nev-er-dy-ing soul to save, And fit it for the sky.

382
A CHARGE to keep I have,
A God to glorify,
A never-dying soul to save,
And fit it for the sky.

2 To serve the present age,
My calling to fulfill,
O may it all my powers engage
To do my Master's will!

3 Arm me with jealous care,
As in thy sight to live;
And O thy servant, Lord, prepare
A strict account to give!

4 Help me to watch and pray,
And on thyself rely,
Assured, if I my trust betray,
I shall forever die.
CHARLES WESLEY.

383
SAVIOUR, thy law we love,
Thy pure example bless,
And with a firm, unwavering zeal,
Would in thy footsteps press.

2 Not to the fiery pains
By which the martyrs bled;
Not to the scourge, the thorn, the cross,
Our favored feet are led;

3 But at this peaceful tide,
Assembled in thy fear,
The homage of obedient hearts
We humbly offer here.
UNKNOWN.

384
MY SOUL, be on thy guard:
Ten thousand foes arise;
The hosts of sin are pressing hard
To draw thee from the skies.

2 O watch, and fight, and pray;
The battle ne'er give o'er;
Renew it boldly every day,
And help divine implore.

3 Ne'er think the victory won,
Nor lay thine armor down;
Thy arduous work will not be done
Till thou obtain thy crown.

4 Fight on, my soul, till death
Shall bring thee to thy God;
He'll take thee, at thy parting breath,
To his divine abode.
GEO. HEATH.

385
Now is th' accepted time,
Now is the day of grace;
Now, sinners, come, without delay,
And seek the Saviour's face.

2 Now is th' accepted time,
The Saviour calls to-day;
To-morrow it may be too late;
Then why should you delay?

3 Now is th' accepted time,
The gospel bids you come;
And every promise in his word
Declares there yet is room.
J. DOBELL.

126

386

In expectation sweet
  We wait, and sing, and pray,
Till Christ's triumphal car we meet,
  And see an endless day.

2 He comes! the Conqueror comes!
  Death falls beneath his sword;
The joyful prisoners burst their tombs,
  And rise to meet their Lord.

3 The trumpet sounds—Awake!
  Ye dead, to judgment come!
The pillars of creation shake,
  While hell receives her doom.

4 Thrice happy morn for those
  Who love the ways of peace;
No night of sorrow e'er shall close
  Upon its perfect bliss.
                              Jos. Swain.

387

Teach me, my God and King,
  Thy will in all to see;
And what I do in any thing,
  To do it as for thee;

2 To scorn the senses' sway,
  While still to thee I tend—
In all I do, be thou the way;
  In all, be thou the end.

3 All may of thee partake;
  Nothing so small can be
But draws, when acted for thy sake,
  Greatness and worth from thee.

4 If done beneath thy laws,
  E'en servile labors shine;
Hallowed is toil, if this the cause;
  The meanest work, divine.
                              Herbert.

388

Sow in the morn thy seed;
  At eve hold not thy hand;
To doubt and fear give thou no heed,
  Broadcast it o'er the land.

2 And duly shall appear,
  In verdure, beauty, strength,
The tender blade, the stalk, the ear,
  And the full corn at length.

3 Thou canst not toil in vain;
  Cold, heat, and moist, and dry,
Shall foster and mature the grain
  For garners in the sky.

4 Then, when the glorious end,
  The day of God, shall come,
The angel reapers shall descend,
  And heaven shout, "Harvest home!"
                              James Montgomery.

389

A parting hymn we sing
  Around thy table, Lord;
Again our grateful tribute bring,
  Our solemn vows record.

2 Here have we seen thy face,
  And felt thy presence here;
So may the savor of thy grace
  In word and life appear.

3 The purchase of thy blood—
  By sin no longer led—
The path our dear Redeemer trod,
  May we, rejoicing, tread.

4 In self-forgetting love,
  Be Christian union shown,
Until we join the Church above,
  And know as we are known.
                              A. R. Wolfe.

390

Servant of God, well done!
  Rest from thy loved employ;
The battle fought, the victory won,
  Enter thy Master's joy.

2 The voice at midnight came;
  He started up to hear:
A mortal arrow pierced his frame;
  He fell, but felt no fear.

3 Tranquil amid alarms,
  It found him on the field,
A veteran slumbering on his arms,
  Beneath his red-cross shield.

4 At midnight came the cry,
  "To meet thy God, prepare!"
He woke, and caught his Captain's eye;
  Then, strong in faith and prayer,

5 His spirit, with a bound,
  Left its encumbering clay;
His tent, at sunrise, on the ground
  A darkened ruin lay.

6 The pains of death are past;
  Labor and sorrow cease,
And, life's long warfare closed at last,
  His soul is found in peace.
                              James Montgomery.

STATE STREET. S. M.   J. C. WOODMAN.

Lord, in this sa-cred hour, With-in thy courts we bend,

And bless thy love, and own thy power, Our Fa-ther and our Friend.

391

LORD, in this sacred hour,
Within thy courts we bend,
And bless thy love, and own thy power,
Our Father and our Friend.

2 But thou art not alone
In courts by mortals trod;
Nor only is the day thine own
When man draws near to God.

3 Thy temple is the arch
Of yon unmeasured sky;
Thy Sabbath the stupendous march
Of grand eternity.

4 Lord, may that holier day
Dawn on thy servants' sight;
And purer worship may we pay
In heaven's unclouded light.
S. G. BULFINCH.

392

TO-MORROW, Lord, is thine,
Lodged in thy sovereign hand;
And if its sun arise and shine,
It shines by thy command.

2 The present moment flies,
And bears our life away;
O make thy servants truly wise,
That they may live to-day.

3 One thing demands our care;
O be it still pursued!
Lest, slighted once, the season fair
Should never be renewed.

4 To Jesus may we fly,
Swift as the morning light,
Lest life's young, golden beams should die
In sudden, endless night.
PHILIP DODDRIDGE.

SHAWMUT. S. M.   Arr. by LOWELL MASON.

How gra-cious and how wise Is our chas-tis-ing God!

And, O how rich the bless-ings are Which blos-som from his rod!

128

GORTON. S. M.   BEETHOVEN.

And is there, Lord, a rest For wea - ry souls de - signed,

Where not a care shall stir the breast, Or sor - row en - trance find ?

393

AND is there, Lord, a rest
For weary souls designed,
Where not a care shall stir the breast,
Or sorrow entrance find ?

2 Is there a blissful home,
Where kindred minds shall meet,
And live, and love, nor ever roam
From that serene retreat ?

3 Forever blessèd they
Whose joyful feet shall stand,
While endless ages waste away,
Amid that glorious land !

4 My soul would thither tend
While toilsome years are given;
Then let me, gracious Lord, ascend,
To sweet repose in heaven.
                              RAY PALMER.

394

How gracious and how wise
Is our chastising God !
And O how rich the blessings are
Which blossom from his rod !

2 He lifts it up on high,
With pity in his heart,
That every stroke his children feel
May grace and peace impart.

3 Instructed thus, they bow
And own his sovereign sway;
They turn their erring footsteps back
To his forsaken way.

4 Our Father, we consent
To discipline divine,
And bless the pain that makes our souls
Still more completely thine.
                              PHILIP DODDRIDGE.

395

"MY TIMES are in thy hand:"
My God, I wish them there ;
My life, my soul, my all, I leave
Entirely to thy care.

2 "My times are in thy hand,"
Whatever they may be,
Pleasing or painful, dark or bright,
As best may seem to thee.

3 "My times are in thy hand"—
Why should I doubt or fear ?
My Father's hand will never cause
His child a needless tear.

4 "My times are in thy hand:"
I'll always trust in thee,
Till I possess the promised land,
And all thy glory see.
                              W. F. LLOYD.

396

GIVE to the Lord thine heart ;
In him all pleasures meet ;
O come and choose the better part,
Low at the Saviour's feet.

2 Hear, and your soul shall live ;
His peace shall be your stay—
Peace which the world can never give,
Can never take away.
                              UNKNOWN.

OLMUTZ. S. M.   Arr. by LOWELL MASON.

Je - sus, I live to thee, The love - li - est and best;

My life in thee, thy life in me, In thy blest love I rest.

397
JESUS, I live to thee,
 The loveliest and best;
My life in thee, thy life in me,
 In thy blest love I rest.

2 Jesus, I die in thee,
 Whenever death shall come;
To die in thee is life to me,
 In my eternal home.

3 Whether to live or die,
 I know not which is best;
To live in thee is bliss to me,
 To die is endless rest.

4 Living or dying, Lord,
 I ask but to be thine;
My life in thee, thy life in me,
 Makes heaven forever mine.
              HENRY HARBAUGH.

398
BLEST Comforter Divine,
 Whose rays of heavenly love
Amid our gloom and darkness shine,
 And point our souls above;

2 Thou, whose inspiring breath
 Can make the cloud of care,
And e'en the gloomy vale of death,
 A smile of glory wear;

3 Thou, who dost fill the heart
 With love to all our race—
Blest Comforter, to us impart
 The blessings of thy grace.
              MRS. L. H. SIGOURNEY.

399
How tender is thy hand,
 O thou most gracious Lord!
Afflictions come at thy command,
 And leave us at thy word.

2 How gentle was the rod
 That chastened us for sin!
How soon we found a smiling God
 Where deep distress had been!

3 A Father's hand we felt,
 A Father's heart we knew:
'Mid tears of penitence we knelt,
 And found his word was true.

4 Now we will bless the Lord,
 And in his strength confide;
Forever be his name adored,
 For there is none beside.
              THOS. HASTINGS.

400
ANOTHER day is past,
 The hours forever fled,
And time is bearing me away,
 To mingle with the dead.

2 My mind in perfect peace
 My Father's care shall keep;
I yield to gentle slumber now,
 For thou canst never sleep.

3 How blessèd, Lord, are they,
 On thee securely stayed!
Nor shall they be in life alarmed,
 Nor be in death dismayed.
              UNKNOWN.

OZREM. S. M. I. B. WOODBURY.

A sweet-ly sol - emn thought Comes to me o'er and o'er;

To - day I'm near-er to my home Than e'er I've been be - fore;

By permission.

401

A SWEETLY solemn thought
 Comes to me o'er and o'er:
To-day I'm nearer to my home
 Than e'er I've been before;

2 Nearer my Father's house,
 Where many mansions be;
And nearer to the great white throne,
 Nearer the crystal sea;

3 Nearer the bound of life,
 Where falls my burden down;
Nearer to where I leave my cross,
 And where I gain my crown.

4 Saviour, confirm my trust,
 Complete my faith in thee;
And let me feel as if I stood
 Close on eternity—

5 Feel as if now my feet
 Were slipping o'er the brink;
For I may now be nearer home,
 Much nearer than I think.
 PHŒBE CARY.

402

O WHERE shall rest be found—
 Rest for the weary soul?
'Twere vain the ocean depths to sound,
 Or pierce to either pole.

2 The world can never give
 The bliss for which we sigh:
'Tis not the whole of life to live,
 Nor all of death to die.

3 Beyond this vale of tears
 There is a life above,
Unmeasured by the flight of years;
 And all that life is love.

4 There is a death, whose pang
 Outlasts the fleeting breath;
O what eternal horrors hang
 Around the second death!

5 Lord God of truth and grace,
 Teach us that death to shun,
Lest we be banished from thy face,
 And evermore undone.
 J. MONTGOMERY.

403

LORD of our highest love,
 Let now thy peace be given;
Fix all our thoughts on things above,
 Our hearts on thee in heaven.

2 And when the loaf we break,
 Thine own rich blessing give;
May all, with loving hearts, partake,
 And all new strength receive.

3 Dear Lord, what memories crowd
 Around the sacred cup:
The upper room—Gethsemane—
 Thy foes—thy lifting up!

4 O scenes of suffering love,
 Enough our souls to win;
Enough to melt our hearts, and prove
 The antidote of sin!
 G. Y. TICKLE.

131

NEW CHRISTIAN

VIGIL. S. M.   "ST. ALBAN'S TUNE-BOOK."

A - rise, ye saints, a - rise! The Lord our lead - er is:

The foe be - fore his ban - ner flies, And vic - to - ry is his.

404

ARISE, ye saints, arise!
  The Lord our leader is:
The foe before his banner flies,
  And vic-to-ry is his.

2 We soon shall see the day
  When all our toils shall cease;
When we shall cast our arms away,
  And dwell in endless peace.

3 This hope supports us here;
  It makes our burdens light;
'Twill serve our drooping hearts to cheer,
  Till faith shall end in sight:

4 Till, of the prize possessed,
  We hear of war no more;
And ever with our Leader rest,
  On yonder peaceful shore.
                        THOMAS KELLY.

405

REST for the toiling hand,
  Rest for the anxious brow,
Rest for the weary, way-worn feet,
  Rest from all labor now.

2 Soon shall the trump of God
  Give out the welcome sound
That shakes thy silent chamber-walls,
  And breaks the turf-sealed ground.

3 Ye dwellers in the dust,
  Awake! come forth and sing;
Sharp has your frost of winter been,
  But bright shall be your spring.

4 'Twas sown in weakness here;
  'Twill then be raised in power:
That which was sown an earthly seed
  Shall rise a heavenly flower.
                        H. BONAR.

406

I HAVE a home above,
  From sin and sorrow free;
A mansion which eternal love
  Designed and formed for me.

2 My Father's gracious hand
  Has built this sweet abode;
From everlasting it was planned—
  My dwelling-place with God.

3 My Saviour's precious blood
  Has made my title sure;
He passed thro' death's dark, raging flood,
  To make my rest secure.

4 The Comforter has come,
  The earnest has been given;
He leads me onward to the home
  Reserved for me in heaven.
                        H. BENNETT.

407

MY SOUL, it is thy God
  Who calls thee by his grace:
Now loose thee from each cumbering load,
  And bend thee to the race.

2 Make thy salvation sure;
  All sloth and slumber shun;
Nor dare a moment rest secure,
  Till thou the goal hast won.

3 Thy crown of life hold fast;
  Thy heart with courage stay;
Nor let one trembling glance be cast
  Along the backward way.

4 Thy path ascends the skies,
  With conquering footsteps bright;
And thou shalt win and wear the prize
  In everlasting light.
                        LEONARD SWAIN.

ELLINWOOD. S. M.

F. B. RICE.

Blest feast of love di - vine! 'Tis grace that makes us free

To feed up - on this bread and wine, In memory, Lord, of thee.

By permission.

408

BLEST feast of love divine!
'Tis grace that makes us free
To feed upon this bread and wine,
In memory, Lord, of thee.

2 That blood which flowed for sin,
In symbol here we see;
And feel the blessèd pledge within,
That we are loved of thee.

3 O if this glimpse of love
Be so divinely sweet,
What will it be, O Lord, above,
Thy gladdening smile to meet!

4 To see thee face to face,
Thy perfect likeness wear;
And all thy ways of wondrous grace
Through endless years declare!
EDWARD DENNY.

409

How various and how new
Are thy compassions, Lord!
Each morning shall thy mercies show,
Each night thy truth record.

2 Thy goodness, like the sun,
Dawned on our early days,
Ere infant reason had begun
To form our lips to praise.

3 Each object we beheld
Gave pleasure to our eyes;
And nature all our senses held
In bands of sweet surprise.

4 But pleasures more refined
Awaited that blest day
When light arose upon our mind
And chased our sins away.

5 How new thy mercies, then!
How sovereign and how free!
Our souls, that had been dead in sin,
Were made alive to thee.
JOSEPH STENNETT.

410

Go to thy rest, fair child;
Go to thy dreamless bed,
While yet so gentle, undefiled,
With blessings on thy head.

2 Before thy heart had learned
In waywardness to stray;
Before thy feet had ever turned
The dark and downward way;

3 Ere sin had seared the breast,
Or sorrow woke the tear;
Rise to thy home of changeless rest
In yon celestial sphere.

4 Because thy smile was fair,
Thy lip and eye so bright;
Because thy loving cradle-care
Was such a dear delight;

5 Shall love, with weak embrace,
Thy upward wing detain?
No! gentle angel, seek thy place
Amid the cherub train.
MRS. L. H. SIGOURNEY.

133

FOREVER WITH THE LORD. S. M. Peculiar.   I. B. WOODBURY.

"For-ev-er with the Lord!" A-men. So let it be. Life from the dead is in that word; 'Tis

im-mor-tal-i - ty. Here in the bod-y pent, Ab-sent from thee I roam; Yet nightly pitch my

moving tent A day's march nearer home, Nearer home, nearer home, A day's march nearer home.

411

"FOREVER with the Lord!"
  Amen. So let it be.
Life from the dead is in that word;
  'Tis immortality.
Here in the body pent,
  Absent from thee I roam;
Yet nightly pitch my moving tent
  A day's march nearer home, Nearer, etc.

2 My Father's house on high,
  Home of my soul, how near,
At times, to faith's aspiring eye
  Thy golden gates appear!

Ah! then my spirit pants
  To reach the land I love,
The bright inheritance of saints,
  Jerusalem above, Home above, etc.

3 Yet doubts still intervene,
  And all my comfort flies;
Like Noah's dove, I flit between
  Rough seas and stormy skies.
Anon the clouds depart,
  The winds and waters cease;
While sweetly o'er my gladdened heart
  Expands the bow of peace, Bow of, etc.
                              J. MONTGOMERY.

ST. IGNATIUS. S. M.   J. H. GAUNTLETT.

While my Re-deem-er's near, My Shep-herd and my Guide,

I bid fare-well to anx-ious fear; My wants are all sup-plied.

OLNEY. S. M.　　　　　　　　　　　　　　　　　LOWELL MASON.

The Lord, who knows full well The heart of ev - ery saint,

In - vites us all our griefs to tell; To pray, and nev - er faint.

412

THE Lord, who knows full well
　The heart of every saint,
Invites us all our griefs to tell;
　To pray, and never faint.

2 He bows his gracious ear;
　We never plead in vain,
Yet we must wait till he appear,
　And pray, and pray again.

3 The Lord will surely hear
　His chosen when they cry;
Yes, though he may awhile forbear,
　He'll help them from on high.

4 Then let us earnest be,
　And never faint in prayer;
He loves our importunity,
　And makes our cause his care.
　　　　　　　　　　WESTON.

413

WHILE my Redeemer's near,
　My Shepherd and my Guide,
I bid farewell to anxious fear;
　My wants are all supplied.

2 To ever-fragrant meads,
　Where rich abundance grows,
His gracious hand indulgent leads,
　And guards my sweet repose.

3 Dear Shepherd, if I stray,
　My wandering feet restore;
To thy fair pastures guide my way,
　And let me rove no more.

4 Unworthy, as I am,
　Of thy protecting care,
Jesus, I plead thy gracious name;
　For all my hopes are there.
　　　　　　　　　　ANNE STEELE.

414

COME to the house of prayer,
　O thou afflicted, come :
The God of peace shall meet thee there;
　He makes that house his home.

2 Come to the house of praise,
　Ye who are happy now;
In sweet accord your voices raise,
　In kindred homage bow.

3 Thou, whose benignant eye
　In mercy looks on all—
Who seest the tear of misery,
　And hear'st the mourner's call—

4 Up to thy dwelling-place
　Bear our frail spirits on,
Till they outstrip time's tardy pace,
　And heaven on earth be won.
　　　　　　　　　　E. TAYLOR.

415

ONCE more, before we part,
　O bless the Saviour's name!
Let every tongue and every heart
　Adore and praise the same.

2 Lord, in thy grace we came,
　That blessing still impart;
We met in Jesus' sacred name,
　In Jesus' name we part.

3 Still on thy holy word
　Help us to feed, and grow,
Still to go on to know the Lord,
　And practice what we know.

4 Now, Lord, before we part,
　Help us to bless thy name;
Let every tongue and every heart
　Adore and praise the same.
　　　　　　　　　　J. HART.

135

NEW CHRISTIAN

WORLEY. S. M. D. J. H. ROSECRANS.

My God, my Strength, my Hope, On thee I cast my care; With humble con-fi-

dence look up, And know thou hear'st my prayer. Give me on thee to wait, Till I can

all things do— On thee, al-might-y to cre-ate, Al-mighty to re-new.

416

My God, my Strength, my Hope,
  On thee I cast my care;
With humble confidence look up,
  And know thou hear'st my prayer.
Give me on thee to wait,
  Till I can all things do—
On thee, almighty to create,
  Almighty to renew.

2 I want a godly fear,
  A quick-discerning eye,
That looks to thee when sin is near,
  And bids the tempter fly;
A spirit still prepared,
  And armed with jealous care,
Forever standing on its guard,
  And watching unto prayer.

3 I rest upon thy word:
  The promise is for me;
My succor and salvation, Lord,
  Shall surely come from thee.
But let me still abide,
  Nor from my hope remove,
Till thou my patient spirit guide
  Into thy perfect love.
                    CHARLES WESLEY.

417

How beauteous are their feet
  Who stand on Zion's hill,
Who bring salvation on their tongues,
  And words of peace reveal!
How charming is their voice!
  How sweet the tidings are:
"Zion, behold thy Saviour King;
  He reigns and triumphs here!"

2 How happy are our ears,
  That hear this joyful sound,
Which kings and prophets waited for,
  And sought, but never found!
How blessed are our eyes,
  That see this heavenly light!
Prophets and kings desired it long,
  But died without the sight.

3 The watchmen join their voice,
  And tuneful notes employ;
Jerusalem breaks forth in songs,
  And deserts learn the joy.
The Lord makes bare his arm
  Through all the earth abroad;
Let every nation now behold
  Their Saviour and their God.
                    ISAAC WATTS.

136

BEALOTH. S. M. D.   ANON.

I love thy kingdom, Lord, The house of thine abode, The Church our blest Re-

deemer saved With his own precious blood; I love thy Church, O God, Her walls be-

fore thee stand, Dear as the ap-ple of thine eye, And graven on thy hand.

418

I LOVE thy kingdom, Lord,
  The house of thine abode,
The Church our blest Redeemer saved
  With his own precious blood;
I love thy Church, O God;
  Her walls before thee stand,
Dear as the apple of thine eye,
  And graven on thy hand.

2 For her my tears shall fall,
  For her my prayers ascend;
To her my cares and toils be given,
  Till toils and cares shall end.
Beyond my highest joy,
  I prize her heavenly ways,
Her sweet communion, solemn vows,
  Her hymns of love and praise.

3 Jesus, thou Friend divine,
  Our Saviour and our King,
Thy hand from every snare and foe
  Shall great deliverance bring.
Sure as thy truth shall last,
  To Zion shall be given
The brightest glories earth can yield,
  And brighter bliss of heaven.
                TIMOTHY DWIGHT.

419

ALL you that have confessed
  That Jesus is the Lord,
And to his people joined yourselves,
  According to his word,
In Zion you must dwell,
  Her altar ne'er forsake;
Must come to all her solemn feasts,
  Of all her joys partake.

2 She must employ your thoughts,
  And your unceasing care;
Her welfare be your constant wish,
  And her increase your prayer.
With humbleness of mind
  Among her sons rejoice—
A meek and quiet spirit is,
  With God, of highest price.

3 Never offend nor grieve
  Your brethren by the way;
But shun the dark abodes of strife,
  Like children of the day.
In all your Saviour's ways
  With willing footsteps move;
Be faithful unto death, and then
  You'll reign with him above.
                UNKNOWN.

NEW CHRISTIAN

LISCHER. H. M.   F. SCHNEIDER.

{ Welcome, delightful morn, Thou day of sa-cred rest! }
{ I hail thy kind return: Lord, make these moments blest. } From the low train of mortal toys,

I soar to reach im-mortal joys, I soar to reach im-mor-tal joys.
I soar to reach

420

WELCOME, delightful morn,
  Thou day of sacred rest!
I hail thy kind return:
  Lord, make these moments blest.
From the low train of mortal toys,
I soar to reach immortal joys.

2 Now may the King descend
  And fill his throne with grace;
The scepter, Lord, extend,
  While saints address thy face;
Let sinners feel thy quickening word,
And learn to know and fear the Lord.
                                    HAYWARD.

WYATT. H. M.   JAS. H. FILLMORE.

Awake, ye saints awake, And hail the sacred day;   Your grateful homage pay:
In loftiest songs of praise

Come bless the day that God hath blest, The type of heaven's e-ter-nal rest.
Come bless   that God

421 [First verse in the music.]

2 On this auspicious morn
  The Lord of life arose,
And burst the bars of death,
  And vanquished all our foes;
And now he pleads our cause above,
And reaps the fruit of all his love.

3 All hail, triumphant Lord!
  Heaven with hosannas rings;
And earth, in humbler strains,
  Thy praise responsive sings:
Worthy the Lamb that once was slain,
Through endless years to live and reign.
                                    THOS. COTTERILL.

138

DARWALL. H. M.   JOHN DARWALL.

Lord of the worlds above, How pleasant and how fair The dwellings of thy love, Thine earthly tem-ples, are! To thine a - bode my heart aspires, With warm desires to see my God.

422

LORD of the worlds above,
  How pleasant and how fair
The dwellings of thy love,
  Thine earthly temples are!
To thine abode my heart aspires,
With warm desires to see my God.

2 O happy souls, who pray
    Where God appoints to hear!
  O happy men, who pay
    Their constant service there!
  They praise thee still; and happy they
  Who love the way to Zion's hill.

3 They go from strength to strength,
    Through this dark vale of tears,
  Till each arrives at length,
    Till each in heaven appears:
  O glorious seat, when God, our King,
  Shall thither bring our willing feet.
                                ISAAC WATTS.

423

CHRIST is our Corner-stone;
  On him alone we build;
With his true saints alone
  The courts of heaven are filled:
On his great love our hopes we place,
Of present grace and joys above.

2 Oh, then with hymns of praise
    These hallowed courts shall ring!
  Our voices we will raise,
    The name of Christ to sing;
  And thus proclaim in joyful song,
  Both loud and long, that glorious Name.
                                J. CHANDLER, tr.

424

IN SWEET, exalted strains,
  The King of glory praise:
O'er heaven and earth he reigns,
  Through everlasting days:
Beneath this roof, O deign to show
How God can dwell with men below.

2 Here may thine ears attend
    Our interceding cries,
  And grateful praise ascend,
    All fragrant, to the skies;
  Here may thy word melodious sound,
  And spread the joys of heaven around.

3 Here may th' attentive throng
    Imbibe thy truth and love;
  And converts join the song
    Of seraphim above;
  And willing crowds surround thy board,
  With sacred joy and sweet accord.

4 Here may our unborn sons
    And daughters sound thy praise,
  And shine like polished stones
    Through long-succeeding days;
  Here, Lord, display thy saving power,
  While temples stand and men adore.
                                BENJ. FRANCIS.

425

TO GOD, the only wise;
  To Jesus Christ, his Son—
Let songs of praise arise,
  From angels round the throne;
Let men unite, in sweet accord,
To praise the goodness of the Lord.
                                L. H. JAMESON.

LENOX. H. M. *Lewis Edson.*

Blow ye the trumpet, blow—The gladly solemn sound; Let all the nations know, To earth's remotest bound,

The year of jubilee is come: Return, ye ransomed sinners, home, Return, ye ransomed sinners, home.

426

Blow ye the trumpet, blow—
 The gladly solemn sound;
Let all the nations know,
 To earth's remotest bound,
The year of jubilee is come:
Return, ye ransomed sinners, home.

2 Exalt the Lamb of God,
 The sin-atoning Lamb;
Redemption by his blood,
 Throughout the world proclaim.
The year of jubilee is come:
Return, ye ransomed sinners, home.

3 Ye slaves of sin and hell,
 Your liberty receive,
And safe in Jesus dwell,
 And blest in Jesus live.
The year of jubilee is come:
Return, ye ransomed sinners, home.

4 Jesus, our great High Priest,
 Has full atonement made:
Ye weary spirits, rest;
 Ye mourning souls, be glad.
The year of jubilee is come:
Return, ye ransomed sinners, home.
 Charles Wesley.

STOW. H. M. *Arr. by Lowell Mason.*

Yes, the Redeemer rose; The Saviour left the dead, And o'er his hellish foes High raised his

conquering head: In wild dismay, the guards a-round Fall to the ground and sink away.

140

HADDAM. H. M.   Arr. by LOWELL MASON.

Come, every pious heart, That loves the Saviour's name, Your noblest powers exert To celebrate his

fame; Tell all a-bove and all be-low The debt of love to him you owe.

427

COME, every pious heart,
  That loves the Saviour's name,
Your noblest powers exert
  To celebrate his fame;
Tell all above and all below
The debt of love to him you owe.

2 He left his starry crown,
  And laid his robes aside;
On wings of love came down,
  And wept, and bled, and died:
What he endured, O who can tell,
To save our souls from death and hell?

3 From the dark grave he rose,
  The mansion of the dead,
And thence his mighty foes
  In glorious triumph led;
Up through the sky the Conqueror rode,
And reigns on high, the Son of God.
                          SAMUEL STENNETT.

428

THE promises I sing,
  Which sovereign love hath spoke—
Nor will th' eternal King
  His words of grace revoke:
They stand secure and steadfast still;
Not Zion's hill abides so sure.

2 The mountains melt away,
  When once the Judge appears;
And sun and moon decay,
  That measure mortal years:
But still the same, in radiant lines,
The promise shines through all the flame.

3 Their harmony shall sound
  Through mine attentive ears,
When thunders cleave the ground,
  And dissipate the spheres:
Midst all the shock of that dread scene,
I stand serene, thy word my rock.
                          PHILIP DODDRIDGE.

429

YES, the Redeemer rose;
  The Saviour left the dead,
And o'er his hellish foes
  High raised his conquering head;
In wild dismay the guards around
Fall to the ground and sink away.

2 Lo! the angelic bands
  In full assembly meet,
To wait his high commands,
  And worship at his feet;
Joyful they come, and wing their way
From realms of day to Jesus' tomb.

3 Then back to heaven they fly,
  The joyful news to bear;
Hark! as they soar on high,
  What music fills the air!
Their anthems say, "Jesus who bled
Has left the dead—he rose to-day."

4 All hail! triumphant Lord,
  Who saved us by thy blood;
Wide be thy name adored,
  Thou reigning Son of God!
With thee we rise, with thee we reign,
And kingdoms gain beyond the skies.
                          PHILIP DODDRIDGE.

141

DORT. 6s & 4s. LOWELL MASON.

Sound, sound the truth abroad; Bear ye the word of God Thro' the { Tell what our Lord has done,
wide world; { Tell how the day is won,

Tell from his loft-y throne Satan is hurled.

430

SOUND, sound the truth abroad;
Bear ye the word of God
  Through the wide world;
Tell what our Lord has done,
Tell how the day is won,
Tell from his lofty throne
  Satan is hurled.

2 Far over sea and land,
Go, at your Lord's command;
  Bear ye his name—
Bear it to every shore,
Regions unknown explore,
Enter at every door:
  Silence is shame.

3 Speed on the wings of love—
Jesus, who reigns above,
  Bids us to fly—
They who his message bear
Should neither doubt nor fear;
He will their Friend appear,
  He will be nigh.

THOS. KELLY.

ITALIAN HYMN. 6s & 4s. F. GIARDINI.

Rise, glorious Leader, rise Into thy native skies—Assume thy { And where, in many a fold,
right; { The clouds are backward rolled,

Pass thro' those gates of gold, And reign in light.

431

RISE, glorious Leader, rise
Into thy native skies—
  Assume thy right;
And where, in many a fold,
The clouds are backward rolled,
Pass through those gates of gold,
  And reign in light.

2 Victor o'er death and hell,
Cherubic legions swell
  Thy radiant train;
Praises all heaven inspire;
Each angel sweeps his lyre,
And waves his wings of fire,
  Thou Lamb once slain!

3 Enter, incarnate God:
No feet but thine have trod
  The serpent down.
Blow the full trumpet—blow!
Wider your portals throw!
Saviour, triumphant go,
  And take thy crown!

M. BRIDGES.

AMERICA. 6s & 4s.　　　　　　　　　　　　　　HENRY CAREY.

My country, 'tis of thee, Sweet land of lib-er-ty, Of thee I sing; Land where my fathers died, Land of the pilgrims' pride; From ev-ery mountain side Let free-dom ring.

432

My country, 'tis of thee,
Sweet land of liberty,
　Of thee I sing;
Land where my fathers died,
Land of the pilgrims' pride:
From every mountain side
　Let freedom ring.

2 My native country, thee,
Land of the noble free—
　Thy name I love;
I love thy rocks and rills,
Thy woods and templed hills;
My heart with rapture thrills
　Like that above.

3 Let music swell the breeze,
And ring from all the trees
　Sweet freedom's song;
Let mortal tongues awake,
Let all that breathe partake,
Let rocks their silence break—
　The sound prolong.

4 Our fathers' God! to thee,
Author of liberty,
　To thee we sing:
Long may our land be bright
With freedom's holy light;
Protect us by thy might,
　Great God, our King!
　　　　　　　　　　　S. F. SMITH.

433

GOD bless our native land!
Firm may she ever stand
　Through storm and night;

When the wild tempests rave,
Ruler of wind and wave,
Do thou our country save
　By thy great might.

2 For her our prayer shall rise
To God above the skies;
　On him we wait.
Thou who art ever nigh,
Guarding with watchful eye,
To thee aloud we cry,
　God save the State!
　　　　　　　　　　　J. S. DWIGHT.

434

THE God of harvest praise;
In loud thanksgiving, raise
　Hand, heart, and voice;
The valleys smile and sing,
Forests and mountains ring,
The plains their tribute bring,
　The streams rejoice.

2 Yes, bless his holy name,
And purest thanks proclaim
　Through all the earth;
To glory in your lot
Is duty—but be not
God's benefits forgot,
　Amidst your mirth.

3 The God of harvest praise;
Hands, hearts, and voices raise
　With sweet accord;
From field to garner throng,
Bearing your sheaves along,
And, in your harvest song,
　Bless ye the Lord.
　　　　　　　　　　　J. MONTGOMERY.

MOZART. 7s. — MOZART.

Christ, the Lord, is risen to-day, Sons of men and an-gels say: Raise your joys and triumphs high; Sing, ye heavens; thou earth, reply, Sing, ye heavens; thou earth, reply.

435

CHRIST, the Lord, is risen to-day,
Sons of men and angels say:
Raise your joys and triumphs high;
Sing, ye heavens; thou earth, reply.

2 Love's redeeming work is done;
Fought the fight, the battle won:
Lo! our Sun's eclipse is o'er;
Lo! he sets in blood no more.

3 Vain the stone, the watch, the seal—
Christ hath burst the gates of hell;
Death in vain forbids his rise—
Christ hath opened paradise.

4 Lives again our glorious King:
Where, O death, is now thy sting?
Once he died our souls to save:
Where's thy victory, boasting grave?
CHARLES WESLEY.

EASTER HYMN. 7s. — J. WORGAN.

Christ, the Lord, is risen to-day: Hal - le-lu - jah! Sons of men and an-gels say: Hal - le-lu - jah! Raise your joys and triumphs high: Hal - le-lu - jah! Sing, ye heavens; thou earth, re - ply: Hal - le-lu - jah!

NOTTINGHAM. 7s.   MOZART.

Songs of praise a-woke the morn When the Prince of peace was born;

Songs of praise a-rose when he Cap-tive led cap-tiv-i-ty.

436

Songs of praise awoke the morn
When the Prince of peace was born;
Songs of praise arose when he
Captive led captivity.

2 Heaven and earth must pass away—
Songs of praise shall crown the day;
God will make new heavens and earth—
Songs of praise shall hail their birth.

3 Saints below, with heart and voice,
Still in songs of praise rejoice,
Learning here, by faith and love,
Songs of praise to sing above.

4 Borne upon the latest breath,
Songs of praise shall conquer death;
Then, amidst eternal joy,
Songs of praise their powers employ.
                                        J. MONTGOMERY.

437

God with us! O glorious name!
Let it shine in endless fame;
God and man in Christ unite—
O mysterious depth and height!

2 God with us! amazing love
Brought him from his courts above:
Now, ye saints, his grace admire;
Swell the song with holy fire.

3 God with us! O wondrous grace!
Let us see him face to face,
That we may Immanuel sing,
As we ought, our God and King.
                                        S. SLINN.

438

Now begin the heavenly theme;
Sing aloud in Jesus' name;
Ye who his salvation prove,
Triumph in redeeming love.

2 Ye who see the Father's grace
Beaming in the Saviour's face,
As to Canaan on ye move,
Praise and bless redeeming love.

3 Welcome, all by sin oppressed,
Welcome to his sacred rest!
Nothing brought him from above,
Nothing but redeeming love.

4 Hither, then, your music bring;
Strike aloud each cheerful string;
Mortals, join the host above—
Join to praise redeeming love.
                                        MARTIN MADAN.

439

Thou, from whom we never part,
   Thou, whose love is everywhere,
Thou, who seest every heart,
   Listen to our evening prayer:

2 Father, fill our hearts with love,
   Love unfailing, full and free;
Love that no alarm can move,
   Love that ever rests on thee.

3 Heavenly Father, through the night
   Keep us safe from every ill;
Cheerful as the morning light,
   May we wake to do thy will.
                                        ANON.

13   145

NEW CHRISTIAN

PLEYEL'S HYMN. 7s. I. PLEYEL.

Praise to God, im-mor-tal praise, For the love that crowns our days!

Bounteous Source of ev-ery joy, Let thy praise our tongues em-ploy.

440

PRAISE to God, immortal praise,
For the love that crowns our days!
Bounteous Source of every joy,
Let thy praise our tongues employ.

2 For the blessings of the field,
For the stores the gardens yield,
For the fruits in full supply,
Ripened 'neath the summer sky;

3 Flocks that whiten all the plain,
Yellow sheaves of ripened grain,
Clouds that drop their fattening dews,
Suns that temperate warmth diffuse;

4 All that spring, with bounteous hand,
Scatters o'er the smiling land;
All that liberal autumn pours
From her rich, o'erflowing stores:

5 These to thee, my God, we owe,
Source whence all our blessings flow;
And for these my soul shall raise
Grateful vows and solemn praise.
MRS. A. L. BARBAULD.

441

SHEPHERD of thy little flock,
Lead me to the shadowing rock,
Where the richest pasture grows,
Where the living water flows.

2 By that pure and silent stream,
Sheltered from the scorching beam,
Shepherd, Saviour, Guardian, Guide,
Keep me ever near thy side.
UNKNOWN.

442

LORD of hosts, to thee we raise
Here a house of prayer and praise;
Thou thy people's hearts prepare
Here to meet for praise and prayer.

2 Let the living here be fed
With thy word, the heavenly bread;
Here, in hope of glory blest,
May the dead be laid to rest;

3 Here to thee a temple stand,
While the sea shall gird the land;
Here reveal thy mercy sure,
While the sun and moon endure.

4 Hallelujah!—earth and sky
To the joyful sound reply;
Hallelujah!—hence ascend
Prayer and praise till time shall end.
J. MONTGOMERY.

443

FOR a season called to part,
Let us now ourselves commend
To the gracious eye and heart
Of our ever-present Friend.

2 Jesus, hear our humble prayer;
Tender Shepherd of thy sheep,
Let thy mercy and thy care
All our souls in safety keep.

3 In thy strength may we be strong;
Sweeten every cross and pain;
Give us, if thou wilt, ere long
Here to meet in peace again.
JOHN NEWTON.

146

HENDON. 7s.   C. H. A. Malan.

Lord, we come be-fore thee now; At thy feet we hum-bly bow. O do not our

suit dis - dain! Shall we seek thee, Lord, in vain? Shall we seek thee, Lord, in vain?

444

Lord, we come before thee now;
At thy feet we humbly bow.
O do not our suit disdain!
Shall we seek thee, Lord, in vain?

2 Lord, on thee our souls depend:
In compassion now descend,
Fill our hearts with thy rich grace,
Tune our lips to sing thy praise.

3 In thine own appointed way,
Now we seek thee; here we stay;
Lord, we know not how to go,
Till a blessing thou bestow.

4 Grant that all may seek and find
Thee a God supremely kind;
Heal the sick; the captive free;
Let us all rejoice in thee.
W. Hammond.

445

Sovereign Ruler of the skies,
Ever gracious, ever wise,
All my times are in thy hand,
All events at thy command.

2 Times of sickness, times of health,
Times of penury and wealth—
All must come, and last, and end,
As shall please my heavenly Friend.

3 O thou gracious, wise and just!
In thy hands my life I trust.
Have I somewhat dearer still?
I resign it to thy will.

4 Thee at all times will I bless;
Having thee, I all possess;
How can I bereaved be,
Since I can not part with thee?
John Ryland.

446

To thy temple we repair—
Lord, we love to worship there,
When within the vail we meet
Thee upon the mercy-seat.

2 While thy glorious name is sung,
Tune our lips, unloose our tongue:
Then our joyful souls shall bless
Thee, the Lord our righteousness.

3 While to thee our prayers ascend,
Let thine ear in love attend;
Hear us, for thy Spirit pleads—
Hear, for Jesus intercedes.

4 From thy house when we return,
Let our hearts within us burn,
That at evening we may say:
"We have walked with God to-day."
J. Montgomery.

447

Lord, whom winds and seas obey,
Guide us through the watery way;
In the hollow of thy hand
Hide, and bring us safe to land.

2 Jesus, let our faithful mind
Rest, on thee alone reclined;
Cause each anxious thought to cease;
Keep our souls in perfect peace.

3 Keep the souls whom now we leave:
Bid them to each other cleave;
Bid them walk on life's rough sea;
Bid them come by faith to thee.

4 Save, till all these tempests end,
All who on thy love depend;
Waft our happy spirits o'er,
Land us on the heavenly shore.
Charles Wesley.

NEW CHRISTIAN

UNIVERSITY COLLEGE. 7s.   J. H. GAUNTLETT.

Praise the Lord, his glo-ries show, Saints with-in his courts be-low;

An - gels, round his throne a - bove; All that see and share his love.

448

PRAISE the Lord, his glories show,
Saints within his courts below ;
Angels, round his throne above ;
All that see and share his love.

2 Earth to heaven, and heaven to earth,
Tell his wonders, sing his worth ;
Age to age, and shore to shore,
Praise him, praise him, evermore.

3 Praise the Lord, his mercies trace ;
Praise his providence and grace—
All that he for man hath done,
All he sends us through his Son.

4 Strings and voices, hands and hearts,
In the concert bear your parts ;
All that breathe, your Lord adore ;
Praise him, praise him, evermore.
H. F. LYTE.

449

SWELL the anthem, raise the song—
Praises to our God belong—
Saints and angels join to sing
Praises to the heavenly King.

2 Blessings from his liberal hand
Flow around this happy land ;
Kept by him, no foes annoy ;
Peace and freedom we enjoy.

3 Here, beneath a virtuous sway,
May we cheerfully obey ;
Never feel oppression's rod,
Ever own and worship God.

4 Hark ! the voice of nature sings
Praises to the King of kings :
Let us join the choral song,
And the grateful notes prolong.
NATHAN STRONG.

SEYMOUR. 7s.   "GREATOREX COLL."

Sav-iour, teach me, day by day, Love's sweet les - son to o - bey:

Sweet-er les-son can not be— Lov-ing him who first loved me.

By permission.
148

FLOWER. 7s.   J. H. FILLMORE.

Stealing from the world a-way, We are come to seek thy face;

Kind-ly meet us, Lord, we pray; Grant us thy re-viv-ing grace.

450

STEALING from the world away,
　We are come to seek thy face;
Kindly meet us, Lord, we pray;
　Grant us thy reviving grace.

2 Yonder stars that gild the sky
　Shine but with a borrowed light;
We, unless thy light be nigh,
　Wander, wrapt in gloomy night.

3 Sun of Righteousness, dispel
　All our darkness, doubts, and fears;
May thy light within us dwell,
　Till eternal day appears.
　　　　　　　　　RAY PALMER.

451

SAVIOUR, teach me, day by day,
Love's sweet lesson to obey:
Sweeter lesson can not be—
Loving him who first loved me.

2 With a child-like heart of love,
At thy bidding may I move;
Prompt to serve and follow thee—
Loving him who first loved me.

3 Teach me all thy steps to trace,
Strong to follow in thy grace;
Learning how to love from thee—
Loving him who first loved me.

4 Love in loving finds employ—
In obedience all her joy;
Ever new that joy will be—
Loving him who first loved me.
　　　　　　　　　UNKNOWN.

452

JESUS, Lord, we look to thee:
Let us in thy name agree;
Show thyself the Prince of peace;
Bid our jars forever cease.

2 By thy reconciling love,
Every stumbling-block remove;
Each to each unite, endear;
Come, and spread thy banner here.

3 Make us of one heart and mind—
Courteous, pitiful, and kind;
Lowly, meek, in thought and word—
Altogether like our Lord.
　　　　　　　　　CHARLES WESLEY.

453

SOFTLY now the light of day
Fades upon my sight away:
Free from care, from labor free,
Lord, I would commune with thee.

2 Thou, whose all-pervading eye
Naught escapes, without, within,
Pardon each infirmity—
Open fault, and secret sin.

3 Soon, for me, the light of day
Shall forever pass away:
Then, from sin and sorrow free,
Take me, Lord, to dwell with thee.

4 Thou who, sinless, yet hast known
All of man's infirmity,
Then, from thine eternal throne,
Jesus, look with pitying eye.
　　　　　　　　　G. W. DOANE.

NEW CHRISTIAN

MONKLAND. 7s.JOHN P. WILKES.

Sleep not, sol-dier of the cross: Foes are lurk-ing all a-round;

Look not here to find re-pose: This is but thy bat-tle-ground.

454

SLEEP not, soldier of the cross:
  Foes are lurking all around;
Look not here to find repose:
  This is but thy battle-ground.

2 Up! and take thy shield and sword;
  Up! it is the call of heaven;
Shrink not faithless from the Lord;
  Nobly strive, as he hath striven.

3 Break through all the force of ill;
  Tread the might of passion down,
Struggling onward, onward still,
  To thy conquering Saviour's crown.

4 Through the midst of toil and pain,
  Let this thought ne'er leave thy breast:
Every triumph thou dost gain
  Makes more sweet thy coming rest.
                          MRS. E. C. GASKELL.

455

OFT in sorrow, oft in woe,
Onward, Christian, onward go;
Fight the fight, maintain the strife,
Strengthened with the bread of life.

2 Onward, Christian, onward go;
Join the war, and face the foe.
Will you flee in danger's hour?
Know you not your Captain's power?

3 Let your drooping heart be glad;
March, in heavenly armor clad;
Fight, nor think the battle long:
Soon shall victory tune your song.

4 Let not sorrow dim your eye:
Soon shall every tear be dry;
Let not fears your course impede:
Great your strength, if great your need.
          H. K. WHITE, MISS F. F. MAITLAND.

HATFIELD. 7s.   W. T. PORTER.

Prince of peace, con-trol my will; Bid this struggling heart be still;

Bid my fears and doubtings cease; Hush my spir-it in-to peace.

MERCY. 7s.

Arr. from L. M. GOTTSCHALK.

'Tis my hap-pi-ness be-low Not to live without the cross,

But the Saviour's power to know Sanc-ti-fy-ing ev-ery loss.

456

'Tis my happiness below
  Not to live without the cross,
But the Saviour's power to know
  Sanctifying every loss.

2 Trials must and will befall;
  But, with humble faith, to see
Love inscribed upon them all—
  This is happiness to me.

3 Trials make the promise sweet;
  Trials give new life to prayer;
Trials bring me to his feet,
  Lay me low, and keep me there.
  WM. COWPER.

457

PRINCE of peace, control my will;
Bid this struggling heart be still;
Bid my fears and doubtings cease;
Hush my spirit into peace.

2 Thou hast bought me with thy blood,
Opened wide the gate of God:
Peace I ask—but peace must be,
Lord, in being one with thee.

3 May thy will, not mine, be done;
May thy will and mine be one;
Chase these doubtings from my heart—
Now thy perfect peace impart.

4 Saviour, at thy feet I fall;
Thou, my Life, my God, my All.
Let thy happy servant be,
One for evermore with thee.
  MARY A. S. BARBER.

458

BLESSÈD fountain, full of grace—
  Grace for sinners, grace for me—
To this source alone I trace
  What I am, and hope to be:

2 What I am, as one redeemed,
  Saved and rescued by the Lord,
Hating what I once esteemed,
  Loving what I once abhorred;

3 What I hope to be ere long,
  When I take my place above,
When I join the heavenly throng,
  When I see the God of love.

4 Then I hope like him to be,
  Who redeemed his saints from sin,
Whom I now obscurely see,
  Through a vail that stands between.
  T. KELLY.

459

Now the shades of night are gone;
Now the morning light is come:
Lord, may I be thine to-day;
Drive the shades of sin away;

2 Fill my soul with heavenly light,
Banish doubt, and cleanse my sight;
In thy service, Lord, to-day,
Help me labor, help me pray.

3 When my work of life is past,
O receive me, then, at last:
When I reach the heavenly shore,
Night of sin will be no more.
  UNKNOWN.

SABBATH. 7s. 6 l.   LOWELL MASON.

Safe-ly through an-oth-er week God has brought us on our way: Let us
each a blessing seek, Waiting in his courts to-day— Day of all the week the best,
Emblem of e-ter-nal rest, Day of all the week the best, Emblem of e-ter-nal rest.

460

SAFELY through another week
  God has brought us on our way:
Let us each a blessing seek,
  Waiting in his courts to-day—
Day of all the week the best,
Emblem of eternal rest.

2 While we seek supplies of grace,
  Through the blest Redeemer's name,
Show thy reconciling face,
  Take away our sin and shame;
From our worldly care set free,
May we rest this day in thee.

3 Here we come, thy name to praise:
  Let us feel thy presence near;
May thy glory meet our eyes,
  While we in thy house appear;
Here afford us, Lord, a taste
Of our everlasting rest.

4 May the gospel's joyful sound
  Conquer sinners, comfort saints,
Make the fruits of grace abound,
  Bring relief to all complaints;
Thus let all our worship prove,
Till we join thy courts above.

JOHN NEWTON.

FLOYD. 7s. 6 l.   A. D. FILLMORE.

{Glo - ry, glo - ry to our King! Crowns un-fad - ing wreathe his head! }
{Je - sus is the name we sing—Je - sus, ris - en from the dead; }
Je - sus, Vic - tor of the grave; Je - sus, might-y now to save.

DIX. 7s. 6 l.   Arr. by W. H. Monk.

{ As with gladness men of old   Did the guid-ing star be-hold; }
{ As with joy they hailed its light,   Lead-ing on-ward, beaming bright; }

So, most gracious Lord, may we   Ev - er-more be   led to thee.

461

As WITH gladness men of old
Did the guiding star behold;
As with joy they hailed its light,
Leading onward, beaming bright;
So, most gracious Lord, may we
Evermore be led to thee.

2 As with joyful steps they sped,
Saviour, to thy manger bed,
There to bend the knee before
Thee, whom heaven and earth adore;
So may we with willing feet
Ever seek the mercy-seat.

3 As they offered gifts most rare
At thy cradle, rude and bare;
So may we, with holy joy,
Pure and free from sin's alloy,
All our costliest treasures bring,
Christ, to thee our heavenly King.

4 Blessèd Jesus, every day
Keep us in the narrow way;
And, when earthly things are past,
Bring our ransomed souls at last
Where they need no star to guide,
Where no clouds thy glory hide.
                              W. C. DIX.

462

GLORY, glory to our King!
Crowns unfading wreathe his head!
Jesus is the name we sing—
Jesus, risèn from the dead:
Jesus, Victor of the grave;
Jesus, mighty now to save.

2 Now behold him high enthroned,
Glory beaming from his face,
By adoring angels owned
God of holiness and grace.
O for hearts and tongues to sing,
Glory, glory to our King!

3 Jesus, on thy people shine;
Warm our hearts and tune our tongues,
That with angels we may join—
Share their bliss, and swell their songs.
Glory, honor, praise, and power,
Lord, be thine for evermore!
                          THOMAS KELLY.

463

IF 'TIS sweet to mingle where
Christians meet for social prayer;
If 'tis sweet with them to raise
Songs of holy joy and praise,
Passing sweet that state must be
Where they meet eternally.

2 Saviour, may these meetings prove
Antepasts to that above;
While we worship in this place,
May we go from grace to grace,
Till we each, in his degree,
Fit for endless glory be.
                          UNKNOWN.

464

GLORY be to God on high—
God, whose glory fills the sky!
Glory to the Lamb be given—
Glory in the highest heaven!
Wisdom, riches, praise, and power
Be to God for evermore!

NEW CHRISTIAN

AMBOY. 7s. D.   LOWELL MASON.

{ An-gels, roll the rock a-way; Death, yield up thy might-y prey: }
{ See, the Sav-iour leaves the tomb, Glow-ing with im-mor-tal bloom. }
D. C. Let the earth's re-mot-est bound Ech-o with the bliss-ful sound.

Hark! the won-dering an-gels raise Loud-er notes of joy-ful praise:

465

ANGELS, roll the rock away;
Death, yield up thy mighty prey:
See, the Saviour leaves the tomb,
Glowing with immortal bloom.
Hark! the wondering angels raise
Louder notes of joyful praise:
Let the earth's remotest bound
Echo with the blissful sound.

2 Now, ye saints, lift up your eyes;
See him high in glory rise:
Ranks of angels, on the road,
Hail him—the incarnate God.
Heaven unfolds its portals wide:
See the Conqueror through them ride!
King of glory, mount thy throne—
Boundless empire is thine own.
THOMAS SCOTT.

ARIMATHEA. 7s, with Hallelujah.   C. F. R.

Morning breaks upon the tomb; Jesus dissipates its gloom; Day of triumph through the skies—

See the glorious Saviour rise. Hal-le-lu-jah! hal-le-lu-jah! See the glorious Saviour rise.

By permission of F. J. Huntington & Co.

466

MORNING breaks upon the tomb;
Jesus dissipates its gloom;
Day of triumph through the skies—
See the glorious Saviour rise.
  Hallelujah! hallelujah!
  See the glorious Saviour rise.

2 Drive your anxious cares away;
See the place where Jesus lay;

Ye, who are of death afraid,
Triumph in the scattered shade:
  Hallelujah! hallelujah!
  Triumph in the scattered shade.

3 Christians, dry your flowing tears;
Chase those unbelieving fears:
Look on his deserted grave;
Doubt no more his power to save:
  Hallelujah! hallelujah!
  Doubt no more his power to save.
W. B. COLLYER.

ELTHAM. 7s. D.   LOWELL MASON.

{ Has-ten, Lord, the glorious time, When, be-neath Mes-si-ah's sway, }
{ Ev-ery na-tion, ev-ery clime, Shall the gos-pel call o-bey. }
D. C. Sa-tan and his host, o'er-thrown, Bound in chains, shall hurt no more.

Mightiest kings his power shall own, Heathen tribes his name a-dore;

467

HASTEN, Lord, the glorious time,
  When, beneath Messiah's sway,
Every nation, every clime,
  Shall the gospel call obey.
Mightiest kings his power shall own,
  Heathen tribes his name adore;
Satan and his host, o'erthrown,
  Bound in chains, shall hurt no more,

2 Then shall wars and tumults cease,
  Then be banished grief and pain;
Righteousness, and joy, and peace,
  Undisturbed shall ever reign.
Bless we, then, our gracious Lord;
  Ever praise his glorious name;
All his mighty acts record,
  All his wondrous love proclaim.
                          HARRIET AUBER.

468

PEACE! the welcome sound proclaim;
Dwell with rapture on the theme;
Loud, still louder swell the strain—
Peace on earth, good-will to men!
Breezes, whispering soft and low,
Gently murmur, as ye blow,
Now, when war and discord cease,
Praises to the God of peace.

2 Ocean's billows, far and wide
Rolling in majestic pride,
Loud, still louder swell the strain:
Peace on earth, good-will to men!

Vocal songsters of the grove,
Sweetly chant in notes of love,
Now, when war and discord cease,
Praises to the God of peace.
                          UNKNOWN.

469

THOU who roll'st the year around,
  Crowned with mercies large and free,
Rich thy gifts to us abound,
  Warm our praise shall rise to thee.
Kindly to our worship bow,
  While our grateful thanks we tell,
That, sustained by thee, we now
  Bid the parting year farewell.

2 All its numbered days are sped,
  All its busy scenes are o'er,
All its joys forever fled,
  All its sorrows felt no more.
Mingled with th' eternal past,
  Its remembrance shall decay—
Yet to be revived at last
  At the solemn judgment-day.

3 All our follies, Lord, forgive;
  Cleanse us from each guilty stain;
Let thy grace within us live,
  That we spend not years in vain.
Then, when life's last eve shall come,
  Happy spirits, may we fly
To our everlasting home,
  To our Father's house on high.
                          RAY PALMER.

155

BENEVENTO. 7s. D.   S. WEBBE.

Brethren, while we sojourn here, Fight we must, but should not fear; Foes we have, but we've a Friend.
D. S. Soon the joyful news will come,

Fine.   D. S.

One that loves us to the end, Forward, then, with courage go: Long we shall not dwell below;
"Child, your Father calls: come home."

470

BRETHREN, while we sojourn here,
Fight we must, but should not fear;
Foes we have, but we've a Friend,
One that loves us to the end.
Forward, then, with courage go:
Long we shall not dwell below;
Soon the joyful news will come,
"Child, your Father calls: come home."

2 In the way a thousand snares
Lie, to take us unawares;
Satan, with malicious art,
Watches each unguarded part;

But from Satan's malice free,
Saints shall soon victorious be;
Soon the joyful news will come,
"Child, your Father calls: come home."

3 But of all the foes we meet,
None so oft mislead our feet—
None betray us into sin
Like the foes that dwell within.
Yet let nothing spoil our peace:
Christ shall also conquer these;
Soon the joyful news will come,
"Child, your Father calls: come home."
J. SWAIN.

HOLLINGSIDE. 7s. D.   J. B. DYKES.

Je-sus, merciful and mild, Lead me as a helpless child; On no oth-er arm but thine
D. S. Guide the wanderer, day by day,

Fine.   D. S.

Would my wea-ry soul recline, Thou art ready to forgive, Thou canst bid the sinner live:
In the strait and narrow way.

IVES. 7s. D.   ELAM IVES.

Who are these in bright array, This exulting, happy throng, Round the altar night and day,
D. S. Wisdom, rich-es, to ob - tain,

Hymning one triumphant song? "Worthy is the Lamb once slain, Blessing, honor, glory, power,
New do-min-ion every hour."

471

Who are these in bright array,
  This exulting happy throng,
Round the altar night and day,
  Hymning one triumphant song?
"Worthy is the Lamb once slain,
  Blessing, honor, glory, power,
Wisdom, riches, to obtain,
  New dominion every hour."

2 These through fiery trials trod;
  These from great affliction came;
Now, before the throne of God,
  Sealed with his almighty name,
Clad in raiment pure and white,
  Victor-palms in every hand,
Through their great Redeemer's might,
  More than con-quer-ors they stand.

3 Hunger, thirst, disease unknown,
  On immortal fruits they feed;
Them the Lamb, amidst the throne,
  Shall to living fountains lead;
Joy and gladness banish sighs,
  Perfect love dispels all fears;
And forever from their eyes
  God shall wipe away the tears.
                            J. MONTGOMERY.

472

Jesus, merciful and mild,
Lead me as a helpless child :
On no other arm but thine
Would my weary soul recline;

Thou art ready to forgive,
Thou canst bid the sinner live :
Guide the wanderer, day by day,
In the strait and narrow way.

2 Thou canst fit me, by thy grace,
For the heavenly dwelling-place;
All thy promises are sure,
Ever shall thy love endure.
Then what more could I desire?
How to greater bliss aspire?
All I need, in thee I see;
Thou art all in all to me.
                            THOS. HASTINGS.

473

Thine forever—God of love,
Hear us from thy throne above—
Thine forever may we be,
Here and in eternity.
Thine forever—Lord of life,
Shield us through our earthly strife;
Thou, the Life, the Truth, the Way,
Guide us to the realms of day.

2 Thine forever—Saviour, keep
These thy frail and trembling sheep;
Safe alone beneath thy care,
Let us all thy goodness share.
Thine forever—thou our Guide,
All our wants by thee supplied,
All our sins by thee forgiven,
Lead us, Lord, from earth to heaven.
                            MRS. MARY F. MAUDE.

157

WARING. 7s & 6s.   MENDELSSOHN.

In heavenly love a-bid-ing, No change my heart shall fear; And safe is such con-fid-ing, For nothing changes here. The storm may roar without me, My heart may low be laid, But God is round a-bout me—And can I be dismayed? can . . . . I be dismayed?

474

In HEAVENLY love abiding,
  No change my heart shall fear;
And safe is such confiding,
  For nothing changes here.
The storm may roar without me,
  My heart may low be laid,
But God is round about me—
  And can I be dismayed?

2 Wherever he may guide me,
  No want shall turn me back;
My Shepherd is beside me,
  And nothing can I lack.
His wisdom ever waketh,
  His sight is never dim;
He knows the way he taketh,
  And I will walk with him.

3 Green pastures are before me,
  Which yet I have not seen;
Bright skies will soon be o'er me,
  Where the dark clouds have been.
My hope I can not measure,
  My path to life is free;
My Saviour has my treasure,
  And he will walk with me.
                    ANNA L. WARING.

475

GOD is my strong salvation:
  What foe have I to fear?
In darkness and temptation,
  My light, my help, is near.
Though hosts encamp around me,
  Firm in the fight I stand:
What terror can confound me,
  With God at my right hand?

2 Place on the Lord reliance;
  My soul, with courage wait;
His truth be thine affiance
  When faint and desolate.
His might thy heart shall strengthen,
  His love thy joy increase;
Mercy thy days shall lengthen;
  The Lord will give thee peace.
                    J. MONTGOMERY.

EWING. 7s & 6s. ALEXANDER EWING.

Je - ru - sa - lem, the gold-en, With milk and honey blest, Beneath thy contem-

pla - tion Sink heart and voice oppressed. I know not, O I know not, What

so - cial joys are there, What radiancy of glo - ry, What light beyond compare.

476

JERUSALEM, the golden,
  With milk and honey blest,
Beneath thy contemplation
  Sink heart and voice oppressed.
I know not, O I know not,
  What social joys are there,
What radiancy of glory,
  What light beyond compare.

2 They stand, those halls of Zion,
  All jubilant with song,
And bright with many an angel,
  And all the martyr throng;
The Prince is ever in them,
  The daylight is serene;
The pastures of the blessèd
  Are decked in glorious sheen.

3 There is the throne of David;
  And there, from care released,
The song of them that triumph,
  The shout of them that feast;

And they who, with their Leader,
  Have conquered in the fight,
Forever and forever
  Are clad in robes of white.

                  J. M. NEALE, tr.

477

WE HAVE no home but heaven;
  A pilgrim's garb we wear;
Our path is marked by changes,
  And strewed with many a care;
Surrounded with temptation,
  By varied ills oppressed,
Each day's experience warns us
  That this is not our rest.

2 We have no home but heaven—
  We want no home beside:
O God, our Friend and Father,
  Our footsteps thither guide;
Unfold to us its glory,
  Prepare us for its joy,
Its pure and perfect friendship,
  Its angel-like employ.

                  UNKNOWN.

MISSIONARY HYMN. 7s & 6s. D. LOWELL MASON.

From Greenland's icy mountains,
From India's coral strand;
Where Afric's sunny fountains
Roll down their golden sand;

From many an ancient river,
From many a palmy plain,
They call us to deliver
Their land from error's chain.

478

FROM Greenland's icy mountains,
  From India's coral strand;
Where Afric's sunny fountains
  Roll down their golden sand;
From many an ancient river,
  From many a palmy plain,
They call us to deliver
  Their land from error's chain.

2 What though the spicy breezes
  Blow soft o'er Ceylon's isle—
Though every prospect pleases,
  And only man is vile!
In vain, with lavish kindness,
  The gifts of God are strown;
The heathen, in their blindness,
  Bow down to wood and stone.

3 Shall we, whose souls are lighted
  By wisdom from on high—
Shall we, to man benighted,
  The lamp of life deny?
Salvation! O salvation!
  The joyful sound proclaim,
Till earth's remotest nation
  Has learned Messiah's name.

4 Waft—waft, ye winds, his story;
  And you, ye waters, roll,
Till, like a sea of glory,
  It spreads from pole to pole;
Till, o'er our ransomed nature,
  The Lamb, for sinners slain,
Redeemer, King, Creator,
  In bliss returns to reign.
                          R. HEBER.

MENDEBRAS. 7s & 6s. D. Arr. by LOWELL MASON.

Hail to the Lord's anointed, Great David's greater Son!
Hail, in the time ap-point-ed, His reign on earth begun! He comes to break oppression,
To set the cap-tive free, To take a-way transgression, And rule in eq-ui-ty.

JEWETT. 6s. D.   C. M. VON WEBER

My Saviour, as thou wilt— O may thy will be mine! In-to thy hand of love
I would my all re-sign. Through sorrow, or through joy, Con-duct me
as thine own, And help me still to say, My Lord, thy will be done!

479

MY SAVIOUR, as thou wilt—
　O may thy will be mine!
Into thy hand of love
　I would my all resign.
Through sorrow, or through joy,
　Conduct me as thine own,
And help me still to say,
　My Lord, thy will be done!

2 My Saviour, as thou wilt—
　If needy here and poor,
Give me thy people's bread,
　Their portion rich and sure;

The manna of thy word,
　Let my soul feed upon,
And, if all else should fail,
　My Lord, thy will be done!

3 My Saviour, as thou wilt:
　If among thorns I go,
Still sometimes here and there
　Let a few roses blow.
But thou, on earth, along
　The thorny path hast gone:
Then lead me after thee;
　My Lord, thy will be done!
JANE BORTHWICK—*tr.*

480

HAIL to the Lord's anointed,
　Great David's greater Son!
Hail, in the time appointed,
　His reign on earth begun!
He comes to break oppression,
　To set the captive free,
To take away transgression,
　And rule in equity.

2 He comes, with succor speedy,
　To those who suffer wrong;
To help the poor and needy,
　And bid the weak be strong;

To give them songs for sighing,
　Their darkness turn to light,
Whose souls, condemned and dying,
　Were precious in his sight.

3 He shall come down like showers
　Upon the fruitful earth,
And love, and joy, like flowers,
　Spring in his path to birth.
Before him, on the mountains,
　Shall peace, the herald, go,
And righteousness in fountains
　From hill to valley flow.
J. MONTGOMERY.

14　　　　161

PEREZ. 8s & 7s, with Hallelujah. ANON.

Praise the Lord; ye heavens, adore him; Praise him, angels in the height;
Sun and moon, rejoice before him;
Sun and moon, rejoice before him;

A - - men.

Praise him, all ye stars of light. Hal-le-lujah! Amen, A-men, Amen, A - men.
Praise   him, all ye stars of light. Hal-le-lu-jah!

481

PRAISE the Lord; ye heavens, adore him;
Praise him, angels in the height;
Sun and moon, rejoice before him;
Praise him, all ye stars of light.

2 Praise the Lord: for he hath spoken;
Worlds his mighty voice obeyed;
Laws which never shall be broken,
For their guidance he hath made.

3 Praise the Lord: for he is glorious;
Never shall his promise fail;
God hath made his saints victorious;
Sin and death shall not prevail.

4 Praise the God of our salvation;
Hosts on high his power proclaim;
Heaven and earth, and all creation,
Laud and magnify his name.
J. KEMPTHORNE.

SKENE. 8s, 7s & 4. JAS. H. FILLMORE.

Praise the Lord; ye saints, adore him; All u - nite with one accord; Bring your offerings,

come be - fore him— O praise the Lord! (praise the Lord!) O praise the Lord!

482

PRAISE the Lord; ye saints, adore him;
All unite with one accord;
Bring your offerings, come before him—
O praise the Lord!

2 Praise the Lord, who every blessing
On our heads hath richly poured;
Sing aloud, his love confessing—
O praise the Lord!

3 Praise the Lord! Who would not praise him?
He hath us to grace restored:
To the highest honors raise him—
O praise the Lord!

4 Praise the Lord, your songs excelling
Worldly music's richest chord;
Sing- your Saviour's glory telling—
O praise the Lord!
BENJ. SKENE.

SOLNEY. 8s & 7s.   I. A. P. SCHULZ.

Praise to thee, thou great Cre-a-tor! Praise to thee from ev-ery tongue!

Join, my soul, with ev-ery crea-ture; Join the u-ni-ver-sal song.

483

PRAISE to thee, thou great Creator!
  Praise to thee from every tongue!
Join, my soul, with every creature;
  Join the universal song.

2 Father, Source of all compassion,
  Pure, unbounded grace is thine:
Hail the God of our salvation;
  Praise him for his love divine.

3 For ten thousand blessings given,
  For the hope of future joy,
Sound his praise thro' earth and heaven,
  Sound Jehovah's praise on high.

4 Joyfully on earth adore him,
  Till in heaven our song we raise;
Then enraptured fall before him,
  Lost in wonder, love, and praise.
          J. FAWCETT.

484

WE ARE living, we are dwelling
  In a grand and awful time,
In an age on ages telling;
  To be living is sublime.

2 Hark the onset! will ye fold your
  Faith-clad arms in lazy lock?
Up! O up! thou drowsy soldier;
  Worlds are charging to the shock.

3 Worlds are charging, heaven beholding;
  Thou hast but an hour to fight;
Now, the blazoned cross unfolding,
  On! right onward for the right.

4 On! let all the soul within you
  For the truth's sake go abroad;
Strike! let every nerve and sinew
  Tell on ages—tell for God!
          A. C. COXE.

485

WORSHIP, honor, glory, blessing,
  Be to him who reigns above;
Young and old thy name confessing,
  Saviour, let us share thy love.

2 As the saints in heaven adore thee,
  We would bow before thy throne;
As thine angels bow before thee,
  So on earth thy will be done.
          UNKNOWN.

ESSEX. 8s & 7s.   THOMAS CLARK.

We are liv-ing, we are dwe'ling In a grand and aw-ful time, In an age on

a-ges tell-ing; To be liv-ing is sublime, To be liv-ing is sublime.

RATHBUN. 8s & 7s. I. CONKEY.

In the cross of Christ I glo-ry, Towering o'er the wrecks of time;

All the light of sa - cred sto-ry Gathers round its head sublime.

486

IN THE cross of Christ I glory,
  Towering o'er the wrecks of time ;
All the light of sacred story
  Gathers round its head sublime.

2 When the woes of life o'ertake me,
  Hopes deceive, and fears annoy,
Never shall the cross forsake me ;
  Lo! it glows with peace and joy.

3 When the sun of bliss is beaming
  Light and love upon my way,
From the cross the radiance, streaming,
  Adds more luster to the day.

4 Bane and blessing, pain and pleasure,
  By the cross are sanctified ;
Peace is there, that knows no measure,
  Joys that through all time abide.
                                J. BOWRING.

487

CROWN his head with endless blessing,
  Who, in God the Father's name,
With compassions never ceasing,
  Comes, salvation to proclaim.

2 Hail, ye saints, who know his favor,
  Who within his gates are found—
Hail, ye saints, th' exalted Saviour ;
  Let his courts with praise abound.

3 Jesus, thee our Saviour hailing ;
  Thee our God in praise we own ;
Highest honors, never failing,
  Rise eternal round thy throne.

4 Now, ye saints, his power confessing,
  In your grateful strains adore ;
For his mercy, never ceasing,
  Flows and flows for evermore.
                            WILLIAM GOODE.
                              BEETHOVEN.

SARDIS. 8s & 7s.

Crown his head with end - less bless-ing, Who, in God the Fa-ther's name,

With com - pas - sions nev - er ceas - ing, Comes, sal - va - tion to pro - claim.

SICILY. 8s & 7s.   Sicilian Melody.

Onward, Christian, though the region Where thou art be drear and lone:

God has set a guardian le-gion Ver-y near thee: press thou on.

488

ONWARD, Christian, though the region
  Where thou art be drear and lone :
God has set a guardian legion
  Very near thee : press thou on.

2 By the thorn-road, and none other,
  Is the mount of vision won ;
Tread it without shrinking, brother—
  Jesus trod it—press thou on.

3 Be this world the wiser, stronger,
  For thy life of pain and peace ;
While it needs thee, O no longer
  Pray thou for thy quick release.

4 Pray thou, Christian, daily rather,
  That thou be a faithful son ;
By the prayer of Jesus, " Father,
  Not my will, but thine, be done."
                                    S. JOHNSON.

489

PRAISE the Saviour, all ye nations,
  Praise him, all ye hosts above ;
Shout, with joyful acclamations,
  His divine, victorious love.

2 Be his kingdom now promoted,
  Let the earth her Monarch know ;
Be my all to him devoted :
  To my Lord my all I owe.

3 With my substance I will honor
  My Redeemer and my Lord ;
Were ten thousand worlds my manor,
  All were nothing to his word.

4 While the heralds of salvation
  His abounding grace proclaim,
Let his friends of every station
  Gladly join to spread his fame.
                                    BENJ. FRANCIS.

490

CAST thy bread upon the waters,
  Thinking not 'tis thrown away :
God himself saith, thou shalt gather
  It again some future day.

2 Cast thy bread upon the waters :
  Wildly though the billows roll,
They but aid thee as thou toilest
  Truth to spread from pole to pole.

3 As the seed by billows floated,
  To some distant island lone,
So to human souls benighted,
  That thou flingest may be borne.

4 Cast thy bread upon the waters.
  Why wilt thou still doubting stand ?
Bounteous shall God send the harvest,
  If thou sow'st with liberal hand.
                                    J. H. HANAFORD.

491

LORD, dismiss us with thy blessing;
  Bid us now depart in peace ;
Still on heavenly manna feeding,
  Let our faith and love increase.

2 Fill each breast with consolation :
  Up to thee our hearts we raise ;
When we reach our blissful station,
  Then we'll give thee nobler praise.
                                    E. SMYTHE.

NEW CHRISTIAN

STOCKWELL, 8s & 7s. — D. E. JONES.

Silent - ly the shades of even - ing Gath - er round my low - ly door;

Si - lent - ly they bring be - fore me Fac - es I shall see no more.

492

SILENTLY the shades of evening
  Gather round my lowly door;
Silently they bring before me
  Faces I shall see no more.

2 O the lost, the unforgotten,
  Though the world be oft forgot!
O the shrouded and the lonely!
  In our hearts they perish not;

3 Living in the silent hours,
  Where our spirits only blend—
They, unlinked with earthly trouble;
  We, still hoping for its end.

4 How such holy memories cluster,
  Like the stars when storms are past;
Pointing up to that far heaven
  We may hope to gain at last
                              C. C. COXE.

493

SAVIOUR, breathe an evening blessing,
  Ere repose our spirits seal.
Sin and want we come confessing:
  Thou canst save, and thou canst heal.

2 Though destruction walk around us,
  Though the arrows past us fly,
Angel guards from thee surround us—
  We are safe if thou art nigh.

3 Though the night be dark and dreary,
  Darkness can not hide from thee;
Thou art he who, never weary,
  Watchest where thy people be.

4 Should swift death this night o'ertake us,
  And our couch become our tomb,
May the morn in heaven awake us,
  Clad in bright and deathless bloom.
                              J. EDMESTON.

THOMAS, 8s & 7s. — FRED. A. FILLMORE.

He that go - eth forth with weeping, Bear-ing precious seed in love,

Nev - er tir - ing, nev - er sleeping, Findeth mer - cy from a - bove.

DORRNANCE. 8s & 7s.　　　　　　　　　　　I. B. WOODBURY.

Je - sus on - ly, when the morn-ing Beams up - on the path I tread;

Je - sus on - ly, when the dark-ness Gathers round my wea-ry head;

494

Jesus only, when the morning
　Beams upon the path I tread;
Jesus only, when the darkness
　Gathers round my weary head;

2 Jesus only, when the billows
　Cold and sullen o'er me roll;
Jesus only, when the trumpet
　Rends the tomb and wakes the soul;

3 Jesus only, when, adoring,
　Saints their crowns before him bring;
Jesus only, I will, joyous,
　Through eternal ages sing.
　　　　　　　　　　　E. NASON.

495

HE THAT goeth forth with weeping,
　Bearing precious seed in love,
Never tiring, never sleeping,
　Findeth mercy from above.

2 Soft descend the dews of heaven;
　Bright the rays celestial shine;
Precious fruits will thus be given,
　Through the influence all divine.

3 Sow thy seed; be never weary;
　Let no fears thy soul annoy:
Be the prospect ne'er so dreary,
　Thou shalt reap the fruits of joy.

4 Lo! the scene of verdure brightening;
　See the rising grain appear;
Look again: the fields are whitening,
　For the harvest-time is near.
　　　　　　　　　　　THOS. HASTINGS.

496

ONE there is, above all others,
　Well deserves the name of Friend;
His is love beyond a brother's,
　Costly, free, and knows no end.

2 Which of all our friends, to save us,
　Could or would have shed his blood?
But our Jesus died to have us
　Reconciled in him to God.

3 When he lived on earth abased,
　Friend of sinners was his name;
Now, above all glory raised,
　He rejoices in the same.

4 O for grace our hearts to soften!
　Teach us, Lord, at length, to love;
We, alas! forget too often
　What a friend we have above.
　　　　　　　　　　　J. NEWTON.

497

TAKE my heart, O Father; mold it
　In obedience to thy will;
And as ripening years unfold it,
　Keep it true and childlike still.

2 Father, keep it pure and lowly,
　Strong and brave, yet free from strife,
Turning from the paths unholy
　Of a vain or sinful life.

3 Ever let thy might surround it;
　Strengthen it with power divine,
Till thy cords of love have bound it,
　Father, wholly unto thine.
　　　　　　　　　　　UNKNOWN.

NEW CHRISTIAN

BARTIMEUS. 8s & 7s. STEPHEN JENKS.

While in sweet com-munion feed-ing On this earthly bread and wine,

Sav-iour, may we see thee bleeding On the cross, to make us thine.

498

WHILE in sweet communion feeding
   On this earthly bread and wine,
Saviour, may we see thee bleeding
   On the cross, to make us thine.

2 Though unseen, now be thou near us;
   With the still small voice of love,
Whispering words of peace to cheer us,
   Every doubt and fear remove.

3 Bring before us all the story
   Of thy life and death of woe;
And, with hopes of endless glory,
   Wean our hearts from all below.
                    EDWARD DENNY.

499

SWEET the moments, rich in blessing,
   Which before the cross we spend,
Life, and health, and peace possessing,
   From the sinner's dying Friend.

2 Here we feel our sins forgiven,
   While upon the Lamb we gaze;
And our thoughts are all of heaven,
   And our lips o'erflow with praise.

3 Still in ceaseless contemplation,
   Fix our hearts and eyes on thee,
Till we taste thy full salvation,
   And, unvailed, thy glories see.
                    J. ALLEN.

STEARNS. 8s & 7s. JOSEPH MAZZINGHI.

Sweet the moments, rich in blessing, Which be-fore the cross we spend.

Life, and health, and peace possessing. From the sin-ner's dy-ing Friend.

168

CARTER. 8s & 7s.   E. S. CARTER.

Al-ways with us, al-ways with us—Words of cheer and words of love;

Thus the ris-en Saviour whispers, From his dwelling-place a-bove:

500

ALWAYS with us, always with us—
  Words of cheer and words of love;
Thus the risen Saviour whispers,
  From his dwelling-place above :

2 With us when we toil in sadness,
  Sowing much and reaping none,
Telling us that in the future
  Golden harvests shall be won ;

3 With us when the storm is sweeping
  O'er our pathway dark and drear,
Waking hope within our bosoms,
  Stilling every anxious fear ;

4 With us in the lonely valley,
  When we cross the chilling stream—
Lighting up the steps to glory
  With salvation's radiant beam.
                              E. H. NEVIN.

WILSON. 8s & 7s.
                                              MENDELSSOHN.

Come, thou long-ex-pect-ed Je-sus, Born to set thy peo-ple free;

From our fears and sins re-lease us, Let us find our rest in thee.

501

COME, thou long-expected Jesus,
  Born to set thy people free ;
From our fears and sins release us,
  Let us find our rest in thee.

2 Israel's Strength and Consolation,
  Hope of all the saints thou art ;
Dear Desire of every nation,
  Joy of every longing heart.

3 Born, thy people to deliver,
  Born a child, and yet a King,
Born to reign in us forever,
  Now thy gracious kingdom bring.

4 By thine own eternal Spirit,
  Rule in all our hearts alone ;
By thine all-sufficient merit,
  Raise us to thy glorious throne.
                              CHARLES WESLEY.

NEW CHRISTIAN

ST. SYLVESTER. 8s & 7s.   J. B. DYKES.

Fa - ther, hear the prayer we of - fer: Not for ease that prayer shall be,

But for strength, that we may ev - er Live our lives courag - eous - ly.

502

FATHER, hear the prayer we offer:
  Not for ease that prayer shall be,
But for strength, that we may ever
  Live our lives courageously.

2 Not forever by still waters
  Would we idly quiet stay;
But would smite the living fountains
  From the rocks along our way.

3 Be our strength in hours of weakness;
  In our wanderings, be our guide;
Through endeavor, failure, danger,
  Father, be thou at our side.
                                    ANON.

503

LIKE the eagle, upward, onward,
  Let my soul in faith be borne;
Calmly gazing, skyward, sunward,
  Let my eye unshrinking turn.

2 Where the cross, God's love revealing,
  Sets the fettered spirit free;
Where it sheds its wondrous healing,
  There, my soul, thy rest shall be.

3 O may I no longer, dreaming,
  Idly waste my golden day,
But, each precious hour redeeming,
  Upward, onward, press my way.
                                    H. BONAR.

DIJON. 8s & 7s.   German.

Like the ea - gle, up-ward, on - ward, Let my soul in faith be borne;

Calm - ly gaz - ing, sky-ward, sunward, Let my eye un - shrink-ing turn.

MILWAUKEE. 8s & 7s.   J. ZUNDEL.

Hum - ble souls, who seek sal - va - tion Through the Lamb's redeeming blood,

Hear the voice of rev - e - la - tion, Tread the path that Je - sus trod.

504

HUMBLE souls, who seek salvation
  Through the Lamb's redeeming blood,
Hear the voice of revelation,
  Tread the path that Jesus trod.

2 Hear the blest Redeemer call you;
  Listen to his heavenly voice;

Dread no ills that can befall you,
  While you make his way your choice.

3 Plainly here his footsteps tracing,
  Follow him without delay,
Gladly his command embracing:
  Lo! your Captain leads the way.
                  JOHN FAWCETT.

MOUNT VERNON. 8s & 7s.
                          LOWELL MASON.

Sis - ter, thou wast mild and love - ly, Gen - tle as the sum-mer breeze,

Pleas-ant as the air of even - ing, When it floats a - mong the trees.

505

SISTER, thou wast mild and lovely,
  Gentle as the summer breeze,
Pleasant as the air of evening,
  When it floats among the trees.

2 Peaceful be thy silent slumber—
  Peaceful in the grave so low.
Thou no more wilt join our number;
  Thou no more our songs shalt know.

3 Dearest sister, thou hast left us;
  Here thy loss we deeply feel;
But 'tis God that hath bereft us;
  He can all our sorrows heal.

4 Yet again we hope to meet thee,
  When the day of life is fled;
Then in heaven with joy to greet thee,
  Where no farewell tear is shed.
                  S. F. SMITH.

AUSTRIA. 8s & 7s. D. HAYDN.

{ Hear what God, the Lord, hath spoken: O my people, faint and few, }
{ Com-fort-less, af-flic-ted, bro-ken, Fair abodes I build for you; } Scenes of heartfelt tribulation

Shall no more perplex your ways; You shall name your walls "Salvation,"
And your gates shall all be "Praise."

506

HEAR what God, the Lord, hath spoken:
  O my people, faint and few,
Comfortless, afflicted, broken,
  Fair abodes I build for you;
Scenes of heartfelt tribulation
  Shall no more perplex your ways;
You shall name your walls "Salvation,"
  And your gates shall all be "Praise."

2 There, like streams that feed the garden,
  Pleasures without end shall flow,
For the Lord, your faith rewarding,
  All his bounty shall bestow.

Still, in undisturbed possession,
  Peace and righteousness shall reign,
Never shall you feel oppression,
  Hear the voice of war again.

3 Ye, no more your suns descending,
  Waning moons no more shall see;
But, your griefs forever ending,
  Find eternal noon in me.
God shall rise, and, shining o'er you,
  Change to day the gloom of night;
He, the Lord, shall be your Glory,
  God, your everlasting Light.

WM. COWPER.

LOVE DIVINE. 8s & 7s. D. JOHN ZUNDEL.

Love divine, all love excelling, Joy of heaven, to earth come down, Fix in us thy humble dwelling,
D. S. Vis-it us with thy sal-va-tion,

Fine. D. S.

All thy faithful mercies crown, Jesus, thou art all compassion, Pure, unbounded love thou art:
En-ter ev-ery trembling heart.

GREENVILLE. 8s & 7s. D.   J. J. ROSSEAU.

{ Glo - rious things of thee are spok-en, Zi - on, cit - y of our God; }
{ He, whose word can not be brok-en, Formed thee for his own a - bode. }
D. C. With sal - va-tion's wall sur-round-ed, Thou mayest smile at all thy foes.

On the Rock of A - ges founded, What can shake thy sure re - pose?

507

GLORIOUS things of thee are spoken,
  Zion, city of our God;
He, whose word can not be broken,
  Formed thee for his own abode.
On the Rock of Ages founded,
  What can shake thy sure repose?
With salvation's wall surrounded,
  Thou mayest smile at all thy foes.

2 See the streams of living waters,
  Springing from eternal love,
Well supply thy sons and daughters,
  And all fear of drought remove.
Who can faint, while such a river
  Ever flows their thirst to assuage—
Grace, which, like the Lord, the Giver,
  Never fails from age to age?

3 Blest inhabitants of Zion,
  Washed in the Redeemer's blood,
Jesus, whom their souls rely on,
  Makes them kings and priests to God.
'Tis his love his people raises
  With himself to reign as kings;
And, as priests, his solemn praises
  Each for a thank-offering brings.

4 Saviour, since of Zion's city
  I through grace a member am,
Let the world deride or pity,
  I will glory in thy name.
Fading is the worldling's treasure,
  All his boasted pomp and show;
Solid joy and lasting pleasure
  None but Zion's children know.
                              JOHN NEWTON.

508

LOVE divine, all love excelling,
  Joy of heaven, to earth come down,
Fix in us thy humble dwelling,
  All thy faithful mercies crown.
Jesus, thou art all compassion,
  Pure, unbounded love thou art:
Visit us with thy salvation,
  Enter every trembling heart.

2 Breathe, O breathe thy loving Spirit
  Into every troubled breast;
Let us all in thee inherit,
  Let us find the promised rest.
Take away the love of sinning,
  Take our load of guilt away;
End the work of thy beginning—
  Bring us to eternal day.
                              CHARLES WESLEY.

509

CALL Jehovah thy salvation,
  Rest beneath th' Almighty's shade;
In his secret habitation
  Dwell, and never be dismayed.
There no tumult shall alarm thee;
  Thou shalt dread no hidden snare.
Guile nor violence can harm thee,
  In eternal safeguard there.

2 Since with pure and firm affection
  Thou on God hast set thy love,
With the wings of his protection
  He will shield thee from above.
Thou shalt call on him in trouble;
  He will hearken; he will save;
Here for grief reward thee double;
  Crown with life beyond the grave.
                              J. MONTGOMERY.

NEW CHRISTIAN

AUTUMN. 8s & 7s. D.   MARECHIO.

Gently, Lord, O gently lead us Thro' this gloomy vale of tears; Thro' the changes thou'st decreed us,
D. S. Let thy goodness never fail us,

Till our last great change appears. When temptation's darts assail us,
Lead us in thy perfect way. When in devious paths we stray,

510

GENTLY, Lord, O gently lead us
  Through this gloomy vale of tears;
Through the changes thou'st decreed us,
  Till our last great change appears.
When temptation's darts assail us,
  When in devious paths we stray,
Let thy goodness never fail us,
  Lead us in thy perfect way.

2 In the hour of pain and anguish,
  In the hour when death draws near,
Suffer not our hearts to languish,
  Suffer not our souls to fear.
Let thy promise to be near us
  Fill our hearts with joy and peace;
May thy presence sweetly cheer us,
  Till our conflicts all shall cease.

3 When this mortal life is ended,
  Bid us in thine arms to rest,
Till, by angel bands attended,
  We awake among the blest.
Then, O crown us with thy blessing,
  Through the triumphs of thy grace;
Then shall praises, never ceasing,
  Echo through thy dwelling-place.
          THOS. HASTINGS.

511

HAIL, thou God of grace and glory,
  Who thy name hast magnified,
By redemption's wondrous story,
  By the Saviour crucified!

Thanks to thee for every blessing,
  Flowing from the Fount of love;
Thanks for present good unceasing,
  And for hopes of bliss above.

2 Bind thy people, Lord, in union,
  With the sevenfold cord of love;
Breathe a spirit of communion
  With the glorious hosts above;
Let thy work be seen progressing;
  Bow each heart, and bend each knee,
Till the world, thy truth possessing,
  Celebrates its jubilee.
          T. W. AVELING.

512

EARTHLY joys no longer please us;
  Here would we renounce them all,
Seek our only rest in Jesus,
  Him our Lord and Master call.
Faith, our languid spirits cheering,
  Points to brighter worlds above;
Bids us look for his appearing,
  Bids us triumph in his love.

2 May our lights be always burning,
  And our loins be girded round,
Waiting for our Lord's returning,
  Longing for the welcome sound.
Thus the Christian life adorning,
  Never will we be afraid,
Should he come at night or morning,
  Early dawn or evening shade.
          C. L. FORD.

174

513

ONLY waiting till the shadows
Are a little longer grown;
Only waiting till the glimmer
Of the day's last beam is flown;
Till the night of earth is faded
From the heart once full of day;
Till the stars of heaven are breaking
Through the twilight soft and gray.

2 Only waiting till the reapers
Have the last sheaf gathered home;
For the summer-time is faded,
And the autumn winds have come.
Quickly, reapers, gather quickly
The last ripe hours of my heart;
For the bloom of life is withered,
And I hasten to depart.

3 Only waiting till the shadows
Are a little longer grown;
Only waiting till the glimmer
Of the day's last beam is flown;
Then, from out the gathered darkness,
Holy, deathless stars shall rise,
By whose light my soul shall gladly
Tread its pathway to the skies.

MRS. F. L. MACE.

514

THEY are going—only going—
Jesus called them long ago;
All the wintry time they're passing,
Softly as the falling snow.
When the violets, in the spring-time,
Catch the azure of the sky,
They are carried out to slumber
Sweetly where the violets lie.

2 They are going—only going—
When with summer earth is dressed,
In their cold hands holding roses
Folded to each silent breast;
When the autumn hangs red banners
Out above the harvest sheaves,
They are going—ever going—
Thick and fast, like falling leaves.

3 Little hearts forever stainless,
Little hands as pure as they,
Little feet by angels guided,
Never a forbidden way—
They are going, ever going,
Leaving many a lonely spot;
But 'tis Jesus who has called them:
Suffer and forbid them not.

FABEN. 8s & 7s. D.   J. H. WILCOX.

They are go-ing—on-ly going— Jesus called them long a-go; All the wintry time they're pass-ing, Soft-ly as the falling snow. When the violets, in the spring-time, Catch the a-zure of the sky, They are car-ried out to slumber Sweetly where the violets lie.

MIDDLETOWN. 8s & 7s. D.　　　　　　　　　　　　English.

{ O how kind-ly hast thou led me, Heaven-ly Fa - ther, day by day; }
{ Found my dwelling, clothed and fed me, Furnished friends to cheer my way! }
D. C. 'Twas that still my step might has-ten Homeward, heavenward, to my God.

Didst thou bless me, didst thou chasten, With thy smile or with thy rod,

515

O how kindly hast thou led me,
　Heavenly Father, day by day;
Found my dwelling, clothed and fed me,
　Furnished friends to cheer my way!
Didst thou bless me, didst thou chasten,
　With thy smile or with thy rod,
'Twas that still my step might hasten
　Homeward, heavenward, to my God.

2 O how slowly have I often
　Followed where thy hand would draw!
How thy kindness failed to soften!
　How thy chastening failed to awe!
Make me for thy rest more ready,
　As thy path is longer trod;
Keep me in thy friendship steady,
　Till thou call me home, my God.
　　　　　　　　　　　　　　GRINFIELD.

GUIDANCE. 8s & 7s. D.　　　　　　　　　　　　FLOTOW.

O how kind-ly hast thou led me, Heavenly Fa-ther, day by day; Found my dwelling,

clothed and fed me, Furnished friends to cheer my way! Didst thou bless me, didst thou chasten,

With thy smile or with thy rod, 'Twas that still my step might hasten
　　　　　　　　　　　　　　Homeward, heavenward, to my God.

WOLFORD. 8s & 7s. D. English Melody.

Lord, with glowing heart I'll praise thee For the bliss thy love bestows;
For the pardoning grace that saves me,
D. S. Thou must light the flame, or never

And the peace that from it flows. Help, O Lord, my weak endeavor; This dull soul to rapture raise:
Can my love be warmed to praise.

516

Lord, with glowing heart I'll praise thee
For the bliss thy love bestows;
For the pardoning grace that saves me,
And the peace that from it flows.
Help, O Lord, my weak endeavor:
This dull soul to rapture raise;
Thou must light the flame, or never
Can my love be warmed to praise.

2 Praise, my soul, the God that sought thee,
Wretched wanderer, far astray,
Found thee lost, and kindly brought thee
From the path of death away;
Praise, with love's devoutest feeling,
Him who saw thy guilt-born fear,
And, the light of hope revealing,
Bade the blood-stained cross appear.

3 Lord, this bosom's ardent feeling
Vainly would my lips express;
Low before thy footstool kneeling,
Deign thy suppliant's prayer to bless;
Let thy grace, my soul's chief treasure,
Love's pure flame within me raise;
And since words can never measure,
Let my life show forth thy praise.
S. F. KEY.

517

Take me, O my Father, take me—
Take me, save me, through thy Son;
That which thou wouldst have me, make me;
Let thy will in me be done.

Long from thee my footsteps straying,
Thorny proved the way I trod;
Weary come I now, and praying—
Take me to thy love, my God.

2 Fruitless years with grief recalling,
Humbly I confess my sin;
At thy feet, O Father, falling,
To thy household take me in.
Freely now to thee I proffer
This relenting heart of mine;
Freely, life and soul I offer,
Gift unworthy love like thine.

3 Once the world's Redeemer, dying,
Bore our sins upon the tree;
On that sacrifice relying,
Now I look in hope to thee.
Father, take me! all forgiving,
Fold me to thy loving breast:
In thy love forever living,
I must be forever blest.
RAY PALMER.

518

Praise the God of all creation;
Praise the Father's boundless love;
Praise the Lamb, our expiation—
Priest and King, enthroned above;
Praise the Author of salvation—
Him by whom our spirits live;
Undivided adoration
To the one Jehovah give.
UNKNOWN.

CLARINGTON. 8s. D.
ANON. Fine.

{ The angels that watched round the tomb, Where low the Redeemer was laid, }
{ When deep in mor-tal-i-ty's gloom He hid for a season his head; }
D. S. witnessed his ris-ing, and swept The chords with the triumphs of joy.

D. S.

That vailed their fair face while he slept, And ceased their sweet harps to employ, Have

519

THE angels that watched round the tomb,
Where low the Redeemer was laid,
When deep in mortality's gloom
He hid for a season his head;
That vailed their fair face while he slept,
And ceased their sweet harps to employ,
Have witnessed his rising, and swept
The chords with the triumphs of joy.

2 You saints, who once languished below,
But long since have entered your rest,
I pant to be glorified too,
To lean on Immanuel's breast.
The grave in which Jesus was laid
Has buried my guilt and my fears;
And while I contemplate its shade,
The light of his presence appears.

3 O sweet is the season of rest,
When life's weary journey is done!
The blush that spreads over its west,
The last lingering ray of its sun!
Though dreary the empire of night,
I soon shall emerge from its gloom,
And see immortality's light
Arise on the shades of the tomb.

4 Then welcome the last rending sighs,
When these aching heart-strings shall break,
When death shall extinguish these eyes,
And moisten with dew the pale cheek.
No terror the prospect begets—
I am not mortality's slave;
The sunbeam of life, as it sets,
Paints a rainbow of peace o'er the grave.
WM. B. COLLYER.

DE FLEURY. 8s. D.
LEWIS EDSON. Fine.

{ My gra-cious Re-deem-er I love; His prais-es a-loud I'll pro-claim, }
{ And join with the ar-mies a-bove, To shout his a-dor-a-ble name. }
D. C. And feel them in-ces-sant-ly shine, My boundless, in-ef-fa-ble joy.

D. C.

To gaze on his glo-ries di-vine Shall be my e-ter-nal employ,

SMART. 8s. D.   JAS. H. FILLMORE.

{ How shall I my Saviour set forth? How shall I his beau-ties de-clare? }
{ O how shall I speak of his worth, Or what his chief dig-ni-ties are? }

His an-gels can nev-er ex-press, Nor saints who sit near-est his throne,

How rich are his treas-ures of grace— No, this is a se-cret unknown.

520

How shall I my Saviour set forth?
  How shall I his beauties declare?
O how shall I speak of his worth,
  Or what his chief dignities are?
His angels can never express,
  Nor saints who sit nearest his throne,
How rich are his treasures of grace—
  No, this is a secret unknown.

2 In him all the fullness of God
  Forever transcendently shines;
Though once like a mortal he stood,
  To finish his gracious designs.

Though once he was nailed to the cross,
  Vile rebels like me to set free,
His glory sustained no loss,
  Eternal his kingdom shall be.

3 O sinners, believe and adore
  This Saviour, so rich to redeem :
No creature can ever explore
  The treasures of goodness in him.
Come, all you who see yourselves lost,
  And feel yourselves burdened with sin,
Draw near, while with terror you're tossed ;
  Obey, and your peace shall begin.
                              MAXWELL.

521

MY GRACIOUS Redeemer I love ;
  His praises aloud I'll proclaim,
And join with the armies above,
  To shout his adorable name.
To gaze on his glories divine
  Shall be my eternal employ,
And feel them incessantly shine,
  My boundless, ineffable joy.

2 You palaces, scepters and crowns,
  Your pride with disdain I survey ;
Your pomps are but shadows and sounds,
  And pass in a moment away.
The crown that my Saviour bestows
  Yon permanent sun shall outshine ;
My joy everlastingly flows—
  My God, my Redeemer, is mine.
                              B. FRANCIS.

OLIPHANT. 8s, 7s & 4s.   Arr. by LOWELL MASON.

God is in his holy temple; All the earth keep silence here; Worship him in truth and spirit,

Reverence him with godly fear. Ho - ly, ho - ly, Ho - ly, ho - ly, Lord of hosts, our

Lord, appear, Lord of hosts, our Lord, appear.

522

God is in his holy temple:
  All the earth keep silence here;
Worship him in truth and spirit,
  Reverence him with godly fear.
    Holy, holy,
  Lord of hosts, our Lord, appear.

2 God in Christ reveals his presence,
  Throned upon the mercy-seat:
Saints, rejoice! and sinners, tremble!
  Each prepare his God to meet;
    Lowly, lowly,
  Bow adoring at his feet.

3 Hail him here with songs of praises;
  Him with prayers of faith sur-
      round;
Hearken to his glorious gospel,
  While the preacher's lips ex-
      pound:
    Blessèd, blessèd,
  They who know the joyful sound.
                        J. MONTGOMERY.

ZION. 8s, 7s & 4s.   THOS. HASTINGS.

{ On the mountain's top appear-ing, Lo! the sa - cred herald stands, }
{ Welcome news to Zi - on bear-ing—Zi - on, long in hos-tile lands. } Mourning

captive, God himself will loose thy bands, Mourning captive, God himself will loose thy bands.

HARWELL. 8s, 7s & 4s, or 8s & 7s. D.   LOWELL MASON.

(Hark! ten thousand harps and voices Sound the note of praise above;)
(Jesus reigns, and heaven rejoices—Jesus reigns, the God of love.) See, he sits on yonder throne See, he sits

Jesus rules the world alone. Halle-lu-jah! halle-lu-jah! Jesus rules the world alone.
Jesus rules   the world alone.

523

Hark! ten thousand harps and voices
  Sound the note of praise above;
Jesus reigns, and heaven rejoices—
  Jesus reigns, the God of love.
See, he sits on yonder throne;
Jesus rules the world alone.
  Hallelujah! hallelujah!
  Jesus rules the world alone.

2 Jesus, hail! whose glory brightens
  All above, and gives it worth:
Lord of life, thy smile enlightens,
  Cheers, and charms thy saints on earth;
When we think of love like thine,
Lord, we own it love divine.
  Hallelujah! hallelujah!
  Lord, we own it love divine.

3 King of glory, reign forever—
  Thine an everlasting crown:
Nothing from thy love shall sever
  Those whom thou hast made thine own;
Happy objects of thy grace,
Destined to behold thy face.
  Hallelujah! hallelujah!
  Destined to behold thy face.

4 Saviour, hasten thine appearing;
  Bring, O bring the glorious day,
When, the awful summons hearing,
  Heaven and earth shall pass away.
Then, with golden harps, we'll sing,
" Glory, glory to our King!"
  Hallelujah! hallelujah!
  Glory, glory to our King!
             THOS. KELLY.

524

On the mountain's top appearing,
  Lo! the sacred herald stands,
Welcome news to Zion bearing—
  Zion, long in hostile lands.
  Mourning captive,
God himself will loose thy bands.

2 Has thy night been long and mournful?
  Have thy friends unfaithful proved?
Have thy foes been proud and scornful,
  By thy sighs and tears unmoved?
  Cease thy mourning:
Zion still is well beloved.

3 God, thy God, will now restore thee;
  He himself appears thy Friend;
All thy foes shall flee before thee;
  Here their boasts and triumphs end;
  Great deliverance
Zion's King will surely send.

4 Peace and joy shall now attend thee;
  All thy warfare now be past;
God, thy Saviour, will defend thee;
  Vic-to-ry is thine at last;
  All thy conflicts
End in everlasting rest.
             THOS. KELLY.

CORONAL. 8s, 7s & 4s. M. S., In "Lute of Zion."

Look, ye saints: the sight is glorious—See the Man of Sorrows now
From the fight returned victorious: Every knee to him shall bow.

Crown him, crown him: Crowns become the Victor's brow, Crowns become the Victor's brow.

525

Look, ye saints: the sight is glorious—
See the Man of Sorrows now
From the fight returned victorious:
Every knee to him shall bow.
  Crown him, crown him:
  Crowns become the Victor's brow.

2 Crown the Saviour, angels, crown him!
Rich the trophies Jesus brings:
In the seat of power enthrone him,
  While the heavenly concert rings;
  Crown him, crown him:
  Crown the Saviour King of kings.

3 Sinners in derision crowned him,
Mocking thus the Saviour's claim:
Saints and angels, crowd around him,
Own his title, praise his name;
  Crown him, crown him;
  Spread abroad the Victor's name.

4 Hark, those bursts of acclamation!
Hark, those loud, triumphant chords!
Jesus takes the highest station:
O what joy the sight affords!
  Crown him, crown him
  King of kings, and Lord of lords.
                    Thos. Kelly.

MARTON. 8s, 7s & 4s. Anon.

O'er the gloomy hills of darkness, Look, my soul; be still and gaze:
All the promises do travail With a glorious day of grace. Blessed jubilee, Let thy glorious

morning dawn, Blessed jubilee, Let thy glorious morning dawn, Let thy glorious morning dawn.

CALVARY. 8s, 7s & 4s.   SAMUEL STANLEY.

Hark! the voice of love and mer- cy Sounds a - loud from Cal - va - ry;

See, it rends the rocks a - sun-der, Shakes the earth, and vails the sky.

"It is finished!" "It is fin-ished!" Hear the dy- ing Sav-iour cry.

526 [First verse in the music.]

2 It is finished : O what pleasure
  Do these precious words afford!
Heavenly blessings without measure
  Flow to us from Christ the Lord.
    It is finished:
  Saints, the dying words record.

3 Finished all the types and shadows
  Of the ceremonial law!
Finished all that God had promised!
  Death and hell no more shall awe.
    It is finished:
  Saints, from this your comfort draw.
                              J. EVANS.

527

O'ER the gloomy hills of darkness,
  Look, my soul; be still and gaze:
All the promises do travail
  With a glorious day of grace.
    Blessèd jubilee,
  Let thy glorious morning dawn.

2 Let the Indian, let the negro,
  Let the rude barbarian see
That divine and glorious conquest
  Once obtained on Calvary;
    Let the gospel
  Loud resound from pole to pole.

3 Kingdoms wide that sit in darkness,
  Grant them, Lord, the glorious light,
And from eastern coast to western
  May the morning chase the night,
    And redemption,
  Freely purchased, win the day.

4 Fly abroad, thou mighty gospel;
  Win and conquer, never cease;
May thy lasting, wide dominion
  Multiply and still increase.
    Sway thy scepter,
  Saviour, all the world around.
                            W. WILLIAMS.

PERON. 8s, 7s & 4s. ANON.

Guide me, O thou great Je - ho vah, Pilgrim through this bar-ren land:
I am weak, but thou art might-y : Hold me with thy powerful hand;

Bread of heav-en, bread of heav-en, Feed me till I want no more.

528

GUIDE me, O thou great Jehovah,
  Pilgrim through this barren land:
I am weak, but thou art mighty :
  Hold me with thy powerful hand;
  Bread of heaven,
  Feed me till I want no more.

2 Open thou the crystal fountain
  Whence the healing waters flow;
Let the fiery, cloudy pillar
  Lead me all my journey through ;
  Strong Deliverer,
  Be thou still my strength and shield.

3 When I tread the verge of Jordan,
  Bid my anxious fears subside;
Bear me through the swelling current,
  Land me safe on Canaan's side :
  Songs of praises
  I will ever give to thee.
                          W. WILLIAMS.

529

PRAISE, my soul, the King of heaven;
  To his feet thy tribute bring;
Ransomed, healed, restored, forgiven,
  Who like thee his praise should sing?
  Praise him, praise him,
  Praise the everlasting King.

2 Praise him for his grace and favor
  To our fathers in distress;
Praise him, still the same forever,
  Slow to chide and swift to bless;
  Praise him, praise him,
  Glorious in his faithfulness.

3 Father-like he tends and spares us;
  Well our feeble frame he knows;
In his hands he gently bears us—
  Rescues us from all our foes :
  Praise him, praise him,
  Widely as his mercy flows.
                          H. F. LYTE.

REGENT SQUARE. 8s, 7s & 4s. HENRY SMART.

Praise, my soul, the King of heav-en :
To his feet thy tribute bring:
Ransomed, healed, restored, forgiv-en,

Who like thee his praise should sing?
Praise him, praise him, Praise him, praise him, Praise the ev-er-last-ing King.

SIBERIA. 8s, 7s & 4s. S. B. POND.

Lord, dismiss us with thy blessing, Fill our hearts with joy and peace; Let us each, thy love possessing,

Triumph in re - deem-ing grace; O refresh us, O refresh us, Traveling thro' this wilderness.

530

LORD, dismiss us with thy blessing,
  Fill our hearts with joy and peace;
Let us each, thy love possessing,
  Triumph in redeeming grace;
    O refresh us,
  Traveling through this wilderness.

2 Thanks we give, and adoration,
  For the gospel's joyful sound:
May the fruits of thy salvation
  In our hearts and lives abound;
    May thy presence
  With us evermore be found.

3 So, whene'er the signal's given
  Us from earth to call away,
Borne on angels' wings to heaven,
  Glad the summons to obey,
    May we, ready,
  Rise and reign in endless day.
                        SHIRLEY.

531

YES, we trust the day is breaking,
  Joyful times are near at hand;
God, the mighty God, is speaking
  By his word, in every land.
    Mark his progress:
  Darkness flies at his command.

2 While the foe becomes more daring,
  While he "enters like a flood,"
God the Saviour is preparing
  Means to spread his truth abroad;
    Every language
  Soon shall tell the love of God.

3 God of Jacob, high and glorious,
  Let thy people see thy hand;
Let the gospel be victorious
  Through the world, in every land;
    Let the idols
  Perish, Lord, at thy command.
                      THOS. KELLY.

532

LO! HE comes, with clouds descending,
  Once for favored sinners slain;
Thousand thousand saints attending,
  Swell the triumph of his train.
    Hallelujah!
  Jesus now shall ever reign.

2 Every eye shall now behold him
  Robed in dreadful majesty;
Those who set at naught and sold him,
  Pierced and nailed him to the tree,
    Deeply wailing,
  Shall the true Messiah see.

3 Every island, sea, and mountain,
  Heaven and earth, shall flee away;
All who hate him, must, confounded,
  Hear the trump proclaim the day:
    Come to judgment;
  Come to judgment, come away.

4 Now redemption, long expected,
  See in solemn pomp appear:
All his saints, by man rejected,
  Now shall meet him in the air.
    Hallelujah!
  See the day of God appear.
                    CHARLES WESLEY.

16   185

NEW CHRISTIAN

CHALLEN. 8s & 7s. Peculiar.   JAMES CHALLEN.

Jesus wept: those tears are over, But his heart is still the same; Kinsman, Friend, and Elder Brother,

Is his ev-erlasting name. Saviour, who can love like thee, Gracious One of Beth-an-y?

533

Jesus wept: those tears are over,
  But his heart is still the same;
Kinsman, Friend, and Elder Brother,
  Is his everlasting name.
Saviour, who can love like thee,
Gracious One of Bethany?

2 When the pangs of trial seize us,
  When the waves of sorrow roll,
I will lay my head on Jesus—
  Pillow of the troubled soul.
Truly, none can feel like thee,
Weeping One of Bethany.

3 Jesus wept, and still, in glory,
  He can mark each mourner's tear—
Living to retrace the story
  Of the hearts he solaced here.
Lord, when I am called to die,
Let me think of Bethany.

4 Jesus wept: that tear of sorrow
  Is a legacy of love;
Yesterday, to-day, to-morrow,
  He the same shall ever prove.
Thou art all in all to me,
Living One of Bethany.
                    EDWARD DENNY.

IOWA. 8s.   A. D. FILLMORE.

We speak of the realms of the blest, That country so bright and so fair, And oft are its

glories confessed: But what must it be to be there? But what must it be to be there!

186

SORROWS. 6s, 5s & 7.   J. P. POWELL.

Night, with eb-on pinion, Brooded o'er the vale; All around was si-lent,

Save the night-wind's wail, When Christ, the Man of Sorrows, In tears and

sweat and blood, Prostrate in the gar-den, Raised his voice to God.

By permission.

534

NIGHT, with ebon pinion,
  Brooded o'er the vale;
All around was silent,
  Save the night-wind's wail,
When Christ, the Man of Sorrows,
  In tears and sweat and blood,
Prostrate in the garden,
  Raised his voice to God.

2 Smitten for offenses
  Which were not his own,
He, for our transgressions,
  Had to weep alone;

No friend with words to comfort,
  Nor hand to help was there,
When the Meek and Lowly
  Humbly bowed in prayer.

3 Abba, Father, Father,
  If indeed it may,
Let this cup of anguish
  Pass from me, I pray.
Yet, if it must be suffered
  By me, thine only Son,
Abba, Father, Father,
  Let thy will be done.
                              L. H. JAMESON.

535

WE SPEAK of the realms of the blest,
  That country so bright and so fair,
And oft are its glories confessed:
  But what must it be to be there!

2 We speak of its pathways of gold,
Of its walls decked with jewels so rare,
Of its wonders and pleasures untold:
  But what must it be to be there!

3 We speak of its freedom from sin,
  From sorrow, temptation and care,

From trials without and within:
  But what must it be to be there!

4 We speak of its service of love,
  The robes which the glorified wear,
The Church of the First-born above:
  But what must it be to be there!

5 O Lord, in this valley of woe,
  Our spirits for heaven prepare;
Then shortly we also shall know
  And feel what it is to be there.
                              MRS. E. MILLS.

RAYNOLDS. 10s.　　　　　　　　　　　　　　　MENDELSSOHN.

Here, O my Lord, I see thee face to face; Here would I touch and handle things unseen;

Here grasp with firmer hand th'eternal grace,　And all my wea-ri-ness up-on thee lean.

536

HERE, O my Lord, I see thee face to face;
　Here would I touch and handle things unseen;
Here grasp with firmer hand th' eternal grace,
　And all my weariness upon thee lean.

2 Here would I feed upon the bread of God;
　Here drink with thee the royal wine of heaven;
Here would I lay aside each earthly load,
　Here taste afresh the calm of sin forgiven.

3 Too soon we rise; the symbols disappear;
　The feast, though not the love, is passed and gone;
The bread and wine remove, but thou art here—
　Nearer than ever—still my Shield and Sun.

4 Feast after feast thus comes and passes by;
　Yet, passing, points to the glad feast above—
Giving sweet foretaste of the festal joy,
　The Lamb's great bridal feast of bliss and love.

HORATIUS BONAR.

MT. BLANC. P. M.　　　　　　　　　　　　　English Melody.

We are on our journey home, Where Christ, our Lord, is gone; We shall meet around his throne,

When he makes his peo-ple one, In the new, In the new　Je - ru - sa - lem.
In the new Je-ru-sa-lem.

EVENTIDE. 10s.   W. H. MONK.

A-bide with me: fast falls the e-ven- tide ; The darkness deep-ens : Lord, with me a-bide ;

When oth-er help- ers fail, and comforts flee, Help of the helpless, O a-bide with me.

537

ABIDE with me: fast falls the eventide ;
The darkness deepens : Lord, with me abide ;
When other helpers fail, and comforts flee,
Help of the helpless, O abide with me.

2 Swift to its close ebbs out life's little day ;
Earth's joys grow dim, its glories pass away ;
Change and decay in all around I see :
O thou who changest not, abide with me.

3 I need thy presence every passing hour :
What but thy grace can foil the tempter's power?
Who, like thyself, my guide and stay can be?
Through cloud and sunshine, O abide with me.

4 Hold thou thy cross before my closing eyes ;
Shine through the gloom, and point me to the skies :
Heaven's morning breaks, and earth's vain shadows flee :
In life, in death, O Lord, abide with me.

H. F. LYTE.

538

WE ARE on our journey home,
 Where Christ, our Lord, is gone ;
We shall meet around his throne,
When he makes his people one,
 In the new Jerusalem.

2 We can see that distant home,
 Though clouds rise dark between ;
Faith views the radiant dome,
 And a luster flashes keen
 From the new Jerusalem.

3 O holy, heavenly home !
 O rest eternal there !
When shall the exiles come
 Where they cease from earthly care,
 In the new Jerusalem?

4 Our hearts are breaking now
 Those mansions fair to see :
O Lord, thy heavens bow,
 And raise us up with thee—
 To the new Jerusalem.

CHARLES BEECHER.

NEW CHRISTIAN

WESLEY. 11s & 10s.   LOWELL MASON.

Hail to the brightness of Zion's glad morning! Joy to the lands that in darkness have lain!

Hushed be the accents of sorrow and mourning: Zi-on in triumph be-gins her mild reign.

539

HAIL to the brightness of Zion's glad morning!
Joy to the lands that in darkness have lain!
Hushed be the accents of sorrow and mourning:
Zion in triumph begins her mild reign.

2 Hail to the brightness of Zion's glad morning,
Long by the prophets of Israel foretold!
Hail to the millions from bondage returning!
Gentiles and Jews, the blest vision behold.

3 Lo! in the desert rich flowers are springing;
Streams ever copious are gliding along;
Loud from the mountain-tops echoes are ringing;
Wastes rise in verdure and mingle in song.

4 See from all lands—from the isles of the ocean—
Praise to Jehovah ascending on high;
Fall'n are the engines of war and commotion,
Shouts of salvation are rending the sky.
                                        THOS. HASTINGS.

FREDERICK. 11s.   GEO. KINGSLEY.

I would not live always; I ask not to stay Where storm after storm rises dark o'er the way;

The few cloudy mornings that dawn on us here Are enough for life's woes, full enough for its cheer.

COMFORT. 10s & 11s.   FROM "SOCIAL HYMN AND TUNE-BOOK."

Though troubles assail, and dangers affright, Though friends should all fail, and foes all unite;

Yet one thing secures us, what-ev-er betide— The Scripture assures us, the Lord will provide.

540

THOUGH troubles assail and dangers affright,
Though friends should all fail, and foes all unite;
Yet one thing secures us, whatever betide,
The Scripture assures us, the Lord will provide.

2 The birds, without barn or store-house are fed:
From them let us learn to trust for our bread;
His saints what is fitting shall ne'er be denied,
So long as 'tis written, the Lord will provide.

3 We may, like the ships, by tempests be tossed
On perilous deeps, but can not be lost;
Though Satan enrages the wind and the tide,
The promise engages, the Lord will provide.

4 His call we obey, like Abram of old,
Not knowing our way, but faith makes us bold;
For though we are strangers, we have a good Guide,
And trust, in all dangers, the Lord will provide.
JOHN NEWTON.

541

I WOULD not live always; I ask not to stay
Where storm after storm rises dark o'er the way;
The few cloudy mornings that dawn on us here
Are enough for life's woes, full enough for its cheer.

2 I would not live always; no, welcome the tomb!
Since Jesus has lain there, I dread not its gloom;
There sweet be my rest, till he bid me arise,
To hail him in triumph descending the skies.

3 Who, who would live always, away from his God,
Away from yon heaven, that blissful abode,
Where the rivers of pleasure flow o'er the bright plains,
And the noontide of glory eternally reigns;

4 Where the saints of all ages in harmony meet,
Their Saviour and brethren transported to greet;
While the anthems of rapture unceasingly roll,
And the smile of the Lord is the feast of the soul?
W. A. MUHLENBERG.

191

SLEEP THY LAST SLEEP. 10s. (Quartet.)   JOSEPH BARNBY.

Sleep thy last sleep, free from care and sorrow; Rest, where none weep, till th'eternal morrow:

Though dark waves roll o'er the si - lent riv - er, Thy fainting soul Jesus can deliver.

542

SLEEP thy last sleep, free from care and sorrow;
Rest, where none weep, till th' eternal morrow:
Though dark waves roll o'er the silent river,
Thy fainting soul Jesus can deliver.

2 Life's dream is past, all its sin, its sadness;
Brightly at last dawns a day of gladness:
Under the sod, earth, receive our treasure,
To rest in God, waiting all his pleasure.

3 Though we may mourn those in life the dearest,
They shall return, Christ, when thou appearest;
Soon shall thy voice comfort those now weeping,
Bidding rejoice all in Jesus sleeping.

E. A. DAYMAN.

SILENT NIGHT. 6, 6, 9, 9, 6.   German Melody.

Si-lent night! hallowed night! Land and deep silent sleep! { Soft-ly glitters bright Beckoning Isra - el's

Bethlehem's star, } eye from a - far, { Where the Saviour is born, Where the Saviour is born.

THOU ART GONE TO THE GRAVE. 12s & 11s.

Thou art gone to the grave; but we will not de-plore thee, Though sorrows and dark-ness en - compass the tomb; The Saviour has passed thro' its por-tals be - fore thee, And the lamp of his love is thy guide thro' the gloom.

543

Thou art gone to the grave, but we will not deplore thee,
  Though sorrows and darkness encompass the tomb;
The Saviour has passed through its portals before thee,
  And the lamp of his love is thy guide through the gloom.

2 Thou art gone to the grave; we no longer behold thee,
  Nor tread the rough paths of the world by thy side;
But the wide arms of mercy are spread to enfold thee,
  And sinners may hope, since the Saviour has died.

3 Thou art gone to the grave, and, its mansion forsaking,
  Perchance thy weak spirit in doubt lingered long;
But the sunshine of heaven beamed bright on thy waking,
  And the sound thou didst hear was the seraphim's song.

4 Thou art gone to the grave, but we will not deplore thee,
  Since God was thy Ransom, thy Guardian, thy Guide;
He gave thee, he took thee, and he will restore thee;
  And death has no sting, since the Saviour has died.   R. Heber.

544

Silent night! hallowed night!
  Land and deep silent sleep!
Softly glitters bright Bethlehem's star,
Beckoning Israel's eye from afar,
  Where the Saviour is born.

2 Silent night! hallowed night!
  On the plain wakes the strain,
Sung by heavenly harbingers bright,
Fraught with tidings of boundless delight:
  Christ the Saviour has come.

3 Silent night! hallowed night!
  Earth awake, silence break;
High your anthems of melody raise,
Heaven and earth in full chorus of praise:
  Peace forever shall reign.
                        Unknown.

DYKES. 7s. 6 l.   J. B. DYKES.

Rock of A - ges, cleft for me, Let me hide my-self in thee;

Let the wa - ter and the blood, From thy riv - en side which flowed,

Be of sin the doub-le cure, Cleanse me from its guilt and power.

545   *[To other tune, No. 600.]*

Rock of Ages, cleft for me,
Let me hide myself in thee;
Let the water and the blood,
From thy rivén side which flowed,
Be of sin the double cure,
Cleanse me from its guilt and power.

2 Not the labor of my hands
Can fulfill the law's demands;
Could my zeal no respite know,
Could my tears forever flow,
All for sin could not atone;
Thou must save, and thou alone.

3 While I draw this fleeting breath,
When my heart-strings break in death,
When I soar to worlds unknown,
See thee on thy judgment throne,
Rock of Ages, cleft for me,
Let me hide myself in thee.

       A. M. TOPLADY.

546

"TILL he come:" O let the words
Linger on the trembling chords;
Let the little while between
In their golden light be seen;
Let us think how heaven and home
Lie beyond that—"Till he come."

2 When the weary ones we love
Enter on their rest above,
Seems the earth so poor and vast,
All our life-joy overcast?
Hush! be every murmur dumb:
It is only—"Till he come."

3 See, the feast of love is spread:
Drink the wine, and break the bread—
Sweet memorials—till the Lord
Call us round his heavenly board—
Some from earth, from glory some,
Severed only—"Till he come."

      E. H. BICKERSTETH.

LUX BENIGNA. 10s & 4s.

J. B. DYKES.

Lead, kindly Light! amid th'encircling gloom, Lead thou me on. The night is dark, and I am far from home: Lead thou me on. Keep thou my feet: I do not ask to see The dis-tant scene; one step e-nough for me.

547

LEAD, kindly Light! amid th' encircling gloom,
  Lead thou me on.
The night is dark, and I am far from home:
  Lead thou me on.
Keep thou my feet: I do not ask to see
The distant scene; one step enough for me.

2 I was not ever thus, nor prayed that thou
    Shouldst lead me on.
I loved to choose and see my path; but now
    Lead thou me on.
I loved the garish day, and, spite of fears,
Pride ruled my will.   Remember not past years.

3 So long thy power has blest me, sure it still
    Will lead me on,
O'er moor and fen, o'er crag and torrent, till
    The night is gone,
And with the morn those angel faces smile
Which I have loved long since, and lost awhile.

J. H. NEWMAN.

FADING, STILL FADING. P. M., with Refrain.

F. V. WEISENTHAL.

Fading, still fading, the last beam is shining; Father in heaven, the day is de-clining:

Safety and innocence flee with the light, Temptation and danger walk forth with the night.

From the fall of the shade till the morning bells chime, Shield us from danger, keep us from crime.

REFRAIN.

2nd verse.

Father, have mercy, Father, have mercy, Father, have mercy, thro' Jesus Christ our Lord. Amen.

548

FADING, still fading, the last beam is shining;
Father in heaven, the day is declining:
Safety and innocence flee with the light,
Temptation and danger walk forth with the night.
From the fall of the shade till the morning bells chime,
Shield us from danger, keep us from crime.—REF.

2 Father in heaven, O hear when we call;
Hear, for Christ's sake, who is Saviour of all.
Feeble and fainting, we trust in thy might;
In doubting and darkness thy love be our light;
Let us sleep on thy breast while the night taper burns,
Wake in thine arms when morning returns.—REF.

SELINA HUNTINGTON.

REJOICE AND BE GLAD. P. M., with Refrain.   English Melody.

Rejoice and be glad: the Redeemer has come. Go look on his cradle, his cross, and his tomb.

REFRAIN.   1st.   2nd.

{ Sound his praises, tell the sto - ry   Of   him who was slain: He liv-eth a - gain.
{ Sound his praises, tell with gladness,   *(For last verse.)*   He com-eth a - gain.

549   *(First verse in the music.)*

2 Rejoice and be glad: for the blood has been shed;
Redemption is finished, the price has been paid.

3 Rejoice and be glad: for the Lamb that was slain,
O'er death is triumphant, and liveth again.

4 Rejoice and be glad: for our King is on high;
He pleadeth for us on his throne in the sky.

5 Rejoice and be glad: for he cometh again—
He cometh in glory, the Lamb that was slain.

H. BONAR.

550

WE PRAISE thee, O God, for the Son of thy love,
For Jesus who died, and is now gone above.

2 We praise thee, O God, for thy Spirit of light,
Who has shown us our Saviour, and scattered our night.

3 All glory and praise to the Lamb that was slain,
Who has borne all our sins, and has cleansed every stain!

4 All glory and praise to the God of all grace,
Who has bought us, and sought us, and guided our ways!

5 Revive us again; fill each heart with thy love;
May each soul be rekindled with fire from above.

W. P. MACKEY.

HE LEADETH ME. L. M., with Refrain, or L. M. D.   Wm. B. Bradbury.

He leadeth me: O bless-ed thought! O words with heavenly comfort fraught! Whate'er I do, wher-

REFRAIN.

e'er I be, Still 'tis God's hand that lead-eth me. He leadeth me, he lead-eth me; By

his own hand he leadeth me; His faithful follower I would be, For by his hand he leadeth me.

By permission of Biglow & Main.

551

HE LEADETH me: O blessèd thought!
O words with heavenly comfort fraught!
Whate'er I do, where'er I be,
Still, 'tis God's hand that leadeth me.—Ref.

2 Sometimes 'mid scenes of deepest gloom,
Sometimes where Eden's bowers bloom,
By waters still, o'er troubled sea—
Still, 'tis God's hand that leadeth me.—Ref.

3 Lord, I would clasp thy hand in mine,
Nor ever murmur or repine;
Content, whatever lot I see,
Since 'tis my God that leadeth me.—Ref.

4 And when my task on earth is done,
When by thy grace the victory's won,
E'en death's cold wave I will not flee,
Since God thro' Jordan leadeth me.—Ref.

J. H. Gilmore.

552

The Lord himself doth condescend
To be my Shepherd and my Friend;
I on his faithfulness rely,
His care shall all my wants supply.

In pastures green he doth me lead,
And there in safety makes me feed;
Refreshing streams are ever nigh,
My thirsty soul to satisfy.

2 When strayed, or languid, I complain,
His grace revives my soul again;
For his name's sake in ways upright
He makes me walk with great delight.
Yea, when death's gloomy vale I tread,
With joy, e'en there, I'll lift my head;
From fear and dread he'll keep me free,
His rod and staff shall comfort me.

3 Thou spread'st a table, Lord, for me,
While foes with spite thy goodness see;
Thou dost my head with oil anoint,
And a full cup for me appoint.
Goodness and mercy shall to me,
Through all my life extended be;
And when my pilgrimage is o'er,
I'll dwell with thee for evermore.

New York Dutch Reformed Collection of Psalms.

SWEET HOUR OF PRAYER. L. M. D. Wm. B. Bradbury.

Sweet hour of prayer, sweet hour of prayer, That calls me from a world of care, And bids me, at my
D. S. And oft escaped the
Father's throne, Make all my wants and wishes known: { In seasons of distress and grief
tempter's snare, By thy return, sweet hour of prayer. { My soul has oft-en found re - lief, }

By permission of Bigdow & Main.

553

Sweet hour of prayer, sweet hour of prayer,
That calls me from a world of care,
And bids me, at my Father's throne,
Make all my wants and wishes known!
In seasons of distress and grief
My soul has often found relief,
And oft escaped the tempter's snare,
By thy return, sweet hour of prayer.

2 Sweet hour of prayer, sweet hour of prayer,
The joy I feel, the bliss I share
Of those whose anxious spirits burn
With strong desires for thy return!
With such I hasten to the place
Where God, my Saviour, shows his face,
And gladly take my station there,
And wait for thee, sweet hour of prayer.

3 Sweet hour of prayer, sweet hour of prayer,
Thy wings shall my petition bear
To him whose truth and faithfulness
Engage the waiting soul to bless;
And since he bids me seek his face,
Believe his word, and trust his grace,
I'll cast on him my every care,
And wait for thee, sweet hour of prayer.
W. W. Walford.

554

And is the gospel peace and love?
Such let our conversation be—
The serpent blended with the dove,
Wisdom and meek simplicity.
Whene'er the angry passions rise
And tempt our thoughts or tongues to strife,
On Jesus let us fix our eyes,
Bright pattern of the Christian life.

2 O how benevolent and kind!
How mild! how ready to forgive!
Be his the temper of our mind,
And his the rules by which we live.
To do his heavenly Father's will
Was his employment and delight;
Humility, and love, and zeal
Shone through his life divinely bright.

3 Dispensing good where'er he came,
The labors of his life were love:
O if we love the Saviour's name,
Let his divine example move!
Thy fair example may we trace,
To teach us what we ought to be;
Make us, by thy transforming grace,
Lord Jesus, daily more like thee.
Anne Steele.
Anon.

YOUNG. L. M. D.

LOVING KINDNESS. L. M.

American Melody.

Awake, my soul, to joyful lays,
And sing the great Redeemer's praise:
He justly claims a song from me—
His loving kindness, O how free!
His loving kindness, loving kindness,
His loving kindness, O how free!

555

AWAKE, my soul, to joyful lays,
And sing the great Redeemer's praise:
He justly claims a song from me—
His loving kindness, O how free!

2 He saw me ruined in the fall,
Yet loved me, notwithstanding all;
He saved me from my lost estate—
His loving kindness, O how great!

3 Though numerous hosts of mighty foes,
Though earth and hell my way oppose,
He safely leads my soul along;—
His loving kindness, O how strong!

4 When trouble, like a gloomy cloud,
Has gathered thick and thundered loud,
He near my soul has always stood—
His loving kindness, O how good!

SAMUEL MEDLEY.

HAPPY DAY. L. M., with Chorus.

E. F. RIMBAULT.

CHORUS.

O happy day, that fixed my choice On thee, my Saviour and my God!
Well may this glowing heart rejoice, And tell its raptures all abroad.
Hap-py day, hap-py day,
D. S. Happy day, happy day,

Fine.

When Je - sus washed my sins a - way;
When Je - sus washed my sins a - way!
He taught me how to watch and pray,
And live re-joic-ing ev - ery day.

D. S.

556

O HAPPY day, that fixed my choice
On thee, my Saviour and my God!
Well may this glowing heart rejoice,
And tell its raptures all abroad. —CHO.

2 O happy bond, that seals my vows
To him who merits all my love!
Let cheerful anthems fill his house,
While to that sacred shrine I move. —CHO.

3 'Tis done, the great transaction's done;
I am my Lord's and he is mine;
He drew me, and I followed on,
Charmed to confess the voice divine. —CHO.

4 Now rest, my long-divided heart,
Fixed on this blissful center, rest;
Here have I found a nobler part,
Here heavenly pleasures fill my breast. —CHO.

PHILIP DODDRIDGE.

WOODWORTH. L. M.   WM. B. BRADBURY.

just as I am, with-out one plea, But that thy blood was shed for me,

And that thou bidd'st me come to thee, O Lamb of God, I come, I come.

By permission of Biglow & Main.

557

JUST as I am, without one plea,
But that thy blood was shed for me,
And that thou bidd'st me come to thee,
   O Lamb of God, I come, I come.

2 Just as I am, and waiting not
To rid my soul of one dark blot;
To thee, whose blood can cleanse each spot,
   O Lamb of God, I come, I come.

3 Just as I am, though tossed about
With many a conflict, many a doubt;
With fears within, and foes without—
   O Lamb of God, I come, I come.

4 Just as I am, poor, wretched, blind,—
Sight, riches, healing of the mind,
Yea, all I need, in thee to find—
   O Lamb of God, I come, I come.

5 Just as I am—thou wilt receive,
Wilt welcome, pardon, cleanse, relieve,
Because thy promise I believe—
   O Lamb of God, I come, I come.

6 Just as I am—thy love unknown,
Has broken every barrier down;
Now to be thine, yea, thine alone,
   O Lamb of God, I come, I come.
              CHARLOTTE ELLIOTT.

RETREAT. L. M.   THOS. HASTINGS.

From ev-er-y storm-y wind that blows, From ev-er-y swell-ing tide of woes,

There is a calm, a sure re-treat; 'Tis found be-neath the mer-cy - seat.

558   [First verse in the music]

2 There is a place where Jesus sheds
The oil of gladness on our heads—
A place than all besides more sweet;
It is the blood-bought mercy-seat.

3 There is a scene where spirits blend,
Where friend holds fellowship with friend;
Though sundered far, by faith they meet
Around one common mercy-seat.

4 Ah! whither could we flee for aid,
When tempted, desolate, dismayed;

Or how the host of hell defeat,
Had suffering souls no mercy-seat?

5 There, there on eagle wings we soar,
And sin and sense seem all no more;
And heaven comes down our souls to greet,
And glory crowns the mercy-seat.

6 O let my hand forget her skill,
My tongue be silent, cold, and still,
This bounding heart forget to beat,
Ere I forget the mercy-seat.
            H. STOWELL.

CHESTNUT STREET. L. M.   M. C. RAMSEY.

Life is the time to serve the Lord, The time t' insure the great reward; And while the lamp holds

ont to burn, O has-ten, sin - ner, to re - turn, O has-ten, sin - ner, to re - turn.

559

LIFE is the time to serve the Lord,
The time t' insure the great reward;
And while the lamp holds out to burn,
O hasten, sinner, to return.

2 Life is the hour that God has given
T' escape from hell, and fly to heaven;
The day of grace, when mortals may
Secure the blessings of the day.

3 Then what my thoughts design to do,
My hands, with all your might, pursue:
Since no device nor work is found,
Nor faith, nor hope, beneath the ground.

4 There are no acts of pardon passed
In the cold grave to which we haste:
O may we all receive thy grace,
And see with joy thy smiling face.
                                   ISAAC WATTS.

560

O DO not let the word depart,
And close thine eyes against the light;
Poor sinner, harden not thine heart:
Thou wouldst be saved: why not to-night?

2 To-morrow's sun may never rise,
To bless thy long deluded sight;
This is the time: O then be wise—
Thou wouldst be saved: why not to-night?

3 Our God in pity lingers still,
And wilt thou thus his love requite?
Renounce at once thy stubborn will:
Thou wouldst be saved: why not to-night?

4 Our blessèd Lord refuses none
Who would to him their souls unite;
Believe, obey him, and 'tis done:
Thou wouldst be saved: why not to-night?
                                   UNKNOWN.

ROSECRANS. L. M., with Refrain.   J. H. FILLMORE.

O do not let the word depart, Poor sinner, harden not thine heart:
And close thine eyes against the light;

REFRAIN.
Repeat ppp.   Cres.

Thou wouldst be saved: why not to-night?   Thou wouldst be saved: why not to-night?
Why not to-night?   why not

THE FOUNDATION-STONE. L. M., with Chorus.

T. C. O'KANE.

There stands a Rock, on shores of time, That rears to heaven its head sub-lime;

That Rock is cleft, and they are blest Who find with-in this cleft a rest.

CHORUS.

Some build their hopes on the ever-drifting sand, Some on their fame or their treasure or their land;

Mine's on the Rock that for-ev-er shall stand, Je-sus, tho "Rock of A-ges."

By permission.

561

THERE stands a Rock, on shores of time,
That rears to heaven its head sublime;
That Rock is cleft, and they are blest
Who find within this cleft a rest.

CHO.—Some build their hopes on the
    ever-drifting sand,
Some on their fame or their treasure
    or their land;
Mine's on the Rock that forever shall stand,
  Jesus, the " Rock of Ages."

2 That Rock's a cross, its arms outspread,
Celestial glory bathes its head;
To its firm base my all I bring,
And to the Cross of Ages cling.—Cho.

3 That Rock's a Tower, whose lofty
    height,
Illumed with heaven's unclouded light,
Opes wide its gates beneath the dome,
Where saints find rest with Christ at
    home.—Cho.

S. S. Journal.

FOUNTAIN. C. M.

American Melody.

There is a fountain filled with blood, Drawn from Immanuel's veins; And sinners, plunged beneath that flood, Lose all their guilty stains, Lose all their guilty stains, Lose all their guilty stains.

562 *[First verse in the music.]*

2 The dying thief rejoiced to see
That fountain in his day;
And there have I, as vile as he,
Washed all my sins away.

3 O Lamb of God, thy precious blood
Shall never lose its power,
Till all the ransomed Church of God
Be saved, to sin no more.

4 E'er since by faith I saw the stream
Thy flowing wounds supply,
Redeeming love has been my theme,
And shall be till I die.

5 And when this lisping, stammering tongue
Lies silent in the grave,
Then, in a nobler, sweeter song
I'll sing thy power to save.

WM. COWPER.

REMEMBER ME. C. M., with Refrain.

ASA HULL.

Je-sus, thou art the sin-ner's friend; As such I look to thee;
REF. Re-mem-ber me, re-mem-ber me, O Lord, re-mem-ber me;

Now, in the full-ness of thy love, O Lord, re-mem-ber me.

By Permission.

563 *[First verse in the music.]*

2 Remember thy pure word of grace,
Remember Calvary;
Remember all thy promises,
And then remember me.—REF.

3 Thou mighty Advocate with God,
I yield myself to thee:
While thou art sitting on thy throne,
O Lord, remember me.—REF.

[To other tune, No. 26.]

4 I own I'm guilty, own I'm vile;
Yet thy salvation's free:
Then in thy all-abounding grace,
O Lord, remember me.—REF.

5 And when I close my eyes in death,
And creature helps all flee,
Then, O my great Redeemer, Lord,
I pray, remember me.—REF.

RICHARD BURNHAM.

MAITLAND. C. M.

G. N. ALLEN.

Must Je-sus bear the cross a-lone, And all the world go free?

No; there's a cross for ev-er-y one, And there's a cross for me.

564

MUST Jesus bear the cross alone,
    And all the world go free?
No; there's a cross for every one,
    And there's a cross for me.

2 The consecrated cross I'll bear
    Till death shall set me free,
And then go home my crown to wear—
    For there's a crown for me.

3 Upon the crystal pavement, down
    At Jesus' pierced feet,
Joyful I'll cast my golden crown,
    And his dear name repeat.

4 O precious cross! O glorious crown!
    O resurrection day!
Ye angels, from the stars come down,
    And bear my soul away.
                    T. SHEPHERD.

565

RETURN, O wanderer, now return,
    And seek thy Father's face:
Those new desires which in thee burn
    Were kindled by his grace.

2 Return, O wanderer, now return:
    He hears thy humble sigh;
He sees thy softened spirit mourn,
    When no one else is nigh.

3 Return, O wanderer, now return:
    Thy Saviour bids thee live:
Go to his feet, and grateful learn
    How freely he'll forgive.

4 Return, O wanderer, now return,
    And wipe the falling tear:
Thy Father calls—no longer mourn:
    'Tis love invites thee near.
                    W. B. COLLYER.

PASSING AWAY. C. M., with Chorus.

A. D. FILLMORE.

Re-turn, O wan-der-er, now re-turn, And seek thy Fa-ther's face:
Those new de-sires which in thee burn Were kin-dled by his grace.

CHORUS.

We are pass-ing a-way, We are pass-ing a-way;
We are pass-ing a-way To the great judg-ment-day.

NEW CHRISTIAN

MT. PISGAH. C. M.   American Melody.

Am I a sol-dier of the cross, A fol-lower of the Lamb,

And shall I fear to own his cause, Or blush to speak his name?

566

Am I a soldier of the cross,
  A follower of the Lamb,
And shall I fear to own his cause,
  Or blush to speak his name?

2 Must I be carried to the skies
  On flowery beds of ease,
While others fought to win the prize,
  And sailed through bloody seas?

3 Are there no foes for me to face?
  Must I not stem the flood?
Is this vile world a friend to grace,
  To help me on to God?

4 Sure I must fight if I would reign:
  Increase my courage, Lord.
I'll bear the toil, endure the pain,
  Supported by thy word.

5 Thy saints, in all this glorious war,
  Shall conquer, though they die;
They see the triumph from afar,
  With Faith's discerning eye.

6 When that illustrious day shall rise,
  And all thine armies shine,
In robes of victory through the skies,
  The glory shall be thine.
                              Isaac Watts.

567

I'm not ashamed to own my Lord,
  Nor to defend his cause;
Maintain the honor of his word,
  The glory of his cross.

2 Jesus, my Lord, I know his name,
  His name is all my trust;
Nor will he put my soul to shame,
  Nor let my hope be lost.

3 Firm as his throne his promise stands,
  And he can well secure
What I've committed to his hands
  Till the decisive hour.

4 Then will he own my worthless name
  Before his Father's face,
And in the New Jerusalem
  Appoint for me a place.
                              Isaac Watts.

568

Ye men and angels, witness now:
  Before the Lord we speak;
To him we make our solemn vow—
  A vow we dare not break—

2 That, long as life itself shall last,
  Ourselves to Christ we yield;
Nor from his cause will we depart,
  Or ever quit the field.

3 We trust not in our native strength,
  But on his grace rely:
May he, with our returning wants,
  All needful aid supply.

4 O guide our doubtful feet aright,
  And keep us in thy ways;
And, while we turn our vows to prayers,
  Turn thou our prayers to praise.
                              Benj. Beddome.

VAIL. C. M., with Chorus.   S. J. VAIL.

(musical notation)

Alas! and did my Saviour bleed? And did my Sovereign die? Would he devote that sacred head
D. C. Yes, Jesus died for all mankind: Bless God, salvation's free.

CHORUS.   D. C.

(musical notation)

For such a worm as I? Je - sus died for you, Je - sus died for me;

569 *[First verse in the music.]*

2 Was it for crimes that I had done
He groaned upon the tree?
Amazing pity! grace unknown!
And love beyond degree!—Cho.

3 Well might the sun in darkness hide,
And shut his glories in,
When God's own Son was crucified
For man the creature's sin.—Cho.

4 Thus might I hide my blushing face
While his dear cross appears,
Dissolve my heart in thankfulness,
And melt mine eyes to tears. - Cho.

5 But drops of grief can ne'er repay
The debt of love I owe:
Here, Lord, I give myself away—
'Tis all that I can do.—Cho.

ISAAC WATTS.

I BELIEVE. C. M., with Refrain.   Anon.

(musical notation)

Lord, I be - lieve; thy power I own; Thy word I would o - bey;
REF. I do be - lieve, I do be - lieve, That Je - sus died for me;

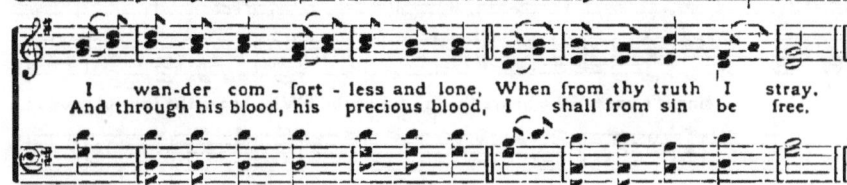

I wan-der com - fort - less and lone, When from thy truth I stray.
And through his blood, his precious blood, I shall from sin be free.

570 *[First verse in the music.]*

2 Lord, I believe; but gloomy fears
Sometimes bedim my sight;
I look to thee with prayers and tears,
And cry for strength and light.—REF.

3 Lord, I believe; but oft, I know,
My faith is cold and weak:

My weakness strengthen, and bestow
The confidence I seek.—REF.

4 Yes, I believe; and only thou
Canst give my soul relief:
Lord, to thy truth my spirit bow;
"Help thou mine unbelief."—REF.

J. R. WREFORD.

NEW CHRISTIAN

WHERE'ER THOU GOEST. C. M., with Chorus.

T. E. HALL.

Wher-e'er thou goest I will go: Dear Saviour, lead the way: Just where, or how, I do not know,
D. S. Where'er thou goest I will go,

Fine. CHORUS. D. S.

But thou'lt not lead a-stray. Wher-e'er thou goest I will go, Near thee I'll keep each day;
Through all life's weary way.

Copyright, 1879, by Asa Hull.

571

WHERE'ER thou goest I will go:
 Dear Saviour, lead the way:
Just where, or how, I do not know,
 But thou'lt not lead astray.—CHO.

2 Where'er thou goest I will go,
 Though up the mountain steep;
A faithful Guide thou art, I know,
 So close to thee I'll keep.—CHO.

3 Where'er thou goest I will go,
 Though in some lonely dell;
Thou wilt be there—how sweet to know:
 And cheerless hours dispel.—CHO.

4 Where'er thou goest I will go,
 Through all my life's rough way;
And, at its end, I'll pass, I know,
 Into an endless day.—CHO.

T. E. HALL.

COWPER. C. M.

LOWELL MASON.

O what amazing words of grace Are in the gos-pel found, Suit - ed to

ev - ery sinner's case Who hears the joy-ful sound! Who hears the joy-ful sound!

572

O WHAT amazing words of grace
 Are in the gospel found,
Suited to every sinner's case
 Who hears the joyful sound!

2 Come, then, with all your wants and wounds,
 Your every burden bring;
Here love, unchanging love, abounds—
 A deep, celestial spring.

3 This spring with living water flows,
 And heavenly joy imparts:
Come, thirsty souls, your wants disclose,
 And drink with thankful hearts.

4 Millions of sinners, vile as you,
 Have here found life and peace:
Come, then, and prove its virtues, too,
 And drink, adore, and bless.

SAMUEL MEDLEY.

ON JORDAN'S STORMY BANKS. C. M., with Chorus. T. C. O'KANE.

1. On Jor-dan's storm-y banks I stand, And cast a wish-ful eye
2. O'er all those wide-ex-tend-ed plains Shines one e-ter-nal day;

To Ca-naan's fair and hap-py land, Where my pos-ses-sions lie.
There God, the Sun, for-ev-er reigns, And scat-ters night a-way.

CHORUS.

We will rest in the fair and hap-py land, (by and by,) Just a-cross on the

ev-er-green shore . . . . Sing the song of Mo-ses and the
ev-er-green shore,

Lamb, by and by, And dwell with Je-sus ev-er-more,

By permission.

573 [*First and second verses in the music.*]
3 When shall I reach that happy place,
And be forever blest?
When shall I see my Father's face
And in his bosom rest?—CHO.

4 Filled with delight, my raptured soul
Would here no longer stay;
Though Jordan's waves around me roll,
Fearless I'd launch away.—CHO.
SAMUEL STENNETT.

18   209

NEW CHRISTIAN

PURER IN HEART. 6s & 4s. D.   J. H. FILLMORE.

Purer in heart, O God, Help me to be; May I devote my life Wholly to thee.

Watch thou my wayward feet, Guide me with counsel sweet; Purer in heart, Help me to be.

574

Purer in heart, O God,
    Help me to be;
May I devote my life
    Wholly to thee.
Watch thou my wayward feet,
Guide me with counsel sweet;
Purer in heart,
    Help me to be.

2 Purer in heart, O God,
    Help me to be;
Teach me to do thy will
    Most lovingly.

Be thou my Friend and Guide,
Let me with thee abide;
    Purer in heart,
    Help me to be.

3 Purer in heart, O God,
    Help me to be;
That I thy holy face
    One day may see.
Keep me from secret sin,
Reign thou my soul within;
    Purer in heart,
    Help me to be.

                                    MRS. A. L. DAVISON.

MORE LOVE. 6s & 4s. D.   T. F. PERKINS.

More love to thee, O Christ! More love to thee! Hear thou the prayer I make,
D. S. More love, O Christ, to thee,

On bended knee; This is my ear-nest plea—More love, O Christ, to thee!
More love to thee!

BETHANY. 6s & 4s. D.   LOWELL MASON.

Near - er, my God, to thee, Near - er   to   thee; E'en though it be   a cross
D. S. Near - er, my God, to thee,

That rais - eth me! Still all my song shall be, Near-er, my God, to thee!
Near - er   to thee!

By permission.

575

NEARER, my God, to thee,
　Nearer to thee;
E'en though it be a cross
　That raiseth me!
Still all my song shall be,
Nearer, my God, to thee!
　Nearer to thee!

2 Though like the wanderer,
　Daylight all gone,
Darkness be over me,
　My rest a stone;
Yet, in my dreams I'd be
Nearer, my God, to thee,
　Nearer to thee.

3 There let the way appear,
　Steps unto heaven;
All that thou sendest me,
　In mercy given;

Angels to beckon me
Nearer, my God, to thee,
　Nearer to thee.

4 Then, with my waking thoughts
　Bright with thy praise,
Out of my stony griefs
　Bethel I'll raise;
So by my woes to be
Nearer, my God, to thee,
　Nearer to thee.

5 Or if, on joyful wing,
　Cleaving the sky,
Sun, moon, and stars forgot,
　Upward I fly;
Still all my song shall be,
Nearer, my God, to thee!
　Nearer to thee!
　　　　　Mrs. S. F. ADAMS.

576

MORE love to thee, O Christ,
　More love to thee!
Hear thou the prayer I make
　On bended knee:
This is my earnest plea—
More love, O Christ, to thee!
　More love to thee!

2 Once earthly joy I craved—
　Sought peace and rest;
Now thee alone I seek:
　Give what is best.

This all my prayer shall be—
More love, O Christ, to thee;
　More love to thee!

3 Then shall my latest breath
　Whisper thy praise;
This be the parting cry
　My heart shall raise—
This still its prayer shall be,
More love, O Christ, to thee!
　More love to thee!
　　　　　Mrs. E. P. PRENTISS.

NEW CHRISTIAN

I NEED THEE. 6s & 4s., with Refrain.   ROBERT LOWRY.

I need thee every hour, Most gracious Lord; No other voice than thine Can

REFRAIN.

peace af-ford. I need thee, O I need thee; Every hour I need thee. O bless me

Copyright, 1879, by R. Lowry.

now, my Saviour: I come to thee.

577 [First verse in the music.]

2 I need thee every hour:
Stay thou near by—
Temptations lose their power
When thou art nigh.—REF.

3 I need thee every hour,
In joy or pain:
Come quickly and abide,
Or life is vain.—REF.

4 I need thee every hour:
Teach me thy will,
And thy rich promises
In me fulfil.—REF.

5 I need thee every hour,
Most Holy One:
O make me thine indeed,
Thou blessèd Son.
MRS. E. P. PRENTISS.

DEPENDENCE. 6s & 4s. D.   ANON.

{Cling to the Might-y One, Cling in thy grief;}
{Cling to the Ho-ly One, He gives re-lief;} Cling to the Gracious One,

Cling in thy pain; Cling to the Faithful One, He will sus-tain.

212

OLIVET. 6s & 4s. 7 l.   LOWELL MASON.

My faith looks up to thee, Thou Lamb of Cal - va - ry, Sav - iour di - vine:

{ Now hear me while I pray; }
{ Take all my guilt a - way; } O let me, from this day, Be whol - ly thine.

578

My FAITH looks up to thee,
Thou Lamb of Calvary,
  Saviour divine :
Now hear me while I pray;
Take all my guilt away;
O let me, from this day,
  Be wholly thine.

2 May thy rich grace impart
Strength to my fainting heart,
  My zeal inspire;
As thou hast died for me,
O may my love to thee
Pure, warm, and changeless be—
  A living fire.

3 While life's dark maze I tread,
And griefs around me spread,
  Be thou my guide;
Bid darkness turn to day,
Wipe sorrow's tears away,
Nor let me ever stray
  From thee aside.

4 When ends life's transient dream,
When death's cold, sullen stream
  Shall o'er me roll,
Blest Saviour, then, in love,
Fear and distress remove;
O bear me safe above—
  A ransomed soul.
          RAY PALMER.

579

CLING to the Mighty One,
  Cling in thy grief;
Cling to the Holy One,
  He gives relief;
Cling to the Gracious One,
  Cling in thy pain;
Cling to the Faithful One,
  He will sustain.

2 Cling to the Living One,
  Cling in thy woe;
Cling to the Loving One
  Through all below;

Cling to the Pardoning One,
  He speaketh peace;
Cling to the Healing One,
  Anguish shall cease.

3 Cling to the Bleeding One,
  Cling to his side;
Cling to the Risén One,
  In him abide;
Cling to the Coming One,
  Hope shall arise;
Cling to the Reigning One,
  Joy lights thine eyes.
          HENRY BENNETT.

MY PRAYER. 6s & 5s. D.   P. P. BLISS.

More ho - li-ness give me, More strivings with-in; More patience in suffer-ing,

More sor - row for sin; More faith in my Sav-iour, More sense of his care;

By permission of J. Church & Co.

More joy in his service, More purpose in prayer.

2 More gratitude give me,
    More trust in the Lord;
More pride in his glory,
    More hope in his word;
More tears for his sorrows,
    More pain at his grief;
More meekness in trial,
    More praise for relief.

3 More purity give me,
    More strength to o'ercome;
More freedom from earth-stains,
    More longings for home;
More fit for the kingdom,
    More useful I'd be;
More blessèd and holy,
    More, Saviour, like thee.
                        P. P. BLISS.

580

MORE holiness give me,
    More strivings within;
More patience in suffering,
    More sorrow for sin;
More faith in my Saviour,
    More sense of his care;
More joy in his service,
    More purpose in prayer.

EXCELSIOR. 6s & 5s. D.   S. J. VAIL.

Pur - er yet and pur - er   I would be   in mind, Dearer yet and dear-er
D. S. Pa-tient-ly be- liev - ing

Ev - ery du - ty find; Hop-ing still, and trust-ing God with-out a fear,
He will make all clear.

By permission.   214

HOW CAN I BUT LOVE HIM? 6s & 5s, with Refrain. F. S. LORENZ.

So ten - der, so pre-cious, My Sav - iour to me; So true and so gra - cious,

REFRAIN

I've found him to be; How can I but love him? But love him, but love him?

By permission.

There's no friend above him, Poor sinner, for thee.

581

So TENDER, so precious,
  My Saviour to me;
So true and so gracious,
  I've found him to be.—REF.

2 So patient, so kindly
  Toward all of my ways;
I blunder so blindly—
  He love still repays;—REF.

3 Of all friends the fairest
  And truest is he;
His love is the rarest
  That ever can be.—REF.

4 His beauty, though bleeding
  And circled with thorns,
Is then most exceeding,
  For grief him adorns.—REF.
                          J. E. RANKIN.

582

PURER yet and purer
  I would be in mind,
Dearer yet and dearer
  Every duty find;
Hoping still, and trusting
God without a fear,
Patiently believing
He will make all clear.

2 Calmer yet and calmer,
  Trial bear and pain;
Surer yet and surer,
  Peace at last to gain;

Suffering still and doing,
  To his will resigned,
And to God subduing
  Heart and will and mind.

3 Higher yet and higher,
  Out of clouds and night;
Nearer yet and nearer,
  Rising to the light;
Oft these earnest longings
  Swell within my breast;
Yet their inner meaning
  Ne'er can be expressed.
                          UNKNOWN.

NEW CHRISTIAN

SOMETHING FOR JESUS. 6s & 4s. D. ROBERT LOWRY.

Saviour, thy dying love Thou gavest me; Nor should I aught withhold, Dear Lord, from thee:

In love my soul would bow, My heart fulfill its vow, Some offering bring thee now, Something for thee.

Copyright, 1871, by Biglow & Main.

583

SAVIOUR, thy dying love
  Thou gavest me;
Nor should I aught withhold,
  Dear Lord, from thee:
In love my soul would bow,
My heart fulfill its vow,
Some offering bring thee now—
  Something for thee.

2 O'er the blest mercy-seat,
  Pleading for me,
My feeble faith looks up,
  Jesus, to thee;

Help me the cross to bear,
Thy wondrous love declare,
Some song to raise, or prayer—
  Something for thee.

3 Give me a faithful heart—
  Likeness to thee—
That each departing day
  Henceforth may see
Some work of love begun,
Some deed of kindness done,
Some wanderer sought and won—
  Something for thee.

S. D. PHELPS.

JESUS, I WILL TRUST THEE. 6s & 5s. D. J. H. F.

Jesus, I will trust thee, When across my soul, Like a fearful tempest, Doubts and fears shall roll.

Rit.

When the tempter cometh, Surely he will flee When I utter, "Jesus, I am trusting thee!"

VOGEL. 6s & 6s. D.
J. P. POWELL.

Long I was a wanderer—Je-sus now is mine; Yes, I've found a Saviour, Human and Divine.

High he lived in glo-ry—Low to earth he came; Told the wondrous story, Life in Jesus' name!

584

Long I was a wanderer—
  Jesus now is mine;
Yes, I've found a Saviour,
  Human and Divine.
High he lived in glory—
  Low to earth he came;
Told the wondrous story,
  Life in Jesus' name.

2 Equal with the Father—
  Poor like man on earth;
Mighty as Creator—
  Weak as babes at birth;
Hated and rejected,
  For our sins to die;
Buried, risen, ascended,
  Pleads my cause on high.

3 "I will ne'er forsake thee"—
  Thus his promise stands;
"In my hands I'll bear thee
  O'er the burning sands."
Full on him relying,
  Weakness is my strength;
Waiting, toiling, dying,
  Heaven is mine at length.

4 Sweet, so sweet, the service
  Which to him I give:
Hearken—come—dear sinner:
  Now my soul doth live.
Taste the precious Saviour—
  Feel the joy Divine;
Know the love unbounded:
  Jesus now is mine.
PETER VOGEL.

585

Jesus, I will trust thee,
  When across my soul,
Like a fearful tempest,
  Doubts and fears shall roll.
When the tempter cometh,
  Surely he will flee
When I utter, "Jesus,
  I am trusting thee!"

2 Jesus, I will trust thee;
  There is none beside;
In thine arms of mercy
  I will ever hide;

And for my acceptance,
  This my only plea—
Jesus died for sinners,
  Jesus died for me.

3 Jesus, I will trust thee;
  Trust thee even now;
Trust thee when the death-dew
  Gathers on my brow;
Trust thee in the sunshine,
  Trust thee in the shade;
With thy precious shelter,
  I am not afraid.
UNKNOWN.

19

I HEAR THY WELCOME VOICE. S. M., with Chorus. From "Hallowed Songs."

I hear thy welcome voice That calls me, Lord, to thee, For cleansing in thy

CHORUS.

precious blood That flowed on Cal-va - ry. I am com-ing, Lord, Com - ing

now to thee: Wash me, cleanse me in the blood That flowed on Cal - va - ry.

By permission.

586 [First verse in the music.]

2 Though coming weak and vile,
Thou dost my strength assure ;
Thou wilt my vileness fully cleanse,
And make my conscience pure.

3 'Tis Jesus calls me on
To perfect faith and love,
To perfect hope and peace and trust,
For earth and heaven above.

4 'Tis Jesus who confirms
The blesséd work within,
By adding grace to welcomed grace,
Where reigned the power of sin.

5 And he assurance gives
To loyal hearts and true,
That every promise is fulfilled
To those who hear and do.

L. Hartsough.

OAK. 6s & 4s. D.

Lowell Mason, alt.

{ I'm but a stran-ger here, Heaven is my home;
{ Earth is a des-ert drear, Heaven is my home;} Dan-ger and sorrow stand

Round me on ev-ery hand; Heaven is my fa-ther-land—Heaven is my home.

218

HYMN AND TUNE-BOOK.

NEARER MY HOME. S. M., with Chorus.   J. M. Evans.

A crown of glo-ry bright By eyes of faith I see, In realms of un-cre-at-ed light, Laid up in heaven for me. I'm nearer my home, nearer my home, Nearer my home to-day; Yes, nearer my home in heaven to-day Than ever I've been before.

587

A crown of glory bright,
By eyes of faith I see,
In realms of uncreated light,
Laid up in heaven for me.—Cho.

2 O may I faithful prove,
And keep that crown in view,
Sustained by faith and hope and love,
My heavenward way pursue.—Cho.

3 Jesus, be thou my guide;
My every step attend;
By day and night, be near my side,
And keep me to the end.—Cho.

4 Be thou my hiding-place,
My ever-present guard;
And help me, by thy sovereign grace,
To reach my great reward.
Arr. by L. H. Jameson.

588

I'm but a stranger here,
Heaven is my home;
Earth is a desert drear,
Heaven is my home;
Danger and sorrow stand
Round me on every hand;
Heaven is my father-land—
Heaven is my home.

2 What though the tempest rage!
Heaven is my home;
Short is my pilgrimage,
Heaven is my home.

And time's wild wintry blast
Soon will be overpast;
I shall reach home at last—
Heaven is my home.

3 There, at my Saviour's side—
Heaven is my home—
I shall be glorified;
Heaven is my home.
There with the good and blest,
Those I loved most and best,
I shall forever rest—
Heaven is my home.
T. R. Taylor.

ALL TO CHRIST I OWE. 6s & 7.   John T. Grape.

I hear the Saviour say, Thy strength indeed is small: Come to me—I'll be thy stay;

CHORUS.

Find in me thine all in all. Je-sus died for me, All to him I owe—

Sin had left a crimson stain; He washed it white as snow.

By permission.

589

I hear the Saviour say,
  Thy strength indeed is small:
Come to me—I'll be thy stay;
  Find in me thine all in all.—Cho.

2 For nothing good have I
  Whereby thy grace to claim—
Jesus died my soul to save,
  And bless'd be his name.—Cho.

3 When from my dying bed
  My ransomed soul shall rise,
"Jesus died my soul to save,"
  Shall rend the vaulted skies.—Cho.

4 And when, before the throne,
  I stand in him complete,
"Jesus died my soul to save,"
  My lips shall still repeat.

Mrs. E. M. Hall, alt.

SPEER. 6s.   J. H. Fillmore.

My spir-it longs for thee With-in my troub-led breast,

Though I un-worth-y be Of so di-vine a Guest.

I BRING MY SINS TO THEE. 6s & 8s. 61.   P. P. BLISS.

I bring my sins to thee, The sins I can not count, That all may cleans-ed be

In thy once o - pened fount— I bring them, Sav - iour, all to thee;

The bur - den is too great for me, The bur - den is too great for me.

By permission of J. Church & Co.

590

I BRING my sins to thee,
  The sins I can not count,
That all may cleansèd be
  In thy once opened fount—
I bring them, Saviour, all to thee;
The burden is too great for me.

2 I bring my grief to thee,
  The grief I can not tell;
No words shall needed be,
  Thou knowest all so well—
I bring the sorrow laid on me,
O suffering Saviour, all to thee.

3 My joys to thee I bring,
  The joys thy love has given,
That each may be a wing
  To lift me nearer heaven—
I bring them, Saviour, all to thee,
Who hast procured them all for me.

4 My life I bring to thee;
  I would not be my own:
O Saviour, let me be
  Thine ever, thine alone—
My heart, my life, my all I bring
To thee, my Saviour and my King.
            Miss. F. R. HAVERGAL.

591

MY SPIRIT longs for thee
  Within my troubled breast,
Though I unworthy be
  Of so divine a Guest.

2 Of so divine a Guest
  Unworthy though I be,
Yet has my heart no rest
  Unless it come from thee.

3 Unless it come from thee,
  In vain I look around;
In all that I can see
  No rest is to be found.

4 No rest is to be found
  But in thy blessèd love:
O let my wish be crowned,
  And send it from above.
            JOHN BYROM.

NEW CHRISTIAN

HORTON. 7s.   WARTENSEE.

Love for all! and can it be? Can I hope it is for me—

I, who strayed so long a-go; Strayed so far, and fell so low?

592 *[First verse in the music.]*

2 I, the disobedient child,
Wayward, passionate and wild;
I, who left my Father's home,
In forbidden ways to roam;

3 I, who spurned his loving hold;
I, who would not be controlled;
I, who would not hear his call;
I, the willful prodigal—

4 To my Father can I go?
At his feet myself I'll throw;
In his house there yet may be
Place—a servant's place—for me.

5 See! my Father waiting stands;
See! he reaches out his hands:
God is love; I know, I see,
Love for me—yes, even me.
S. LONGFELLOW.

WHITER THAN SNOW. 7s, with Refrain.   K. SHAW. Arr. by J. H. R.

I am sinful; Lord, to thee In my anguish I would flee: To the fountain let me go,

Fine. REFRAIN.   D. S.

Make me whiter than the snow. Whiter than the snow, Whiter than the snow.

593 *[First verse in the music.]*

2 Blind and lost, I call for aid:
Let thy hand on me be laid—
Thou alone canst, Lord, I know,
Make me whiter than the snow.—REF.

3 Cleanse me in thy precious blood,
Love's pure, crimson, streaming flood;
Robes of brightness, Lord bestow,
Make me whiter than the snow.—REF.
K. SHAW.

COOKHAM. 7s. ANON.

Sin - ners, turn—why will you die? God, your Mak - er, asks you why;

God, who did your be - ing give, Made you with him - self to live.

594

SINNERS, turn—why will you die?
God, your Maker, asks you why;
God, who did your being give,
Made you with himself to live.

2 Sinners, turn—why will you die?
Christ, your Saviour, asks you why—
He who did your souls retrieve,
He who died that you might live.

3 Will you let him die in vain?
Crucify your Lord again?
Why, you ransomed sinners, why
Will you slight his grace and die?

4 Will you not his grace receive?
Will you still refuse to live?
O you dying sinners, why—
Why will you forever die?

CHARLES WESLEY.

595

'TIS religion that can give
Sweetest pleasure while we live;
'Tis religion must supply
Solid comfort when we die.

2 After death, its joys will be
Lasting as eternity;
Be the living God my friend,
Then my bliss shall never end.

UNKNOWN.

AMOY. 6s & 4s. LOWELL MASON.

To-day the Saviour calls, Ye wanderers, come : O ye benighted souls, Why longer roam?

596

TO-DAY the Saviour calls,
Ye wanderers, come :
O ye benighted souls,
Why longer roam?

2 To-day the Saviour calls :
O hear him now ;
Within these sacred walls
To Jesus bow.

3 To-day the Saviour calls :
For refuge fly—
The storm of vengeance falls,
And death is nigh.

4 The Saviour calls to-day :
Yield to his power ;
O grieve him not away !
'Tis mercy's hour.

S. F. SMITH.

NEW CHRISTIAN

COMING TO THE CROSS. 7s, with Refrain.

WM. G. FISCHER.

By permission.

I am com-ing to the cross; I am poor and weak and blind; I am counting all but dross;
Ref.—I am trusting, Lord, in thee, Blest Lamb of Cal-va-ry; Humbly at thy cross I bow,

I shall full sal - va - tion find.
Seeking thy sal - va - tion now.

2 Long my heart has sighed for thee,
Long has evil reigned within;
Now thy message comes to me,
"I will cleanse thee from all sin,"—REF.

3 Here I give my all to thee,
Friends and time and earthly store,
Soul and body, thine to be—
Wholly thine for evermore.—REF.

4 Gladly I accept thy grace;
Gladly I obey thy word;
All thy promises embrace,
O my Saviour and my Lord!—REF.

W. McDONALD, *alt.*

597

I AM coming to the cross;
I am poor and weak and blind;
I am counting all but dross;
I shall full salvation find.—REF.

GUIDE. 7s. D.

M. M. WELLS.
Fine.

Bless-ed Je - sus, faith - ful Guide, Ev - er near the Christian's side,
Gen - tly lead us by the hand, Pil - grims in a des - ert land.
D. C. Whispering softly, Wanderer, come; Fol - low me : I'll guide thee home.

D. C.

Wea - ry souls, for - e'er re - joice, While they hear that sweet-est voice,

598

[First verse in the music.]
2 Ever present, truest Friend,
Ever near, thine aid to lend,
Leave us not to doubt and fear,
Groping on in darkness drear;
When the storms are raging sore,
Hearts grow faint and hopes give o'er,
Whisper softly, Wanderer, come;
Follow me : I'll guide thee home.

3 When our days of toil shall cease,
Waiting still for sweet release,
Nothing left but heaven and prayer,
Wondering if our names are there,
Wading deep the dismal flood,
Pleading naught but Jesus' blood,
Whisper softly, Wanderer, come;
Follow me : I'll guide thee home.

M. M. WELLS, *alt.*

224

WONDERFUL WORDS OF LIFE. 8s & 6s.

P. P. Bliss.

Sing them o-ver a-gain to me, Wonder-ful words of life;

Let me more of their beau-ty see, Wonder-ful words of life:

Words of life and beau-ty, Teach me faith and du-ty—

1st 2nd

Beautiful words, wonderful words, Wonderful words of life. life.

By permission of J. Church & Co.

599

Sing them over again to me,
  Wonderful words of life ;
Let me more of their beauty see,
  Wonderful words of life :
Words of life and beauty,
Teach me faith and duty—
  Beautiful words, wonderful words,
  Wonderful words of life.

2 Christ, the blessèd One, gives to all,
  Wonderful words of life :
Sinner, list to the loving call,
  Wonderful words of life,

All so freely given,
Wooing us to heaven—
  Beautiful words, wonderful words,
  Wonderful words of life.

3 Sweetly echo the gospel call,
  Wonderful words of life;
Offer pardon and peace to all,
  Wonderful words of life :
Jesus, only Saviour,
Sanctify forever,
  Beautiful words, wonderful words,
  Wonderful words of life.

P. P. Bliss.

NEW CHRISTIAN

ROCK OF AGES. 7s. 6 l. THOS. HASTINGS.

Rock of Ag-es, cleft for me, Let me hide my-self in thee; Let the wa-ter and the blood,
D.C. Be of sin the double cure—Cleanse me from its guilt and power. From thy rivén side which flowed,

600 [To other tune, No. 545.]

Rock of Ages, cleft for me,
Let me hide myself in thee;
Let the water and the blood,
From thy rivén side which flowed,
Be of sin the double cure—
Cleanse me from its guilt and power.

2 Not the labor of my hands
Can fulfill the law's demands;
Could my zeal no respite know,
Could my tears forever flow,
All for sin could not atone—
Thou must save, and thou alone.

3 Nothing in my hand I bring;
Simply to thy cross I cling;
Naked, come to thee for dress;
Helpless, look to thee for grace;
Foul, I to the fountain fly:
Wash me, Saviour, or I die.

4 While I draw this fleeting breath,
When my heart-strings break in death,
When I soar to worlds unknown,
See thee on thy judgment throne,
Rock of Ages, cleft for me,
Let me hide myself in thee.

A. M. TOPLADY.

PILOT. 7s. 6 l. J. E. GOULD.

Je - sus, Sav - iour, pi - lot me
D. C. Chart and com-pass came from thee: Je - sus, Sav - iour, pi - lot me.
O - ver life's tempestuous sea:

Unknown waves be - fore me roll. Hid - ing rock and treacherous shoal;

By permission.

601 [First verse in the music.]

As a mother stills her child,
Thou canst hush the ocean wild;
Boisterous waves obey thy will
When thou say'st to them, "Be still!"
Wondrous Sovereign of the sea,
Jesus, Saviour, pilot me.

3 When, at last, I near the shore,
And the fearful breakers roar
'Twixt me and the peaceful rest,
Then, while leaning on thy breast,
May I hear thee say to me,
"Fear not: I will pilot thee!"

E. HOPPER.

226

ROSEFIELD. 7s. 6 l.   H. A. C. MALAN.

From the cross, up-lift-ed high, Where the Sav-iour deigns to die,
What me-lo-dious sounds we hear, Burst-ing on the rav-ished ear!

Love's re-deem-ing work is done: Come, and wel-come, sin-ner, come.

602

FROM the cross, uplifted high,
Where the Saviour deigns to die,
What melodious sounds we hear,
Bursting on the ravished ear!
Love's redeeming work is done:
Come, and welcome, sinner, come.

2 Seated on his glorious throne,
Now he makes our cause his own;
Offers pardon through his blood,
Joy of heart, and peace with God.
Bow the knee, embrace the Son;
Come, and welcome, sinner, come.

3 Spread for thee, the festal board,
See, with richest dainties stored;
To thy Father's bosom pressed,
Yet again a child confessed,
Never from his house to roam,
Come, and welcome, sinner, come.

4 Soon the days of life shall end;
Lo! I come, your Saviour, Friend,
Safe your spirit to convey
To the realms of endless day:
Up to my eternal home,
Come, and welcome, sinner, come.
T. HAWEIS.

603

JESUS, Lamb of God, for me
Thou, the Lord of life, didst die:
Whither—whither, but to thee,
Can a trembling sinner fly?
Death's dark waters o'er me roll:
Save, O save my sinking soul.

2 All my soul, by love subdued,
Melts in deep contrition there;
By thy mighty grace renewed,
New-born hope forbids despair.
Lord, thou canst my guilt forgive;
Thou hast bid me look and live.

3 While with broken heart I kneel,
Sinks the inward storm to rest;
Life, immortal life, I feel
Kindled in my throbbing breast;
Thine, forever thine, I am:
Glory to the bleeding Lamb!
RAY PALMER.

604

Now, from labor and from care,
Evening shades have set me free;
In the work of praise and prayer,
Lord, I would converse with thee:
O behold me from above,
Fill me with a Saviour's love.

2 Sin and sorrow, guilt and woe,
Wither all my earthly joys;
Naught can charm me here below,
But my Saviour's melting voice:
Lord, forgive—thy grace restore,
Make me thine for evermore.

3 For the blessings of this day,
For the mercies of this hour,
For the gospel's cheering ray,
For the Spirit's quickening power—
Grateful notes to thee I raise:
O accept my song of praise.
UNKNo

MARTYN. 7s. D.

Fine.

S. B. MARSH.

D. C.

{ Mary to the Saviour's tomb Hasted at the early dawn; }
{ Spice she brought, and sweet perfume; }
{ But the Lord she loved had gone, }
{ For awhile she lingering stood, }
{ Filled with sorrow and surprise; }
D. C. Trembling, while a crystal flood Issued from her weeping eyes.

605

MARY to the Saviour's tomb
  Hasted at the early dawn;
Spice she brought, and sweet perfume;
  But the Lord she loved had gone.
For awhile she lingering stood,
  Filled with sorrow and surprise;
Trembling, while a crystal flood
  Issued from her weeping eyes.

2 Jesus, who is always near,
  Though too often unperceived,
Came, her drooping heart to cheer,
  Kindly asking why she grieved.

Though at first she knew him not,
  When he called her by her name,
She her heavy griefs forgot;
  For she found him still the same.

3 And her sorrows quickly fled,
  When she heard his welcome voice—
Christ had risén from the dead;
  Now he bids her heart rejoice.
What a change his word can make—
  Turning darkness into day!
You who weep for Jesus' sake,
  He will wipe your tears away.

JOHN NEWTON.

REFUGE. 7s. D.

J. P. HOLBROOK.

Je-sus, lov-er of my soul, Let me to thy bo-som fly, While the bil - lows near me

roll, While the tem - pest still is high. Hide me, O my Saviour, hide, Till the storm

of life is past; Safe in - to the ha - ven guide; O receive my soul at last.

By permission.

MERDIN. 7s. D.   LOWELL MASON.

Je - sus, lov - er   of   my soul,   Let me to thy bo - som fly,
While the bil - lows near me roll,   While the tem-pest still is high.

D. C. Safe in - to the ha - ven guide;   O re-ceive my soul at last.

Hide me, O my Saviour, hide,   Till the storm of   life   is past;

606

JESUS, lover of my soul,
  Let me to thy bosom fly,
While the billows near me roll,
  While the tempest still is high;
Hide me, O my Saviour, hide,
  Till the storm of life is past;
Safe into the haven guide;
  O receive my soul at last.

2 Other refuge have I none,
  Hangs my helpless soul on thee:
Leave, O leave me not alone,
  Still support and comfort me.
All my trust on thee is stayed,
  All my help from thee I bring:
Cover my defenseless head
  With the shadow of thy wing.

3 Thou, O Christ, art all I want;
  Boundless love in thee I find:
Raise the fallen, cheer the faint,
  Heal the sick, and lead the blind.
Just and holy is thy name,
  Prince of peace and righteousness—
Most unworthy, Lord, I am;
  Thou art full of love and grace.

4 Plenteous grace with thee is found,
  Grace to pardon all my sin:
Let the healing streams abound;
  Make and keep me pure within.
Thou of life the fountain art:
  Freely let me take of thee;
Spring thou up within my heart,
  Rise to all eternity.
                        CHARLES WESLEY.

607

WHAT could your Redeemer do
More than he has done for you?
To procure your peace with God,
Could he more than shed his blood?
After all this flow of love,
All his drawings from above,
Why will you your Lord deny?
Why will you resolve to die?

2 "Turn," he cries, "O sinner, turn!
By his life your God hath sworn
He would have you turn and live—
He would all the world receive.
If your death were his delight,
Would he thus to life invite?
Would he ask, beseech, and cry,
Why will you resolve to die?"

3 Sinners, turn, while God is near:
He has left you naught to fear;
Now, e'en now, your Saviour stands,
All day long he spreads his hands;
Cries—"You will not happy be;
No, you will not come to me—
Me, who life to none deny:
Why will you resolve to die?"

4 Can you doubt that God is love,
Who thus calls you from above?
Will you not his word receive?
Will you not his oath believe?
See, the suffering Lord appears;
Jesus weeps: believe his tears—
Mingled with his blood, they cry,
"Why will you resolve to die?"
                        CHARLES WESLEY.

WEBB. 7s & 6s. D.   G. J. WEBB.

O when shall I see Je-sus, And dwell with him a-bove, To drink the flowing fountain
D. S. And with my bless-ed Je-sus,

Of ev-er-last-ing love? When shall I be de-liv-ered From this vain world of sin?
Drink endless pleasures in?

608
[First verse in the music.]

2 But now I am a soldier,
  My Captain's gone before;
He's given me my orders,
  And tells me not to fear.
And if I hold out faithful,
  A crown of life he'll give;
And all his valiant soldiers
  Eternal life shall have.

3 Through grace I am determined
  To conquer, though I die;
And then away to Jesus
  On wings of love I'll fly.
Farewell to sin and sorrow—
  I bid them both adieu;
And you, my friends, prove faithful,
  And still your way pursue.

4 O do not be discouraged,
  For Jesus is your Friend;
And if you long for knowledge,
  On him you may depend;
Neither will he upbraid you,
  Though often you request;
He'll give you grace to conquer,
  And take you home to rest.
                          UNKNOWN.

609

STAND up, stand up for Jesus,
  Ye soldiers of the cross;
Lift high his royal banner:
  It must not suffer loss;
From victory unto victory
  His army shall he lead,
Till every foe is vanquished,
  And Christ is Lord indeed.

2 Stand up, stand up for Jesus;
  The trumpet call obey;
Forth to the mighty conflict,
  In this his glorious day.
"Ye that are men, now serve him,"
  Against unnumbered foes;
Let courage rise with danger,
  And strength to strength oppose.

3 Stand up, stand up for Jesus—
  Stand in his strength alone:
The arm of flesh will fail you--
  Ye dare not trust your own:
Put on the gospel armor,
  And, watching unto prayer,
Where duty calls, or danger,
  Be never wanting there.
                          G. DUFFIELD.

610

I saw the cross of Jesus,
  When burdened with my sin;
I sought the cross of Jesus,
  To give me peace within;
I brought my soul to Jesus,
  He cleansed it in his blood;
And in the cross of Jesus,
  I found my peace with God.

2 Sweet is the cross of Jesus!
  There let my weary heart
Still rest in peace unshaken,
  Till with him, ne'er to part;
And then in strains of glory
  I'll sing his wondrous power,
Where sin can never enter,
  And death is known no more.
                          UNKNOWN.

611

THE morning light is breaking;
  The darkness disappears;
The sons of earth are waking
  To penitential tears;
Each breeze that sweeps the ocean
  Brings tidings from afar,
Of nations in commotion,
  Prepared for Zion's war.

2 See heathen nations bending
  Before the God we love,
And thousand hearts ascending
  In gratitude above;

While sinners, now confessing,
  The gospel call obey,
And seek the Saviour's blessing,
  A nation in a day.

3 Blest river of salvation,
  Pursue thine onward way;
Flow thou to every nation,
  Nor in thy richness stay.
Stay not till all the lowly
  Triumphant reach their home:
Stay not till all the holy
  Proclaim, "The Lord is come!"

                         S. F. SMITH.

HO! REAPERS OF LIFE'S HARVEST. 7s & 6s. D.   I. B. WOODBURY.

Ho! reap-ers of life's harvest, Why stand with rusted blade, Until the night draws round thee,
D. S. The gold-en morn is pass-ing:

And day be-gins to fade? Why stand ye i - dle, waiting For reap-ers more to come?
Why sit ye i - dle, dumb?

By permission.

612

Ho! REAPERS of life's harvest,
  Why stand with rusted blade,
Until the night draws round thee,
  And day begins to fade?
Why stand ye idle, waiting
  For reapers more to come?
The golden morn is passing:
  Why sit ye idle, dumb?

2 Thrust in your sharpened sickle,
  And gather in the grain:
The night is fast approaching,
  And soon will come again.
The Master calls for reapers,
  And shall he call in vain?
Shall sheaves lie there ungathered,
  And waste upon the plain?

3 Come down from hill and mountain
  In morning's ruddy glow,
Nor wait until the dial
  Points to the noon below;
And come with stronger sinew,
  Nor faint in heat or cold,
And pause not till the evening
  Draws round its wealth of gold.

4 Mount up the heights of wisdom,
  And crush each error low;
Keep back no word of knowledge
  That human hearts should know.
Be faithful to thy mission,
  In service of the Lord,
And then a golden chaplet
  Shall be thy just reward.

                         I. B. WOODBURY.

NEW CHRISTIAN

I LOVE TO TELL THE STORY. 7s & 6s. D., with Chorus.   WM. G. FISCHER.

I love to tell the sto-ry Of un-seen things above, Of Je-sus and his glo-ry,

Of Je-sus and his love. I love to tell the sto-ry, Be-cause I know 'tis true;

CHORUS.

It sat-is-fies my long-ings, As noth-ing else can do. I love to tell the sto-ry—

'Twill be my theme in glory, To tell the old, old sto-ry Of Je-sus and his love.

By permission.

613   *[First verse in the music]*

2 I love to tell the story;
  More wonderful it seems
Than all the golden fancies
  Of all our golden dreams.
I love to tell the story;—
  It did so much for me—
And that is just the reason
  I tell it now to thee. —CHO.

3 I love to tell the story;
  'Tis pleasant to repeat
What seems, each time I tell it,
  More wonderfully sweet.

I love to tell the story;
  For some have never heard
The message of salvation
  From God's own holy word.—CHO.

4 I love to tell the story;
  For those who know it best
Seem hungering and thirsting
  To hear it, like the rest.
And when, in scenes of glory,
  I sing the new, new song,
'Twill be the old, old story
  That I have loved so long.—CHO.

CATHARINE HANKEY.

JERUSALEM THE GOLDEN, 7s & 6s. D., with Chorus.　　　J. R. MURRAY.

{ Je - ru - sa-lem the Gold-en, I languish for one gleam }
{ Of all thy glo-ry, fold-en In dis-tance and in dream; } My thoughts, like palms in exile,

Climb up to look and pray For a glimpse of that dear country That lies so far a-way.

CHORUS.

Je - ru - sa - lem the Gold-den, My hope, my heaven, my home,

With song of joy and sweet em-ploy, To thee, to thee we come.

By permission.

614　[First verse in the music.]

2 Jerusalem the Golden,
　When sun sets in the west,
It seems the gate of glory,
　Thou City of the Blest;
And midnight's starry torches,
　Through intermediate gloom,
Are waving with their welcome
　To thy eternal home.—CHO.

3 Jerusalem the Golden—
　There all our birds that flew,
Our flowers but half unfolden,
　Our pearls that turned to dew,

And all the glad life-music,
　Now heard no longer here,
Shall come again to greet us,
　As we are drawing near.—CHO.

4 Jerusalem the Golden,
　I toil on, day by day;
Heart-sore each night with longing,
　I stretch my hands and pray
That, midst thy leaves of healing,
　My soul shall find her rest,
Where the wicked cease from troubling,
　The weary are at rest.—CHO.
　　　　　　　　　J. R. MURRAY.

NEW CHRISTIAN

THERE IS NO FRIEND LIKE JESUS. 7s & 6s. D., with Chorus.   J. R. MURRAY.

{ There is no friend like Jesus, When sorrows flood the breast; }
{ He was "a man of sorrows," And had no place to rest. } But when our sorrows vex us,
{ D. S. there's no friend like Jesus, Tho' dear are all the rest; }
{ There is no friend like Jesus, The dearest and the best. }

He gives us sym-pa-thy, And, leaning on his bo-som, He comforts you and me. O

By permission.

615   [First verse in the music.]

2 There is no friend like Jesus;
    Though earthly friends are true,
They can not travel with us
    Our earthly journey through;
But Jesus ne'er will leave us,
    He holds us by the hand,
And guides us in the pathway,
    Toward the better land.—CHO.

3 There is no friend like Jesus;
    In happiness and pain,
In sorrow and in sunshine,
    Our friend he will remain.
To him we turn for comfort,
    To him we look for rest;
And we find them on his bosom—
    On Jesus' loving breast.—CHO.

E. E. REXFORD.

I COULD NOT DO WITHOUT THEE. 7s & 6s. D.   J. R. MURRAY.

I could not do without thee, O Sav-iour of the lost, Whose precious blood redeemed me,
D. S. My on-ly hope and comfort,

At such tremendous cost. Thy righteousness, thy par-don, Thy precious blood must be
My glo-ry and my plea.

By permission of J. Church & Co.

234

IS IT FOR ME? 7s & 6s, with Chorus. T. C. O'KANE.

Is it for me, dear Sav-iour, Thy glo-ry and thy rest— For me, so weak and

CHORUS.

sin-ful? O shall I be so blest? O Sav-iour, my Re-deem-er, What

can I but a-dore, And mag-ni-fy and praise thee, And love thee ever-more?

By permission.

616

Is IT for me, dear Saviour,
Thy glory and thy rest —
For me, so weak and sinful?
O shall I be so blest?—CHO.

2 Is it for me, thy welcome,
Thy gracious "Enter in"—
For me thy "Come, ye blessed,"
For me, so full of sin?—CHO.

3 O Saviour, precious Saviour,
My heart is at thy feet;
I bless thee, and I love thee,
And thee I long to meet.—CHO.

4 I'll be with thee forever,
And never grieve thee more;
Dear Saviour, I must praise thee,
And love thee evermore.—CHO.
MISS F. R. HAVERGAL.

617 *[First verse in the music.]*

2 I could not do without thee,
I can not stand alone;
I have no strength or goodness,
No wisdom of my own.
But thou, beloved Saviour,
Art all in all to me;
And weakness will be power,
If leaning hard on thee.

3 I could not do without thee;
For O the way is long,
And I am often weary,
And sigh replaces song.

How could I do without thee?
I do not know the way;
Thou knowest and thou leadest,
And wilt not let me stray.

4 I could not do without thee;
For years are fleeting fast,
And soon, in solemn loneliness,
The river must be passed.
But thou wilt never leave me;
And though the waves roll high,
I know thou wilt be near me,
And whisper, "It is I."
MISS F. R. HAVERGAL.

235

GOING HOME AT LAST. 7s & 6s, with Chorus.

E. S. LORENZ.

The evening shades are falling, Our sun is sinking fast; The Ho-ly One is

CHORUS.

call-ing, We're going home at last. Go-ing home at last! Go-ing home at last!

The march will soon be o-ver; We're go-ing home at last.

By permission.

618   *[First verse in the music.]*

2 The road's been long and dreary,
   The toils came thick and fast;
In body weak and weary,
   We're going home at last.—CHO.

3 We now are nearing heaven,
   And soon shall be at rest;

Our crowns will soon be given—
   We're going home at last.—CHO.

4 O praise the Lord forever!
   Our sorrows all are past;
We'll part no more—no, never;
   We are at home at last.—CHO.
                              W. GOSSETT.

BY AND BY. 7s & 6s. D.

Arr. from W. T. DALE.

O-ver Jordan we shall meet, By and by, by and by,   In a fellowship so sweet,
                                          D. S. And the Saviour's name adore,

Fine.   D. S.

By and by, by and by; We shall gather on the shore, With our kindred gone before,
By and by, by and by.

O SION, SION. 7s & 6s, with Chorus.

J. H. ROSECRANS.

There is a hab-i-ta-tion, Built by the living God, For all of every

CHORUS.

nation, Who seek that grand abode. O Si - on, Si - on, I long thy gates to
O Si-on, love-ly Si - on,

see: O Si - on, Si - on, When shall I dwell in thee?
O love - ly Si - on, love - ly Si - on,

619

THERE is a habitation,
  Built by the living God,
For all, of every nation,
  Who seek that grand abode.—CHO.

2 A city with foundations,
  Firm as th' eternal throne;
Nor wars, nor desolations
  Shall ever move a stone.—CHO.

3 No night is there, no sorrow,
  No death, and no decay;
No yesterday, no morrow—
  But one eternal day.—CHO.

4 Within its pearly portals,
  Angelic armies sing,
With glorified immortals,
  The praises of its King.—CHO.
L. H. JAMESON.

620

OVER Jordan we shall meet,
  By and by, by and by;
In a fellowship so sweet,
  By and by, by and by;
We shall gather on the shore,
With our kindred gone before,
And the Saviour's name adore,
  By and by, by and by.

2 All our sorrows shall be past,
  By and by, by and by;
We shall reach our home at last,
  By and by, by and by;

With the ransomed we shall stand
There, a holy, happy band,
Crowned with glory in that land,
  By and by, by and by.

3 There we'll join the ransomed throng,
  By and by, by and by,
Chanting love's redeeming song,
  By and by, by and by;
There we'll meet before the throne,
There we'll lay our trophies down,
And receive a shining crown,
  By and by, by and by.
W. T. DALE.

237

WHAT HAST THOU DONE FOR ME? 6s & 8. P. P. BLISS.

I gave my life for thee, My precious blood I shed, That thou might'st ransomed be,

And quickened from the dead. I gave, I gave my life for thee; What hast thou given for me?

By permission of J. Church & Co.

621

I GAVE my life for thee,
  My precious blood I shed,
That thou might'st ransomed be,
  And quickened from the dead.
I gave, I gave my life for thee:
What hast thou given for me?

2 My Father's house of light,
  My glory-circled throne,
I left—for earthly night,
  For wanderings sad and lone.
I left, I left it all for thee:
Hast thou left aught for me?

3 I suffered much for thee—
  More than thy tongue can tell,
Of bitterest agony,
  To rescue thee from hell.
I've borne, I've borne it all for thee:
What hast thou borne for me?

4 And I have brought to thee,
  Down from my home above,
Salvation full and free,
  My pardon and my love.
I bring, I bring rich gifts to thee:
What hast thou brought to me?

MISS F. R. HAVERGAL.

WE SCATTER SEEDS. 8s, 6s & 4s. J. H. ROSECRANS.

We scat-ter seeds with care-less hand, And dream we ne'er shall see them more; But

for a thousand years Their fruit appears, In weeds that mar the land, Or healthful store.

COME, O COME TO ME. 8s, 5s & 9.   FRED. A. FILLMORE.

Far away from home I'm wandering, Far away from thee: Art thou, O my Father, watching? Art thou calling me? Wanderer, wanderer, come, O come to me. In thy Father's house there's welcome, And a home for thee.

622

FAR away from home I'm wandering,
 Far away from thee:
Art thou, O my Father, watching?
 Art thou calling me?
Wanderer, wanderer, come, O come to me.
In thy Father's house there's welcome,
 And a home for thee.

2 Canst thou, wilt thou, O my Father,
 Love me as thy child—
Love me in my sin and sorrow?
 Wretched and defiled?
Wanderer, wanderer, come, O come to me.
In thy wanderings I have loved thee:
 Haste, O haste to me.

3 Canst thou turn my grief to gladness—
 Turn my sighs to praise?
Canst thou grant me free forgiveness?
 Tell me—canst thou save?
Wanderer, wanderer, come, O come to me.
All thy burdens I will carry :
 Come, O come to me.

4 With a broken, contrite spirit,
 Now to thee I flee;
Trusting not upon my merit,
 Trusting only thee.
Saviour, Saviour, hear my fervent cry!
Help, O help me in this conflict—
 Help me, or I die.

       J. S. LOWE.

623

WE SCATTER seeds with careless hand,
 And dream we ne'er shall see them more;
 But for a thousand years
  Their fruit appears,
In weeds that mar the land,
 Or healthful store.

2 The deeds we do, the words we say,
 Into still air they seem to fleet;
 We count them ever past;
  But they shall last—
And in the judgment-day,
 We them shall meet.

3 I charge thee by the years gone by,
 For the love's sake of brethren dear,
 Keep, thou, the one true way
  Through all thy day,
Lest in that world their cry
 Of woe thou hear.

       JOHN DEBLE.

EVERY DAY. 7s & 9s, with Refrain.　　　　　　　W. H. DOANE.

Saviour, more than life to me, I am clinging, clinging close to thee;

Fine.

Ev - er be a present friend, Leave me nev-er, nev-er to the end.
D. S. May thy ten-der love to me Bind me clos-er, clos-er, Lord, to thee.

REFRAIN.　　　　　　　　　　　　　　　　　D. S.

Ev - ery day, ev - ery hour, Let me feel thy cleansing power;
Ev - ery day and hour, ev- ery day and hour,

Copyright, 1870, by Bigelow & Main.

624

SAVIOUR, more than life to me,
I am clinging, clinging close to thee;
Ever be a present friend,
Leave me never, never to the end.—REF.
2 Through this changing world below
Lead me gently, gently as I go:

Trusting thee, I can not stray,
I can never, never lose my way.—REF.
3 Let me love thee more and more,
Till this fleeting, fleeting life is o'er;
Till my soul is lost in love,
In a brighter, brighter world above.—REF.

F. C VAN ALSTYNE.

HE KNOWS IT ALL. 8s & 4.　　　　　　J. H. LESLIE.

He knows the bit - ter, wea-ry way, The endless striving day by day,

The souls that weep, the souls that pray—He knows it all.

Copyright, 1881, by J. H. Leslie.

WE'RE GOING HOME TO-MORROW. 4s & 7s, with Chorus. P. P. BLISS.

We're going home, No more to roam, No more to sin and sor-row; No more to wear

CHORUS.

The brow of care—We're going home to-mor-row. We're go - - ing home,
We're going home, we're going home,

We're going home to-morrow; We're go - ing home, We're going home to-morrow.
We're going home, we're going home,

By permission of J. Church & Co.

625 *[First verse in the music.]*

2 For weary feet,
There waits a street
  Of wondrous pave and golden;
For hearts that ache,
The angels wake
  The story sweet and olden.—Cho.

3 For those who sleep,
And those who weep,
  Above the portals narrow,
The mansions rise
Beyond the skies—
  We're going home to-morrow.—Cho.

4 O joyful song!
O ransomed throng,
  Where sin no more shall sever!
Our King to see,
And, O to be
  With him at home forever!—Cho.
PAULINA.

626

HE knows the bitter, weary way,
The endless striving day by day,
The souls that weep, the souls that pray—
  He knows it all.

2 He knows how hard the fight has been,
The clouds that come our lives between,
The wounds the world has never seen—
  He knows it all.

3 He knows, when, faint and worn, we sink,
How deep the pain, how near the brink
Of dark despair we pause and shrink—
  He knows it all.

4 He knows! O thought so full of bliss!
For though on earth our joys we miss,
We still can bear it, feeling this—
  He knows it all.
UNKNOWN.

COMING NOW. 7s & 6s, with Chorus.

FRED. A. FILLMORE.

Je - sus, I am coming now, Com-ing to the fountain; Pre-cious is th'a-

CHORUS.

ton-ing blood Shed on Calv'ry's mountain. Coming now, coming now, Seeking

grace and fa - vor, That my wea-ry soul may find Rest in thee for-ev - er.

627 [First verse in the music.]

2 Jesus, make me true to thee,
Pure, and meek, and lowly,
While I walk the narrow way
To the city holy.—CHO.

3 Jesus, fill my heart with peace,
Flowing like a river;
Day by day my joy increase,
Till the glad forever.—CHO.

ROBERT MOFFETT.

WHAT A FRIEND. 8s & 7s. D.

C. C. CONVERSE.

What a Friend we have in Jesus, All our sins and griefs to bear! What a privilege to carry
D. S. All because we do not car-ry

Every thing to God in prayer! O what peace we often forfeit, O what needless pain we bear,
Every thing to God in prayer!

By permission.

WE'LL WORK TILL JESUS COMES. C. M., with Chorus.   WM. MILLER.

O land of rest, for thee I sigh! When will the moment come, When I shall lay my

CHORUS.

ar-mor by, And dwell in peace at home? We'll work   till Je - sus comes, We'll
We'll work

work   till Jesus comes, We'll work   till Jesus comes, And we'll be gathered home.
We'll work,   We'll work

628 [To other tune. No. 296.]

O LAND of rest, for thee I sigh:
  When will the moment come,
When I shall lay my armor by,
  And dwell in peace at home?—CHO.

2 No tranquil joys on earth I know,
  No peaceful, sheltering dome;
This world's a wilderness of woe,
  This world is not my home.—CHO.

3 To Jesus Christ I fled for rest;
  He bade me cease to roam,
And lean for succor on his breast,
  Till he conduct me home.—CHO.

4 I sought at once my Saviour's side;
  No more my steps shall roam;
With him I'll brave death's chilling tide,
  And reach my heavenly home.—CHO.
                    ELIZABETH MILLS.

629

WHAT a Friend we have in Jesus,
  All our sins and griefs to bear!
What a privilege to carry
  Every thing to God in prayer!
O what peace we often forfeit,
  O what needless pain we bear,
All because we do not carry
  Every thing to God in prayer!

2 Have we trials and temptations?
  Is there trouble anywhere?
We should never be discouraged:
  Take it to the Lord in prayer.

Can we find a friend so faithful,
  Who will all our sorrows share?
Jesus knows our every weakness:
  Take it to the Lord in prayer.

3 Are we weak and heavy-laden,
  Cumbered with a load of care?
Precious Saviour, still our refuge—
  Take it to the Lord in prayer!
Do thy friends despise, forsake thee?
  Take it to the Lord in prayer;
In his arms he'll take and shield thee;
  Thou wilt find a solace there.
                    H. BONAR.

243

NEW CHRISTIAN

WORK SONG. 7s, 6s & 5s.

LOWELL MASON.

Work, for the night is com-ing; Work thro' the morning hours; Work while the dew is
D. S. Work, for the night is

Fine.

sparkling; Work 'mid springing flowers;
coming, When man's work is done.
Work when the day grows brighter;

Work in the glowing sun;

By permission.

630

Work, for the night is coming;
  Work through the morning hours;
Work while the dew is sparkling;
  Work 'mid springing flowers;
Work when the day grows brighter;
  Work in the glowing sun;
Work, for the night is coming,
  When man's work is done.

2 Work, for the night is coming;
  Work through the sunny noon;
Fill brightest hours with labor—
  Rest comes sure and soon.

Give every flying moment
  Something to keep in store;
Work, for the night is coming,
  When man works no more.

3 Work, for the night is coming,
  Under the sunset skies;
While their bright tints are glowing,
  Work, for daylight flies.
Work till the last beam fadeth,
  Fadeth to shine no more;
Work while the night is darkening,
  When man's work is o'er.

SIDNEY DYER.

PASS ME NOT. 8s & 5s, with Chorus.

W. H. DOANE.

Pass me not, O gen-tle Sav-iour; Hear my humble cry; While on oth-ers thou art
D. S. While on oth-ers thou art

Fine. CHORUS.

smil-ing, Do not pass me by.
call-ing, Do not pass me by.
Sav-iour, Sav-iour, hear my hum-ble cry;

| Copyright, 1870, in "Songs of Devotion." |

211

THE PEARL OF GREATEST PRICE. C. M., with Chorus.   P. P. BLISS.

I've found the pearl of great-est price; My heart doth sing for joy; And sing I

must, for Christ is mine—Christ shall my song employ. I've found the pearl of greatest price;

My heart doth sing for joy; And sing I must, for Christ is mine—Christ shall my song employ.

By permission of J. Church & Co.

631

I've found the pearl of greatest price;
  My heart doth sing for joy;
And sing I must, for Christ is mine—
  Christ shall my song employ.—CHO.

2 Christ is my Prophet, Priest, and King;—
  My Prophet, full of light;
My great High Priest before the throne,
  My King of heavenly might.—CHO.

3 For he, indeed, is Lord of lords,
  And he the King of kings;

He is the Sun of righteousness,
  With healing in his wings.—CHO.

4 Christ is my peace; he died for me;
  For me he shed his blood,
And, as my wondrous Sacrifice,
  Offered himself to God.—CHO.

5 Christ Jesus is my all in all,
  My comfort and my love;
My life below, and he shall be
  My joy and crown above.
               JOHN MASON.

632

PASS me not, O gentle Saviour;
  Hear my humble cry;
While on others thou art smiling,
  Do not pass me by.—CHO.

2 Let me at thy throne of mercy
  Find a sweet relief,
Kneeling there in deep contrition;
  Help mine unbelief.—CHO.

3 Trusting only in thy merit,
  Would I seek thy face:
Heal my wounded, broken spirit,
  Save me by thy grace.—CHO.

4 Thou the Spring of all my comfort,
  More than life to me,
Whom on earth have I beside thee?
  Whom in heaven but thee?—CHO.
            F. C. VAN ALSTYNE.

NEW CHRISTIAN

NEAR THE CROSS. 7s & 6s, with Chorus.   W. H. Doane.

Je-sus, keep me near the cross; There a precious fount-ain, Free to all, a

CHORUS.

healing stream, Flows from Calvary's mountain. In the cross, in the cross, Be my glory

ev - er, Till my rapt-ured soul shall find Rest beyond the riv - er.

Copyright, 1869, in "Bright Jewels."

633

JESUS, keep me near the cross:
  There a precious fountain,
Free to all, a healing stream,
  Flows from Calvary's mountain.—CHO.

2 Near the cross, a trembling soul,
  Love and mercy found me;

There the bright and morning star
  Sheds its beams around me.—CHO.

3 Near the cross! O Lamb of God,
  Bring its scenes before me;
Help me walk from day to day,
  With its shadow o'er me.—CHO.

F. C. VAN ALSTYNE.

BLESSED BIBLE. 8s & 7s. D.   A. D. FILLMORE.

Fine.

Bless - ed Bi - ble, how I love it! How it doth my bo-som cheer!
What hath earth like this to cov - et? O what stores of wealth are here!
D.C. Could he from earth's treasures bor - row, Till his way was cheered by this.

D. C.

Man was lost, and doomed to sor - row; Not one ray of light or bliss

246

SHOUT THE TIDINGS. 8s & 7s, with Chorus. ANON.

Shout the tidings of sal-va-tion To the aged and the young; Till the precious in - vi-

CHORUS.

ta-tion Waken every heart and tongue. Send the sound the earth around, From the rising to the

setting of the sun, Till each gathering crowd shall proclaim aloud, The glorious work is done.

634

Shout the tidings of salvation
  To the aged and the young;
Till the precious invitation
  Waken every heart and tongue.—Cho.

2 Shout the tidings of salvation
  O'er the prairies of the West,
Till each gathering congregation
  With the gospel sound is blest.—Cho.

3 Shout the tidings of salvation,
  Mingling with the ocean's roar,
Till the ships of every nation
  Bear the news from shore to shore.—Cho.

4 Shout the tidings of salvation,
  O'er the islands of the sea,
Till, in humble adoration,
  All to Christ shall bow the knee.—Cho.
  UNKNOWN.

635

Bless-ed Bible, how I love it!
  How it doth my bosom cheer!
What hath earth like this to covet?
  O what stores of wealth are here!
Man was lost, and doomed to sorrow;
  Not one ray of light or bliss
Could he from earth's treasures borrow,
  Till his way was cheered by this.

2 Yes, I'll to my bosom press thee;
  Precious Word, I'll hide thee here;
Sure my very heart will bless thee,
  For thou ever say'st "Good cheer!"

Speak, my heart, and tell thy ponderings,
  Tell how far thy rovings led,
When this book brought back thy wanderings,
  Speaking life as from the dead.

3 Yes, sweet Bible, I will hide thee,
  Hide thee, richly in this heart;
Thou, through all my life, wilt guide me,
  And in death we will not part.
Part in death! no, never, never!
  Through death's vale I'll lean on thee;
Then in worlds above, forever,
  Sweeter still thy truths shall be.
  UNKNOWN.

NEW CHRISTIAN

He Will Hide Me. 8s & 7s, with Chorus. James McGranahan.

When the storms of life are rag-ing, Tem-pests wild on sea and land.

I will seek a place of ref-uge In the shad-ow of God's hand.

CHORUS.

He will hide me, he will hide me, Where no harm can e'er betide me,

He will hide me, safe-ly hide me, In the shad-ow of his hand.

By permission.

636

WHEN the storms of life are raging,
Tempests wild on sea and land,
I will seek a place of refuge
In the shadow of God's hand.

CHO.—He will hide me, he will hide me,
Where no harm can e'er betide me;
He will hide me, safely hide me,
In the shadow of his hand.

2 Though he may send some affliction,
'Twill but make me long for home;

For in love, and not in anger,
All his chastenings will come.—CHO.

3 Enemies may strive to injure,
Satan all his arts employ;
He will turn what seems to harm me
Into everlasting joy.—CHO.

4 So, while here the cross I'm bearing,
Meeting storms and billows wild,
Jesus for my soul is caring;
Naught can harm his Father's child.—CHO.

M. E. SERVOSS.

248

BUCKLE ON THE ARMOR. 8s & 7s, with Chorus. J. H. ROSECRANS.

Life is one con-tin-ued bat-tle, Nev-er end-ed, nev-er o'er;

And the Christian's path to glo-ry Is a con-flict ev-er-more.

CHORUS.

Chris-tian, buck-le on thy ar-mor, Let the weak points strengthened be;

Fight thy fight—all heaven shall greet thee In the hour of vic-to-ry.

637

LIFE is one continued battle,
  Never ended, never o'er;
And the Christian's path to glory
  Is a conflict evermore.

CHO.—Christian, buckle on thy armor,
  Let the weak points strengthened be;
  Fight thy fight—all heaven shall greet thee
  In the hour of vic-to-ry.

2 Satan ever watches round him,
  Seeks to find the weakest part,

And in moments most unheeded
  Quickly throws his fiery dart.—CHO.

3 If perchance thy heart grows weary
  With the struggle and the fight,
And the day seems dark and dreary,
  Little sunshine, little light;—CHO.

4 Be that light but faint and feeble,
  It shall guide thee evermore,
And at every battle leave thee
  Stronger than thou wast before.—CHO.

C. JAY SMITH.

PRECIOUS PROMISE. 8s & 7s, with Refrain.   P. P. Bliss.

Precious prom-ise God hath giv - en To the wea - ry pass - er - by,

On the way from earth to heav-en, "I will guide thee with mine eye."

REFRAIN.

I will guide thee, I will guide thee, I will guide thee with mine eye;

On the way from earth to heav - en, I will guide thee with mine eye.

By permission of J. Church & Co.

638

Precious promise God hath given
  To the weary passer-by,
On the way from earth to heaven,
  "I will guide thee with mine eye."

Ref.—I will guide thee, I will guide thee,
  I will guide thee with mine eye;
On the way from earth to heaven
  I will guide thee with mine eye.

2 When temptations almost win thee,
  And thy trusted watchers fly,

Let this promise ring within thee,
  "I will guide thee with mine eye."—Ref.

3 When thy secret hopes have perished
  In the grave of years gone by,
Let this promise still be cherished,
  "I will guide thee with mine eye."—Ref.

4 When the shades of life are falling,
  And the hour has come to die,
Hear thy trusty Pilot calling,
  "I will guide thee with mine eye."—Ref.
    Nathaniel Niles.

250

ARE YOU READY? 8s & 7s, with Refrain.

E. S. Lorenz.

Soon the evening shadows fall - ing, Close the day of mortal life; Soon the

hand of death appalling, Draws thee from its weary strife. Are you ready?

Are you ready?

REFRAIN.

Are you ready? 'T is the Spir- it calling: why de-lay? Are you

Are you read-y?

ready? Are you ready? Do not linger longer; come to-day.

Are you ready? Are you ready?

639

Soon the evening shadows falling,
　Close the day of mortal life;
Soon the hand of death appalling,
　Draws thee from its weary strife.

Ref.—Are you ready? Are you ready?
　'Tis the Spirit calling: why delay?
　Are you ready? Are you ready?
　Do not linger longer; come to-day.

2 Soon the awful trumpet sounding,
　Calls thee to the judgment-throne;

Now prepare, for love abounding
　Yet has left thee not alone.—Ref.

3 O how fatal 'tis to linger!
　Are you ready—ready now—
Ready, should death's icy finger
　Lay its chill upon thy brow?—Ref.

4 Priceless love and free salvation,
　Freely still are offered thee:
Yield no longer to temptation,
　But from sin and sorrow flee.—Ref.

J. W. Slaughenhaupt.

MY REDEEMER. 8s & 7s, with Chorus.   JAMES McGRANAHAN.

I will sing of my Re-deem-er, And his won-drous love to me;

On the cru-el cross he suffered, From the curse to set me free.

CHORUS.

Sing, O sing . . . . of my Redeem-er; With his
Sing, O sing of my Re-deem-er, Sing, O sing of my Re-deem-er; With his

With his

blood he ransomed me, he ransomed me; . . . On the cross . . he sealed my
blood . . . he ransomed me, he ransomed me; On the cross he sealed my pardon, On the

blood he ransomed me, With his blood he ransomed me;

par - don, Gave his life . . . and made me free. . . .
cross he sealed my pardon, Gave his life and made me free, and made me free, and made me free.

By permission of J. Church & Co.

640

I WILL sing of my Redeemer,
  And his wondrous love to me;
On the cruel cross he suffered,
  From the curse to set me free.

CHO.—Sing, O sing of my Redeemer:
  With his blood he ransomed me;
On the cross he sealed my pardon,
  Gave his life and made me free.

2 I will tell the wondrous story
  How, my lost estate to save,

In his boundless love and mercy,
  He the ransom freely gave.—CHO.

3 I will praise my dear Redeemer;
  His triumphant power I'll tell—
How the vic-to-ry he giveth
  Over sin and death and hell.—CHO.

4 I will sing of my Redeemer,
  And his heavenly love to me;
He from death to life hath brought me,
  Son of God, with him to be.—CHO.

P. P. BLISS.

PRECIOUS NAME. 8s & 7s, with Chorus.   W. H. DOANE.

Take the name of Jesus with you, Child of sorrow and of woe: It will joy and comfort

CHORUS.

give you: Take it, then, where'er you go. Precious name, O how sweet! Hope of
                                         Precious name, O how sweet!

earth and joy of heaven: Precious name, O how sweet! Hope of earth and joy of heaven.
Precious name, O how sweet! how sweet:

641

TAKE the name of Jesus with you,
  Child of sorrow and of woe:
It will joy and comfort give you;
  Take it, then, where'er you go.—CHO.

2 Take the name of Jesus ever,
  As a shield from every snare;
If temptations round you gather,
  Breathe that holy name in prayer.—CHO.

3 O the precious name of Jesus,
  How it thrills our souls with joy,
When his loving arms receive us,
  And his songs our tongues employ!—CHO.

4 At the name of Jesus bowing,
  Falling prostrate at his feet,
King of kings, in heaven we'll crown him,
  When our journey is complete.—CHO.

MRS. LYDIA BAXTER.

253

NEW CHRISTIAN

BEAUTIFUL VALLEY OF EDEN. 8s & 6s, with Refrain.   Wm. F. Sherwin.

Beau-ti-ful val-ley of E-den, Sweet is thy noon-tide calm, O-ver the hearts of the

REFRAIN.

wea-ry, Breath-ing thy waves of balm. Beau-ti-ful val-ley of E-den,

Rit.

Home of the pure and blest, How often amid the wild billows I dream of thy rest—sweet rest!
the pure and blest,

By permission.

642   *[First verse in the music.]*

2 Over the heart of the mourner
  Shineth thy golden day,
Wafting the songs of the angels
  Down from the far-away.—Ref.

3 There is the home of my Saviour;
  There, with the blood-washed throng,
Over the highlands of glory
  Rolleth the great new song.—Ref.

W. O. Cushing.

SHINING SHORE. 8s & 7s, with Chorus.   Geo. F. Root.

My days are gliding swiftly by, And I, a pilgrim stranger, Would not detain them as they fly,
              D. S. just before the shining shore

Fine. CHORUS.   **D. S.**

Those hours of toil and danger; For, O we stand on Jordan's strand, Our friends are passing over; And
We may almost dis-cov-er.

By permission.

254

CHRIST IS PRECIOUS. 8s & 7s, with Chorus.   J. H. FILLMORE.

O the precious love of Je - sus, Grow-ing sweet-er day by day,

Tun-ing all my heart so joy - ous To a heavenly mel - o - dy.

CHORUS.

Christ is precious, Christ is precious, In life's jour-ney he will lead thee;

Christ is precious, Christ is precious, He will lead thee all the way.

643 [First verse in the music.]

2 But we can not know the fullness
  Of the Saviour's wondrous love,
Till we see and know his glory,
  In the heavenly home above.—CHO.

3 Come and taste the love of Jesus,
  At his feet thy burdens lay;
Trust him with thy grief and sorrow,
  Bear this joyful song away.—CHO.
                        ELIZA SHERMAN.

644

MY DAYS are gliding swiftly by,
  And I, a pilgrim stranger,
Would not detain them as they fly,
  Those hours of toil and danger.—CHO.

2 We'll gird our loins, my brethren dear,
  Our distant home discerning;
Our absent Lord has left us word,
  Let every lamp be burning.—CHO.

3 Should coming days be cold and dark,
  We need not cease our singing;
That perfect rest naught can molest,
  Where golden harps are ringing.—CHO.

4 Let sorrow's rudest tempest blow,
  Each cord on earth to sever;
Our King says "Come;" and there's our home,
  Forever, O forever!—CHO.
                        DAVID NELSON.

DRAW ME TO THEE. 8s & 6s, with Chorus.   E. S. LORENZ.

Lord, weak and im-po-tent I stand, As fet-tered by an un-seen hand;

Break thou the strong and sub-tle band, And draw me close to thee.

CHORUS.

Draw me close to thee,   Sav-iour, Draw me close to thee;
close to thee, Sav-iour,   close to thee;

Be-neath thy wing do thou me hide, And draw me close to thee.

By permission.

645

LORD, weak and impotent I stand,
As fettered by an unseen hand:
Break thou the strong and subtle band,
  And draw me close to thee.

CHO.—Draw me close to thee, Saviour,
  Draw me close to thee;
Beneath thy wing do thou me hide,
  And draw me close to thee.

2 In vain I struggle to be free;
I would, but can not, fly to thee:

Ope thou the prison door for me,
  And draw me close to thee.—CHO.

3 O bring me nearer, nearer still,
That thine own peace my soul may fill,
  And I may rest in thy sweet will:
  Lord, draw me close to thee.—CHO.

4 Here, Lord, I would forever bide,
And never wander from thy side:
Beneath thy wing do thou me hide,
  And draw me close to thee.—CHO.
             M. A. W.

ELLESDIE. 8s & 7s. D. — MOZART.

Je-sus, I my cross have tak-en, All to leave, and fol-low thee;

I am poor, despised, for-sak-en—Thou, from hence, my all shalt be.
D. S. Yet how rich is my con-di-tion—God and heaven are still my own!

Per-ish ev-ery fond am-bi-tion, All I've sought and hoped and known:

646 *[First verse in the music.]*

2 Let the world despise and leave me—
It has left my Saviour too;
Human hearts and looks deceive me—
Thou art not, like them, untrue;
Whilst thy graces shall adorn me,
God of wisdom, love, and might,
Foes may hate, and friends may scorn me—
Show thy face, and all is bright.

3 Go, then, earthly fame and treasure,
Come, disaster, scorn and pain;
In thy service, pain is pleasure;
With thy favor, loss is gain.
I have called thee, Abba, Father;
I have set my heart on thee;
Storms may howl, and clouds may gather,
All will work for good to me.

4 Man may trouble and distress me—
'Twill but drive me to thy breast;
Life with trials hard may press me—
Heaven will bring me sweeter rest.

O 'tis not in grief to harm me
While thy love is left to me;
O 'twere not in joy to charm me,
Were that joy unmixed with thee.
H. F. LYTE.

647

SOUL, then know thy full salvation,
Rise o'er sin and fear and care,
Joy to find in every station;
Something still to do or bear;
Think what Spirit dwells within thee,
Think what Father's smiles are thine;
Think that Jesus died to save thee:
Child of heaven, canst thou repine?

2 Haste thee on from grace to glory,
Armed by faith, and winged by prayer;
Heaven's eternal day's before thee—
God's own hand shall guide thee there.
Soon shall close thy earthly mission;
Soon shall pass thy pilgrim days;
Hope shall change to glad fruition,
Faith to sight, and prayer to praise.
H. F. LYTE.

ACROSS THE RIVER. 8s & 7s, with Chorus.

FRED. A FILLMORE.

I have friends a-cross the riv - er, Where for me they glad - ly wait;

Hold a - jar with an - gel fin - gers Yon - der bright and pearl-y gate.
D. S. be the greet-ing Of the Sav-iour whom I love!

CHORUS.

O how sweet will be the meeting In that happy home above !(above !) And how welcome

648 [First verse in the music.]

2 In that home that knows no sorrow,
All our partings will be o'er;
We shall sing the song of glory
On that happy, golden shore.—Cho.

3 Yes, I've friends across the river,
And I hope to greet them there,
When this earthly toil is over,
In that land so bright and fair.—Cho,
EMMA PITT.

WHEN THE MISTS. 8s & 7s. D., with Chorus.

J. H. ANDERSON.

When the mists have rolled in splen-dor From the beau-ty of the hills, And the

sunshine, warm and tender, Falls in kisses on the rills, We may read love's shining letter In the

By permission.

WHEN THE MISTS.—Concluded.

rainbow of the spray; We shall know each oth-er better When the mists have cleared away.

CHORUS.

We shall know as we are known, . . Never - more . . to walk alone, In the
We shall know as we are known, Nevermore to walk alone,

dawn - ing of the morning, When the mists . . have cleared away; In the
In the dawning When the mists have cleared away;

dawn - ing of the morn-ing, When the mists . . . have cleared away.
In the dawning When the mists have cleared away.

Rit.

649 *[First verse in the music.]*

2 If we err in human blindness,
  And forget that we are dust;
If we miss the law of kindness
  When we struggle to be just,
Snowy wings of peace shall cover
  All the plain that hides away,
When the weary watch is over,
  And the mists have cleared away.—Cho.

3 When the silver mist has vailed us
  From the faces of our own,
Oft we deem their love has failed us,
  And we tread our path alone;

We should see them near and truly,
  We should trust them day by day,
Neither love nor blame unduly,
  If the mists were cleared away.—Cho.

4 When the mists have risen above us,
  As our Father knows his own,
Face to face with those that love us,
  We shall know as we are known.
Lo! beyond the orient meadows
  Floats the golden fringe of day;
Heart to heart, we bide the shadows
  Till the mists have cleared away.—Cho.
           ANNIE HERBERT.

ROBINSON. 8s & 7s. D.

THOS. HASTINGS.

Fine.

{ Yes, for me, for me he car-eth With a broth-er's ten-der care;
{ Yes, with me, with me he shareth Ev - ery bur - den, ev - ery fear. }

D. C. Yes, e'en me, e'en me he snatcheth From the per - ils of the way.

D. C.

Yes, o'er me, o'er me he watcheth, Ceaseless watcheth night and day;

650

Yes, for me, for me he careth
With a brother's tender care;
Yes, with me, with me he shareth
Every burden, every fear.
Yes, o'er me, o'er me he watcheth,
Ceaseless watcheth night and day;
Yes, e'en me, e'en me he snatcheth
From the perils of the way.

2 Yes, for me he standeth pleading,
At the mercy-seat above,
Ever for me interceding,
Constant in untiring love.
Yes, in me abroad he sheddeth
Joys unearthly, love and light,
And to cover me he spreadeth
His paternal wing of might.

3 Yes, in me, in me he dwelleth—
I in him, and he in me;
And my empty soul he filleth,
Here and through eternity.
Thus I wait for his returning,
Singing all the way to heaven—
Such the joyful song of morning,
Such the tranquil song of even.
UNKNOWN.

651

HARK! the voice of Jesus calling—
"Who will go and work to-day?
Fields are white, the harvest waiting—
Who will bear the sheaves away?"

Loud and long the Master calleth,
Rich reward he offers free:
Who will answer, gladly saying,
"Here am I, O Lord: send me"?

2 If you can not cross the ocean,
And the heathen lands explore,
You can find the heathen nearer,
You can help them at your door;
If you can not speak like angels,
If you can not preach like Paul,
You can tell the love of Jesus,
You can say he died for all.

3 While the souls of men are dying,
And the Master calls for you,
Let none hear you idly saying,
"There is nothing I can do."
Gladly take the task he gives you,
Let his work your pleasure be;
Answer quickly when he calleth,
"Here am I, O Lord: send me."
D. MARCH.

652

YES, he knows the way is dreary,
Knows the weakness of our frame,
Knows that hand and heart are weary;
He in all points felt the same.
Look to him, and faith shall brighten,
Hope shall soar, and love shall burn,
Peace once more thy heart shall brighten:
Rise: he calleth thee: return.
MISS F. R. HAVERGAL.

NETTLETON. 8s & 7s. D.   ASAHEL NETTLETON.

O thou Fount of every blessing, Tune my heart to sing thy grace: Streams of mercy, never ceasing,

D. S. While the hope of endless glory

Call for songs of loudest praise. Teach me ever to adore thee: May I still thy goodness prove,

Fills my heart with joy and love.

653

O THOU Fount of every blessing,
  Tune my heart to sing thy grace :
Streams of mercy, never ceasing,
  Call for songs of loudest praise.
Teach me ever to adore thee :
  May I still thy goodness prove,
While the hope of endless glory
  Fills my heart with joy and love.

2 Here I'll raise my Ebenezer ;
  Hither by thy help I've come ;
And I hope, by thy good pleasure,
  Safely to arrive at home.
Jesus sought me when a stranger,
  Wandering from thy fold, O God ;
He, to rescue me from danger,
  Interposed his precious blood.

3 O to grace how great a debtor
  Daily I'm constrained to be !
Let thy goodness, like a fetter,
  Bind me closer still to thee.
Never let me wander from thee,
  Never leave thee, whom I love ;
By thy Word and Spirit guide me,
  Till I reach thy courts above.
              R. ROBINSON.

654

SINNER, hear the invitation :
  Mercy calls you from above.
Come, receive this great salvation,
  Purchased by redeeming love.

Jesus calls with sweet compassion,
  "Come, ye weary souls, to me :"
Sinner, heed the invitation ;
  Rise forthwith—he calleth thee.

2 On the rugged cross-tree bleeding,
  Hear the wounded Lamb of God
For transgressors interceding,
  While they shed his precious blood ;
Hear that dying intercession,
  Offered on that bloody tree :
He will pardon your transgression :
  Rise forthwith—he calleth thee.

3 Sinner, soon the day of favor
  Will forever pass away :
Hasten to the bleeding Saviour,
  Hasten while it is to-day.
He will comfort all your sorrow,
  And from every burden free :
Wait not for the coming morrow ;
  Rise forthwith—he calleth thee.
              L. H. JAMESON.

655

MAY the grace of Christ, our Saviour,
  And the Father's boundless love,
With the Holy Spirit's favor,
  Rest upon us from above.
Thus may we abide in union
  With each other and the Lord ;
And possess, in sweet communion,
  Joys which earth can not afford.
              JOHN NEWTON.

MOLUCCA. 8s, 7s & 4s.   ANON.

Sin-ners, will you scorn the message Sent in mer-cy from a-bove?
Ev-ery sentence, O how ten-der! Ev-ery line is full of love.

List-en to it, List-en to it: Ev-ery line is full of love.

656

SINNERS, will you scorn the message
  Sent in mercy from above?
Every sentence, O how tender!
  Every line is full of love.
    Listen to it:
  Every line is full of love.

2 Hear the heralds of the gospel
  News from Zion's King proclaim:
"Pardon to each rebel sinner,
  Free forgiveness in his name."
    O how gracious!
  Free forgiveness in his name.

3 Will you not receive the message—
  Listen to the joyful word—
And embrace the news of pardon
  Offered to you by the Lord?
    Can you slight it—
  Offered to you by the Lord?

4 O ye angels, hovering round us,
  Waiting spirits, speed your way;
Haste ye to the court of heaven;
  Tidings bear without delay:
    Rebel sinners
  Glad the message will obey.

J. ALLEN.

BAVARIA. 8s & 7s. D.   German.
                                                               Fine.

Heav-y-la-den, sad and wea-ry, Lord, we come for help to thee;
All on earth is dark and drear-y: Wilt thou grant our light to be?
D.C. And be pleased to kind-ly hear us, When we bow, and meek-ly pray.

D.C.

With thy pres-ence ev-er cheer us, As we jour-ney on our way;

THE GREAT PHYSICIAN. 8s & 7s, with Chorus.   Arr. by J. H. STOCKTON.

The great Physi-cian now is near, The sympathiz-ing Je-sus; He speaks, the drooping heart to cheer: O hear the voice of Je-sus. "Sweet-est note in ser-aph song,

Sweetest name on mortal tongue, Sweetest car-ol ev-er sung—Je-sus, bless-ed Je-sus!"

657

THE great Physician now is near,
The sympathizing Jesus;
He speaks the drooping heart to cheer:
O hear the voice of Jesus.—CHO.

2 He speaks to us of sins forgiven—
O hear the voice of Jesus—
And how to walk the path to heaven,
And wear a crown with Jesus.—CHO.

3 All glory to the dying Lamb!
I now believe in Jesus;
I love the blessèd Saviour's name,
I love the name of Jesus.—CHO.

4 And when to that bright world above,
We rise to see our Jesus,
We'll sing around the throne of love,
His name, the name of Jesus.—CHO.
WM. HUNTER, alt.

658

HEAVY-LADEN, sad and weary,
Lord, we come for help to thee;
All on earth is dark and dreary:
Wilt thou grant our light to be?
With thy presence, ever cheer us,
As we journey on our way;
And be pleased to kindly hear us,
When we bow, and meekly pray.

2 Many are our sore temptations,
Many are our doubts and fears,
Many are our tribulations,
Many are our bitter tears.

Wilt thou grant to not forsake us,
While we tarry here below,
And, when life is over, take us
Where such sorrows none can know?

3 When we go astray, restrain us
By the drawings of thy love;
From the tempter's power regain us,
For thyself in worlds above;
Every fleeting day and hour
May we live for thee alone;
And may thy almighty power
Bring us near thy glorious throne.
L. H. JAMESON.

NEW CHRISTIAN

ANON.
Fine.

{ Come, ye sin-ners, poor and need-y, Weak and wounded, sick and sore: }
{ Je - sus read-y stands to save you, Full of pit - y, love and power. }
D.C. He is a - ble, He is a - ble, He is will-ing—doubt no more.
D.C. Hearken to the in - vi - ta - tion; O re - ceive his grace to - day.

D. C.

He is a - ble, He is a - ble, He is will-ing—doubt no more,
Cho.*—Turn to the Lord, and seek sal - va - tion; Come, the gos - pel call o - bey;

* The chorus may be used instead of the last two lines of each verse.

659 *[First verse in the music.]*

2 Let not conscience make you linger,
  Nor of fitness fondly dream:
All the fitness he requireth,
  Is to feel your need of him.
    This he gives you;
    'Tis the Saviour's rising beam.

3 Come, you weary, heavy-laden,
  Bruised and mangled by the fall:
If you tarry till you're better,
  You will never come at all;
    Not the righteous—
    Sinners, Jesus came to call.

4 Agonizing in the garden,
  Lo! your Saviour prostrate lies:
On the bloody tree behold him;
  Hear him cry before he dies,
    "It is finished!"
    Sinners, will not this suffice?

5 Lo! the rising Lord ascending,
  Pleads the virtue of his blood:
Venture on him, venture freely,
  Let no other trust intrude.
    None but Jesus
    Can do helpless sinners good.
        CHARLES WESLEY.

OSGOOD. 8s, 7s & 4s.
Arr. from RITTER.

{ List-en, sin - ner: mer - cy hails you; With her sweet-est voice she calls; }
{ Bids you hast-en to the Saviour, Ere the hand of just - ice falls: }

List - en, sin - ner; List - en, sin - ner: 'Tis the voice of mer - cy calls.

HAPPY ZION. 8s, 7s & 4s, or 8s, 7s & 7s. I. B. WOODBURY.

{ Lead us, heavenly Fa-ther, lead us O'er the world's tempestuous sea; }
{ Guard us, guide us, keep us, feed us: For we have no help but thee;}

Yet pos-sess-ing ev - ery bless-ing, If our God our Fa - ther be.

By permission.

660

LEAD us, heavenly Father, lead us
O'er the world's tempestuous sea;
Guard us, guide us, keep us, feed us:
For we have no help but thee;
Yet possessing every blessing,
If our God our Father be.

2 Saviour, breathe forgiveness o'er us:
All our weakness thou dost know;
Thou didst tread this earth before us,
Thou didst feel its keenest woe.
Lone and dreary, faint and weary,
Through the desert thou didst go.

3 Let thy Spirit, now attending,
Fill our hearts with heavenly joy,
Love with every passion blending,
Pleasure that can never cloy.
Thus provided, pardoned, guided,
Nothing can our peace destroy.
JAS. EDMESTON.

661

LISTEN, sinner: mercy hails you;
With her sweetest voice she calls;
Bids you hasten to the Saviour,
Ere the hand of justice falls:
Listen, sinner:
'Tis the voice of mercy calls.

2 See the storm of vengeance gathering
O'er the path you dare to tread;

Hark! the awful thunders rolling
Loud and louder o'er your head;
Flee, O sinner,
Lest the lightnings strike you dead.

3 Haste, O hasten to the Saviour;
Sue his mercy while you may:
Soon the day of grace is over,
Soon your life will pass away:
Hasten, sinner:
You must perish, if you stay.
ANDREW REED.

662

COME to Calvary's holy mountain,
Sinners, ruined by the fall:
Here a pure and healing fountain
Flows, to cleanse the guilty soul,
In a full, perpetual tide,
Opened when the Saviour died.

2 Come in sorrow and contrition,
Wounded, impotent, and blind:
Here the guilty find remission;
Here the lost a refuge find;
Health this fountain will restore;
He that drinks shall thirst no more.

3 Come, ye dying, live forever:
'Tis a soul-reviving flood;
God is faithful—he will never
Break the cov'nant sealed in blood—
Signed when our Redeemer died,
Sealed when he was crucified.
J. MONTGOMERY.

WALES. 8s & 4s.   Welsh Air.

Through the love of God, our Saviour, All will be well; Free and changeless is his fa-vor—
D. S. Strong the hand stretched out to shield us—

All, all is well. Precious is the blood that healed us; Perfect is the grace that sealed us;
All must be well.

663

Through the love of God, our Saviour,
  All will be well;
Free and changeless is his favor—
  All, all is well.
Precious is the blood that healed us;
Perfect is the grace that sealed us;
Strong the hand stretched out to shield us—
  All must be well.

2 Though we pass through tribulation,
  All will be well;
Ours is such a full salvation—
  All, all is well.

Happy, still in God confiding;
Fruitful, if in Christ abiding;
Holy, through the Spirit's guiding—
  All must be well.

3 We expect a bright to-morrow;
  All will be well.
Faith can sing, through days of sorrow,
  All, all is well.
On our Father's love relying,
Jesus every need supplying,
Or in living, or in dying,
  All must be well.

MARY B. PETERS.
WM. B. BRADBURY.

PEACE IS MINE. 8s & 4s.

While I hear life's surg-ing billows, Peace, peace is mine; Why suspend my
D. S. Safe-ly he has

harp on willows? Peace, peace is mine. { I may sing with Christ beside me, }
sworn to guide me; Peace, peace is mine. { Tho' a thousand ills be-tide me; }

LOVE, JOY AND PEACE. 8s & 4s. J. H. FILLMORE.

What care I for fame's o-pin-ion? Love, love is mine; Scorn and hate have lost do-min-ion, Love, love is mine; An-ger's bonds no more enslave me, Je-sus died, in love, to save me, And his Spir-it free-ly gave me; Love, love is mine.

664

WHAT care I for fame's opinion?
　Love, love is mine;
Scorn and hate have lost dominion,
　Love, love is mine;
Anger's bonds no more enslave me,
Jesus died, in love, to save me,
And his Spirit freely gave me;
　Love, love is mine.

2 In my heart is Jesus reigning,
　Joy, joy is mine;
Banished thence is all complaining,
　Joy, joy is mine;

Wrath no more can round me hover,
Dark despair my future cover,
All my fears and doubts are over;
　Joy, joy is mine.

3 As a fruit of promised Spirit,
　Peace, peace is mine,
Which the pure in heart inherit,
　Peace, peace is mine—
Peace at morn, and peace at even;
All my sins have been forgiven,
'Tis a foretaste here of heaven;
　Peace, peace is mine.
D. R. LUCAS.

665

WHILE I hear life's surging billows,
　Peace, peace is mine;
Why suspend my harp on willows?
　Peace, peace is mine.
I may sing with Christ beside me,
Though a thousand ills betide me;
Safely he has sworn to guide me—
　Peace, peace is mine.

2 Every trial draws me nearer—
　Peace, peace is mine;
All his strokes but make him dearer—
　Peace, peace is mine.
Bless I then the hand that smiteth
Gently, and to heal delighteth;
'Tis against my sins he fighteth—
　Peace, peace is mine.
UNKNOWN.

BEULAH LAND. 8s, with Chorus.   JNO. R. SWENEY.

I've reached the land of corn and wine, And all its riches freely mine; Here shines undimmed one

blissful day, For all my night has passed away.   O Beulah Land, sweet Beulah Land, As

on thy highest mount I stand, I look a - way a-cross the sea, Where mansions are pre-

pared for me, And view the shining glory shore, My heaven, my home for evermore.

By permission.

666

I'VE reached the land of corn and
    wine,
And all its riches freely mine ;
Here shines undimmed one blissful
    day,
For all my night has passed away.

CHO.—O Beulah Land, sweet Beulah Land,
    As on thy highest mount I stand,
    I look away, across the sea,
    Where mansions are prepared for me,
    And view the shining glory shore,
    My heaven, my home for evermore.

2 My Saviour comes and walks with me,
And sweet communion here have we;
He gently leads me by his hand,
For this is heaven's border-land.—CHO.

3 A sweet perfume upon the breeze
Is borne from ever-vernal trees,
And flowers that, never fading, grow
Where streams of life forever flow.—CHO.

4 The zephyrs seem to float to me
Sweet sounds of heaven's melody,
As angels with the white-robed throng,
Join in the sweet redemption song.—CHO.

EDGAR PAGE.

THE ROCK THAT IS HIGHER. 8s, with Chorus.   W. G. FISCHER.

O sometimes the shadows are deep, And rough seems the path to the goal;

And sor-rows, how oft-en they sweep, Like tempests, down o-ver the soul!

CHORUS.

O then to the Rock let me fly,   To the Rock that is higher than I:
            let me fly,   is higher than I;

O then to the Rock let me fly,   To the Rock that is higher than I.
            let me fly,

By permission.

667

O SOMETIMES the shadows are deep,
  And rough seems the path to the goal;
And sorrows, how often they sweep,
  Like tempests, down over the soul!

Cho.—O then to the Rock let me fly,
  To the Rock that is higher than I;
O then to the Rock let me fly,
  To the Rock that is higher than I.

2 O sometimes how long seems the day,
  And sometimes how heavy my feet!
But, toiling in life's dusty way,
  The Rock's bless-ed shadow, how sweet!—Cho.

3 O near to the Rock let me keep,
  Or blessings, or sorrows prevail;
Or climbing the mountain-way steep,
  Or walking the shadowy vale.—Cho.
                                    E. JOHNSON.

THE ROCK AND THE SAND. 9s, 8s & 12, with Chorus.   J. H. ROSECRANS.

On what are you building, my brother, Your hopes of an e-ter-nal home? Is it

loose, shifting sand, or the firm, sol-id rock, You are trust-ing for a-ges to come?

CHORUS.

Hearing and do-ing, we build on the Rock; Hearing a-lone, we build on the sand;

Both will be tried by the storm and the flood—On-ly the Rock the tri-al will stand.

By permission.

668   [First verse in the music.]

2 On one or the other, my brother,
  You are building your hopes, day by day;
You are risking your soul on the works that you do:
  Will the dark waters sweep you away?—Cho.

3 Your Saviour has warned you, my brother:
  I pray you, give heed to his voice:
There is life on the rock, but there's death on the sand—
  O, my brother, pray tell me your choice.—Cho.

4 No matter how careful, my brother,
  The sand for your house you prepare,
'Twill be all swept away when the floods shall descend,
  Leaving nothing but death and despair.—Cho.

                      H. R. TRICKETT.

O WHERE ARE THE REAPERS? 10s & 9s, with Chorus.   GEO. F. ROOT.

O where are the reapers that gar-ner in   The sheaves of the good from the fields of sin?

With sick-les of truth must the work be done, And no one may rest till the "harvest home."

CHORUS.

Where are the reapers? O who will come And share in the glo-ry of the "harvest home"?

O who will help us   to gar-ner in   The sheaves of good from the fields of sin?

By permission.

669   [*First verse in the music.*]
2 Go out in the by-ways and search them all—
The wheat may be there, though the weeds are tall—
Then search in the highway, and pass none by,
But gather from all for the home on high.—CHO.

3 The fields all are ripening, and far and wide
The world now is waiting the harvest tide;
But reapers are few, and the work is great,
And much will be lost should the harvest wait.—CHO.

4 So come with your sickles, ye sons of men,
And gather together the golden grain;
Toil on till the Lord of the harvest come,
Then share ye his joy in the "harvest home."—CHO.
                                        EBEN E. REXFORD.

MORE LIKE JESUS. 11s & 8s, with Chorus.

T. C. O'KANE.

More like Je-sus, more like Jesus would I be— More like Je-sus in sub-mis-sion,

Like him trustful, un-re-pin-ing, Patient like him, like him in hu-mil-i-ty.

CHORUS.

More and more, more and more More and more like Jesus every day;
More and more, more and more, More like Jesus every day, every day;

More and more, more and more, more and more, more and more, More like Jesus every day.

Copyright, 1879, by T. C. O'Kane.

670

MORE like Jesus, more like Jesus would I be—
  More like Jesus in submission,
  Like him trustful, unrepining,
Patient like him, like him in humility.—CHO.

2 More like Jesus, more like Jesus would I be—
  More like Jesus, true and steadfast,
  Like him striving, ever doing,
Earnest like him, like him in fidelity.—CHO.

3 Blessèd Jesus, come and make me all like thee—
  All like thee, O blessèd Jesus,
  In the glory of thy manhood,
In the beauty of thy spotless purity.—CHO.

F. MERRICK.

272

ONCE FOR ALL. 10s, 9 & 8, with Chorus.

P. P. BLISS.

Free from the law, O hap-py con - di - tion! Je - sus hath

bled, and there is re - mis - sion; Cursed by the law, and bruised by the

CHORUS.

fall, Grace hath redeemed us once for all. Once for all! O sinner, re-

ceive it; Once for all! O broth-er, be - lieve it; Cling to the

cross: the bur-den will fall, Christ hath redeemed us once for all.

By permission of J. Church & Co.

671 *[First verse in the music.]*

2 Now are we free—there's no condemnation,
Jesus provides a perfect salvation;
"Come unto me!" O hear his sweet call;
Come, and he saves us once for all.—Cho.

3 "Children of God," O g'o-ri-ous calling!
Surely his grace will keep us from falling;
Passing from death to life at his call,
Blessèd salvation, once for all !—Cho.

P. P. BLISS.

WHOSOEVER WILL. 10, 11s & 7, with Chorus. P. P. BLISS.

"Whosoever heareth," shout, shout the sound; Send the bless-ed tidings all the world around;

Spread the joy-ful news wher-ev-er man is found—"Who-so-ev-er will, may come."

CHORUS.

"Who-so-ev-er will, who-so-ev-er will," Send the proc-la-ma-tion ov-er vale and hill;

'Tis a lov-ing Fa-ther calls the wanderer home—"Who-so-ev-er will, may come."

By permission of J. Church & Co.

672

"WHOSOEVER heareth," shout, shout the sound;
Send the blessèd tidings all the world around;
Spread the joyful news wherever man is found—
"Whosoever will, may come."—CHO.

2 Whosoever cometh, need not delay;
Now the door is open: enter while you may:
Jesus is the true, the only Living way—
"Whosoever will, may come."—CHO.

3 "Whosoever will," the promise is secure;
"Whosoever will" forever must endure;
"Whosoever will," 'tis life for evermore—
"Whosoever will, may come."—CHO.

P. P. BLISS.

HYMN AND TUNE-BOOK.

WHITER THAN SNOW. 11s, with Chorus. Wm. G. Fischer.

Lord Jesus, I long to be perfectly whole; I want thee forever to live in my soul: Break down every idol, cast out every foe; Now wash me, and I shall be whiter than snow.

CHORUS.

Whiter than snow—yes, whiter than snow; Now wash me, and I shall be whiter than snow.

By permission.

673 *[First verse in the music.]*

2 Lord Jesus, look down from thy throne in the skies,
And help me to make a complete sacrifice:
I give up myself, and whatever I know:
Now wash me, and I shall be whiter than snow.—Cho.

3 Lord Jesus, for this I most humbly entreat;
I wait, blessèd Lord, at thy crucified feet;
By faith, for my cleansing, I see thy blood flow:
Now wash me, and I shall be whiter than snow.—Cho.

4 Lord Jesus, thou seest I patiently wait:
Come now, and within me a new heart create.
To those who have sought thee, thou never said'st No:
Now wash me, and I shall be whiter than snow.—Cho.

James Nicholson.

275

PORTUGUESE HYMN. 11s.   J. READING.

The Lord is my Shepherd, no want shall I know; I feed in green pastures, safe fold-ed I rest; He leadeth my soul where the still waters flow, Restores me when wandering, redeems when oppressed, Restores me when wandering, redeems when op-[pressed.

674   *[First verse in the music.]*

2 Thro' the valley and shadow of death though I stray,
Since thou art my Guardian, no evil I fear;
Thy rod shall defend me, thy staff be my stay;
No harm can befall, with my Comforter near.

3 In the midst of affliction my table is spread;
With blessings unmeasured my cup runneth o'er;
With perfume and oil thou anointest my head—
O what shall I ask of thy providence more?

4 Let goodness and mercy, my bountiful God,
Still follow my steps till I meet thee above:
I seek, by the path which my forefathers trod,
Through the land of their sojourn, thy kingdom of love.

J. MONTGOMERY.

675

Our Father in heaven, we hallow thy name:
May thy kingdom holy, on earth be the same;
O give to us daily our portion of bread—
It is from thy bounty that all must be fed.

2 Forgive our transgressions, and teach us to know
That humble compassion that pardons each foe;
Keep us from temptation, from weakness and sin,
And thine be the glory forever. Amen.

S. J. HALE.

FOUNDATION. 11s.　　　　　　　　　　　　　　　ANON.

How firm a founda - tion, ye saints of the Lord, Is laid for your faith in his
D. S. You who un - to Je - sus for

ex - cel - lent word! What more can he say than to you he has said,
ref - uge have fled?

676

How firm a foundation, ye saints of the Lord,
Is laid for your faith, in his excellent word!
What more can he say than to you he has said,
You who unto Jesus for refuge have fled?

2 In every condition—in sickness, in health,
In poverty's vale, or abounding in wealth,
At home and abroad, on the land, on the sea—
As your days may demand, so your succor shall be.

3 Fear not: I am with you: O be not dismayed:
I, I am your God, and will still give you aid;
I'll strengthen you, help you, and cause you to stand,
Upheld by my righteous, omnipotent hand.

4 When through the deep waters I cause you to go,
The rivers of sorrow shall not you o'erflow;
For I will be with you, your troubles to bless,
And sanctify to you your deepest distress.

5 When through fiery trials your pathway shall lie,
My grace, all-sufficient, shall be your supply ;
The flame shall not hurt you; I only design
Your dross to consume, and your gold to refine.

6 E'en down to old age all my people shall prove
My sovereign, eternal, unchangeable love;
And when hoary hairs shall their temples adorn,
Like lambs they shall still in my bosom be borne.

7 The soul that on Jesus hath leaned for repose,
I will not, I can not desert to his foes;
That soul, though all hell should endeavor to shake,
I'll never, no never, no never forsake.

GEO. KEITH.

277

NEW CHRISTIAN

GOSHEN. 11s. — Arr. by THOS. HASTINGS.

De - lay not, de - lay not; O sin - ner, draw near: The wa - ters of
D. S. Re - demp - tion is

life are now flow - ing for thee; No price is de-mand-ed, the Saviour is here,
purchased—sal - va - tion is free.

677
[First verse in the music.]

2 Delay not, delay not: why longer abuse
The love and compassion of Jesus, our Lord?
A fountain is opened—how canst thou refuse
To wash and be cleansed in his pardoning blood?

3 Delay not, delay not, O sinner, to come:
For mercy still lingers, and calls thee to-day;
Her voice is not heard in the vale of the tomb;
Her message, unheeded, will soon pass away.

4 Delay not, delay not: the Spirit of grace,
Long grieved and resisted, entreats thee to come:
Beware, lest in darkness thou finish thy race,
And sink to the vale of eternity's gloom.

THOS. HASTINGS.

EXPOSTULATION. 11s. — JOSIAH HOPKINS.

O turn you, O turn you: for why will you die, { When God in his
{ Now Je - sus in -

mer - cy is com - ing so nigh?) And an-gels are waiting to welcome you home.
vites you; the Spir-it says, Come, }

278

EVEN THEE. P. M.   WM. B. BRADBURY.

{ Sin-ners, come to Christ, the Sav-iour; Now his gracious call o-bey; }
{ Come, this is the day of fa-vor; Mer-cy calls: do not de-lay. }

Come to-day, Come to-day: Mer-cy calls: do not de-lay.

Copyright, 1866, in "Golden Shower."

678

SINNERS, come to Christ the Saviour;
Now his gracious call obey;
Come: this is the day of favor;
Mercy calls: do not delay.
Come to-day:
Mercy calls: do not delay.

2 Time, on lightning pinions flying,
Sweeps the sons of earth away;
Every moment men are dying:
Sinner, why do you delay?
Come to-day:
Sinner, why do you delay?

3 Hear the gospel invitation
Ringing in your ears to-day,
Offering pardon and salvation:
Sinner, come, without delay;
Come to-day;
Sinner, come without delay.

4 By the Saviour's earthly pleading,
Be persuaded to obey;
By his heavenly interceding,
Be constrained, do not delay;
Come to-day;
Be constrained, do not delay.
L. H. JAMESON.

679

O TURN you, O turn you: for why will you die,
When God in his mercy is coming so nigh?
Now Jesus invites you; the Spirit says, Come,
And angels are waiting to welcome you home.

2 How vain the delusion that, while you delay,
Your hearts may grow better by staying away!
Come wretched, come starving, come just as you be;
Here streams of salvation are flowing most free.

3 Here Jesus is ready your souls to receive:
O how can you question, since now you believe?
Since sin is your burden, why will you not come?
He now bids you welcome, he now says there's room.

4 In riches, in pleasure, what can you obtain,
To soothe your affliction, or banish your pain;
To bear up your spirit, when summoned to die,
Or waft you to mansions of glory on high?
JOSIAH HOPKINS.

COME, YE DISCONSOLATE. 11s & 10s.   S. WEBBE.

Come, ye disconsolate, where'er you langnish; Come, at the shrine of God fervently kneel;

Here bring your wounded hearts, here tell your anguish;
Earth has no sorrow that heaven can not heal.

680

COME, ye disconsolate, where'er you languish ;
   Come, at the shrine of God fervently kneel ;
Here bring your wounded hearts, here tell your anguish ;
   Earth has no sorrow that heaven can not heal.

2 Joy of the desolate, light of the straying,
   Hope of the penitent, fadeless and pure,
Here speaks the Comforter, tenderly saying,
   Earth has no sorrow that heaven can not cure.

3 Here see the bread of life; see waters flowing
   Forth from the throne of God, pure from above;
Come to the feast of love—come, ever knowing
   Earth has no sorrow but heaven can remove.
                                   THOMAS MOORE.

HOME. 11s, with Chorus.   H. R. BISHOP.
                                        1st.   2nd.

{ 'Mid scenes of confusion and creature complaints,
{ How sweet to my soul is com-mun-ion with   saints; To find   at the banquet of

                                        Fine. CHORUS.   D. S.

mercy there's room, And feel in the presence of Jesus at home! Home! home! sweet, sweet home!
   D. S. Prepare me, dear Saviour, for glory, my home.

HENLEY. 11s & 10s.   LOWELL MASON.

Come un - to me when shadows dark-ly gath-er, When the sad heart is
D. S. Come un - to me, and

Fine.   D. S.

wea - ry and distressed, Seek-ing for com-fort from your heavenly Fa-ther,
I will give you rest.

By permission.

681
[First verse in the music.]

2 Ye who have mourned when the spring flowers were taken;
  When the ripe fruit fell richly to the ground;
When the loved slept, in brighter homes to waken,
  Where their pale brows with spirit-wreaths are crowned.

3 Large are the mansions in your Father's dwelling,
  Glad are the homes that sorrows never dim;
Sweet are the harps in holy music swelling,
  Soft are the tones which raise the heavenly hymn.

4 There, like an Eden, blossoming in gladness,
  Bloom the fair flowers the earth too rudely pressed:
Come unto me, all ye who droop in sadness,
  Come unto me, and I will give you rest.
                                              UNKNOWN.

682

'MID scenes of confusion and creature complaints,
How sweet to my soul is communion with saints;
To find at the banquet of mercy there's room,
And feel in the presence of Jesus at home!—CHO.

2 Sweet bonds that unite all the children of peace!
And thrice blessèd Jesus, whose love can not cease!
Though oft from thy presence in sadness I roam,
I long to behold thee in glory, at home.—CHO.

3 While here in the valley of conflict I stray,
O give me submission and strength as my day;
In all my afflictions to thee would I come,
Rejoicing in hope of my glo-ri-ous home.—CHO.

4 I long, dearest Lord, in thy beauty to shine,
No more as an exile in sorrow to pine;
And in thy dear image arise from the tomb,
With glorified millions, to praise thee at home.—CHO.
                                           DAVID DENHAM.

24   281

NEW CHRISTIAN

WARNING. 12s & 11s.
Wm. B. Bradbury.

Hark, sinner, while God from on high doth en-treat thee, And warnings with
Give ear to his voice, lest in judg-ment he meet thee: (Omit

ac-cents of mer - cy do blend ;
"The harvest is passing, the summer will end."

By permission.

683

HARK, sinner, while God from on high doth entreat thee,
   And warnings with accents of mercy do blend ;
Give ear to his voice, lest in judgment he meet thee:
   "The harvest is passing, the summer will end."

2 Despised and rejected, at length he may leave thee:
   What anguish and horror thy bosom will rend !
Then haste thee, O sinner, while he will receive thee:
   "The harvest is passing, the summer will end."

3 Ere long, and Jehovah will come in his power;
   Our God will arise, with his foes to contend.
Haste, haste thee, O sinner, prepare for that hour:
   "The harvest is passing, the summer will end."

4 The Saviour will call thee in judgment before him :
   O bow to his scepter, and make him thy friend ;
Now yield him thy heart ; make haste to adore him :
   "The harvest is passing, the summer will end."
                                     J. B. Hayne.

PENITENCE. 7s & 6s. Peculiar.
W. H. Oakley.

Time is winging us away To our eternal home; Life is but a winter's day,
D. S. All that's mortal soon shall be

A journey to the tomb. Youth and vigor soon will flee, Blooming beauty lose its charms;
Enclosed in death's cold arms.

LUCAS. 10, 5s & 11s. JAMES LUCAS.

Come, let us a-new Our journey pursue—Roll round with the year, And never stand still till the

Mas-ter appear; His a-dor-a-ble will Let us gladly fulfill, And our talents improve By the

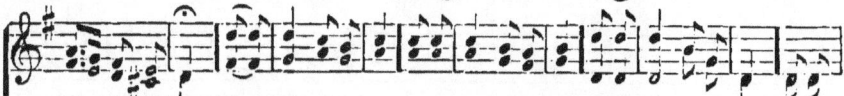

patience of hope, and the labor of love, By the pa-tience of hope and the labor of love.

684

COME, let us anew
Our journey pursue—
Roll round with the year,
And never stand still till the Master
appear;
His adorable will
Let us gladly fulfill,
And our talents improve
By the patience of hope, and the labor of love.

2 Our life is a dream;
Our time, as a stream,
Glides swiftly away,
And the fugitive moment refuses to stay;

The arrow is flown,
The moment is gone,
The millennial year
Rushes on to our view, and eternity's near.

3 O that each, in the day
Of his coming, may say,
"I have fought my way through;
I have finished the work thou didst
give me to do!"
O that each from his Lord
May receive the glad word,
"Well and faithfully done:
Enter into my joy and sit down on my throne"!
CHARLES WESLEY.

685

TIME is winging us away
To our eternal home;
Life is but a winter's day,
A journey to the tomb.
Youth and vigor soon will flee,
Blooming beauty lose its charms;
All that's mortal soon shall be
Enclosed in death's cold arms.

2 Time is winging us away
To our eternal home;
Life is but a winter's day,
A journey to the tomb;
But the Christian shall enjoy
Health and beauty soon above,
Far beyond the world's alloy,
Secure in Jesus' love.
JOHN BURTON.

283

ROWLEY. 11s & 9s.   LOWELL MASON.

How happy are they who their Saviour obey, And have laid up their treasures above! Tongue can not ex-

press the sweet comfort and peace Of a soul in its earliest love, Of a soul in its earliest love.

686 [First verse in the music.]

2 This comfort is mine, since the favor divine
  I have found in the blood of the Lamb.
Since the truth I believed, what a joy I've received,
  What a heaven in Jesus' blest name!

3 'Tis a heaven below my Redeemer to know;
  And the angels can do nothing more
Than to fall at his feet, and the story repeat,
  And the Lover of sinners adore.

4 Jesus all the day long is my joy and my song:
  O that all to this refuge may fly!
He has loved me, I cried; he has suffered and died
  To redeem such a rebel as I!

5 On the wings of his love I am carried above
  All my sin and temptation and pain:
O why should I grieve, while on him I believe?
  O why should I sorrow again?

6 O the rapturous height of that holy delight,
  Which I find in the life-giving blood!
Of my Saviour possessed, I am perfectly blessed,
  Being filled with the fullness of God!

7 Now my remnant of days will I spend to his praise,
  Who has died, me from sin to redeem;
Whether many or few, all my years are his due—
  They shall all be devoted to him.

8 What a mercy is this! what a heaven of bliss!
  How unspeakably happy am I!
Gathered into the fold, with believers enrolled—
  With believers to live and to die!

CHARLES WESLEY.

BRINGING IN THE SHEAVES. 12s & 11s, with Chorus. KNOWLES SHAW.

Sow-ing in the morn-ing, sow-ing seeds of kindness; Sow-ing in the
noon - tide, and the dew - y eves; Wait - ing for the har - vest,
D. S. Wait - ing, etc.
and the time of reaping— We shall come re-joic - ing, bringing in the sheaves.

CHORUS.

Bringing in the golden sheaves, Bringing in the golden sheaves,
the gold-en sheaves, the gold-en sheaves,

687

SOWING in the morning, sowing seeds of kindness;
  Sowing in the noontide, and the dewy eves;
Waiting for the harvest, and the time of reaping—
  We shall come rejoicing, bringing in the sheaves.—CHO.

2 Go and tell the nations now in heathen blindness;
  Tell them Jesus died—now no excuse he leaves;
Bid them come to Jesus—thus prepare the harvest:
  You shall come rejoicing, bringing in the sheaves.—CHO.

3 Sowing in the sunshine, sowing in the shadows;
  Fearing neither clouds nor winter's chilling breeze;
By and by the harvest, and, our labors ended,
  We shall come rejoicing, bringing in the sheaves.—CHO.
                                        KNOWLES SHAW.

HOW STRONG IS THY FAITH? 11s & 5s.   S. M. Lutz.

How strong is thy faith in the Sav-iour di-vine? Say, brother, O say!

How strong is thy hope? Dost thou ev - er re - pine? Say, brother, O say!

How deep in thy heart is the fountain of love? Say, brother, O say!

Is Je - sus enthroned there, all oth-ers a - bove? Say, brother, O say!

688   [First verse in the music.]

2 How much of thy time dost thou give to the Lord?
    Say, brother, O say!
How much of thy time dost thou study his word?
    Say, brother, O say!
How many poor souls art thou leading from sin?
    Say, brother, O say!
How many for Christ art thou striving to win?
    Say, brother, O say!

3 How far on thy journey to heaven art thou?
    Say, brother, O say!
If Jesus should call, are you ready just now?
    Say, brother, O say!
How bright is the crown that is waiting for thee—
    Say, brother, O say!—
When Jesus shall call you across the dark sea?
    Say, brother, O say!   D. R. Lucas.

TO THE WORK. 12s, with Chorus.

W. H. DOANE.

To the work! to the work! We are servants of God: Let us follow the path that our Master has trod;

With the balm of his counsel our strength to renew, Let us do with our might what our hands find to do.

CHORUS.

Toiling on, toil-ing on, toil-ing on, toil-ing on,

Let us hope (and trust), let us watch (and pray), And la-bor till the Mas-ter comes.

By permission of Biglow and Main.

689

[First verse in the music.]

2 To the work! to the work! Let the hungry be fed;
To the fountain of life let the weary be led:
In the cross and its banner our glory shall be,
While we herald the tidings, "Salvation is free!"—Cho.

3 To the work! to the work! There is labor for all;
For the kingdom of darkness and error shall fall,
And the name of Jehovah exalted shall be
In the loud-swelling chorus, "Salvation is free!"—Cho.

4 To the work! to the work, in the strength of the Lord!
And a robe and a crown shall our labor reward,
When the home of the faithful our dwelling shall be,
And we shout with the ransomed, "Salvation is free!"—Cho.

FANNY J. CROSBY.

NEW CHRISTIAN

KNOWLES SHAW.

Is it far to the land of rest, Where the weary feet shall never, never roam;

To the mansions of the pure and the blest, Where we all shall meet at home?

CHORUS.

Is it far? Is it far?
Is it far to that beau-ti-ful home of the blest? Will you

tell me, broth-er pil-grim, is it far? (is it far?) To that mansion of the blest,

Where the wea-ry are at rest? O say, brother pil-grim, is it far?

By permission.

690 *[First verse in the music.]*

2 Is it far to that peaceful shore,
　Where the aching heart shall sorrow not again;
Where the friends who meet shall part nevermore,
　But with Christ forever reign?—Cho.

3 Is it far to the plains of light,
　To that city with its jasper walls aglow,
Where the glory of the Lord is the light?
　To that home, say, will you go?—Cho.　KNOWLES SHAW.

288

TARRY WITH ME. 8s & 7s, with Chorus. KNOWLES SHAW.

Tar-ry with me, O my Sav-iour: For the day is pass ng by;

See, the shades of evening gath-er, And the night is draw-ing nigh.

CHORUS.

Tar-ry with me, bless-ed Sav-iour; Leave me not till morning light:

For I'm lone-ly here without thee: Tar-ry with me thro' the night.

By permission.

691

TARRY with me, O my Saviour:
 For the day is passing by;
See, the shades of evening gather,
 And the night is drawing nigh.

CHO.—Tarry with me, blessèd Saviour;
 Leave me not till morning light:
For I'm lonely here without thee:
 Tarry with me through the night.

2 Many friends were gathered round me
 In the bright days of the past;

But the grave has closed above them,
 And I linger here at last.—CHO.

3 Deeper, deeper grow the shadows,
 Paler now the glowing west;
Swift the night of death advances;
 Shall it be the night of rest?—CHO.

4 Tarry with me, O my Saviour;
 Lay my head upon thy breast
Till the morning; then awake me—
 Morning of eternal rest.—CHO.

MRS. C. S. SMITH.

THE GLORIOUS LAND. 9s & 10s, with Chorus.　　　　A. D. FILLMORE.

The Bi-ble re-veals a Glorious Land, Where an-gels and pu-ri-fied spir-its dwell,

Where pleasures ne'er end, at God's right hand, And anthems of praises for-ev-er swell.

CHORUS.

In that Glo-rious Land, what a hap-py band! Ere long we shall stand, and

sing with them, In the Cit-y of God, Je-ru-sa-lem.

692　*[First verse in the music.]*

2 Outgushing beneath the throne of God,
　And of the blest Lamb at his right hand,
Thence runneth the crystal stream of life,
　A fountain of joy in that Glorious Land.—CHO.

3 In th' midst of the street on either side,
　The tree of life, arching the way, o'ershades,
With health-giving foliage far and wide—
　No sickness this Glo-ri-ous Land invades.—CHO.

4 Twelve manner of fruits hang pendant there,
　And they who partake shall never die:
With Jesus they dwell, and ever share
　The joys of that Glo-ri-ous Land on high.—CHO.

5 Th' afflictions of life are brief and light,
  While faith looks beyond the dark Jordan's strand,
Where splendidly shine the mansions bright,
  Which Jesus prepares in that Glorious Land.—Cho.

6 Then come, my dear brethren, let us haste
  To finish our work with unfaltering hand,
And soon the sweet joys of heaven we'll taste,
  With all the redeemed, in that Glorious Land.—Cho.

A. D. Fillmore.

IS MY NAME WRITTEN THERE? 12s, with Chorus.

W. T. Giffe.

In the Lamb's book of life that is kept in heav-en, Are writ-ten the

CHORUS.

names of those for-giv-en: Is my name written there? Is my name written

there? Is my name written there? In the Lamb's book of life, Is my name written there?

By permission.

693

In the Lamb's book of life that is kept in heaven,
Are written the names of those forgiven:
  Is my name written there?—Cho.

2 All the good that I do is there recorded,
And in heaven by grace I'll be rewarded:
  Is my name written there?—Cho.

3 Though my life may be fraught with afflictions fearful,
I can bear with it all, and my heart be cheerful,
  If my name's written there.—Cho.

W. T. Giffe.

NEW CHRISTIAN

ONLY WAITING. 8s & 7s, with Chorus.

JAS. H. FILLMORE.

1. I am wait-ing for the morn-ing Of the bless-ed day to dawn,
2. I am wait-ing, worn and wea-ry With the bat-tle and the strife,

When the sor-row and the sad-ness Of this change-ful life are gone.
Hop-ing, when the war-fare's o-ver, To re-ceive a crown of life.

CHORUS.

I am wait - - - ing, on-ly wait-ing, Till this
I am wait-ing, wait-ing, wait-ing, on-ly wait-ing on-ly wait-ing

wea - - - ry life is o'er; On-ly wait - - - ing
wea-ry, wea-ry, wea-ry—till this wea-ry life is o'er; On-ly waiting, waiting, waiting

for my welcome, From my Sav-iour on the oth-er shore.
for my welcome, for my welcome,

694 [First and second verses in the music.]

3 Waiting, hoping, trusting ever,
  For a home of boundless love;
Like a pilgrim, looking forward
  To the land of bliss above.—CHO.

4 Hoping soon to meet the loved ones
  Where the "many mansions" be;
Listening for the happy welcome
  Of my Saviour calling me.—CHO.

W. G. IRVIN.

SUMMER-LAND. 12s, 10 & 7, with Refrain.   Dr. A. B. Everett.

Beyond this land of parting, los-ing and leaving, Far be-yond the loss-es, dark-en-ing this,

And far be-yond the tak-ing and the be-reav-ing Lies the summer-land of bliss.

REFRAIN.

Land be - yond, so fair and bright! Land be - yond, where is no night!
Land be-yond, so fair and bright!   Land be-yond, where is no night!

Summer land, God is its Light, O hap-py summer-land of bliss!
Sum-mer land,

By permission.

695   *[First verse in the music.]*

2 Beyond this land of toiling, sowing, and reaping,
  Far beyond the shadows, darkéning this,
And far beyond the sighing, moaning, and weeping,
  Lies the summer-land of bliss.—Ref.

3 Beyond this land of sinning, fainting, and falling,
  Far beyond the doubtings, darkéning this,
And far beyond the griefs and dangers befalling,
  Lies the summer-land of bliss.—Ref.

4 Beyond this land of waiting, seeking, and sighing,
  Far beyond the sorrows, darkéning this,
And far beyond the pain and sickness and dying,
  Lies the summer-land of bliss.—Ref.

Mrs. M. B. C. Slade.

NEW CHRISTIAN

THE THOUSAND YEARS. 9s & 8s. D.

HENRY C. WORK.

Be of good cheer, ye friends of Je - sus; Nev-er suc-cumb to doubts and fears;

Cherish the great and precious promise, "To reign with Christ a thousand years."
D.S. This is the Father's pre-cious promise, "To reign with Christ a thousand years."

To reign a thou-sand years with Je - sus, Free from all tri - als, toils and tears—

By permission.

696

Be of good cheer, ye friends of Jesus;
  Never succumb to doubts and fears;
Cherish the great and precious promise.
  "To reign with Christ a thousand
    years."
To reign a thousand years with Jesus,
  Free from all trials, toils and tears—
This is the Father's precious promise,
  "To reign with Christ a thousand
    years."

2 Be of good cheer: earth's night of
    sorrow
  Shortly will close, with all its fears;
Then shall arise the glorious morrow,
  The reign with Christ a thousand years.
To reign a thousand years with Jesus
  More than requites for all our tears;
This is the sure and gracious promise,
  "To reign with Christ a thousand
    years."

3 Be of good cheer: time's painful
    conflicts
  All will be done when Christ appears;
Then will begin the glorious era,
  The reign with Christ a thousand years.
To reign a thousand years with Jesus,
  Far from the tempter's lures and snares,
With the redeemed of every nation
  Reigning with Christ a thousand
    years.

4 Be of good cheer: ten thousand ages
  Perfect in bliss and free from tears,
Soon will begin their endless cycle,
  Reigning with Christ a thousand
    years.
Ten thousand times ten thousand ages,
  Freedom from sin and death and tears—
What an "eternal weight of glory"
  Comes with that reign of a thousand
    years!

L. H. JAMESON.

294

697 Sweet By-and-By.

THERE'S a land that is fairer than day,
And by faith we can see it afar;
For the Father waits over the way,
To prepare us a dwelling-place there.

CHO.—In the sweet by-and-by,
We shall meet on that beautiful shore;
In the sweet by-and-by,
We shall meet on that beautiful shore.

2 We shall sing on that beautiful shore
The melodious songs of the blest;
And our spirits shall sorrow no more—
Not a sigh for the blessing of rest.

3 To our bountiful Father above
We will offer the tribute of praise,
For the glorious gifts of his love,
And the blessings that hallow our days
S. FILLMORE BENNETT.

698 The Home Over There.

O THINK of the home over there,
By the side of the river of light,
Where the saints, all immortal and fair,
Are robed in their garments of white—
Over there, over there,
O think of the home over there.

2 O think of the friends over there,
Who before us the journey have trod,
Of the songs that they breathe on the air,
In their home in the palace of God—
Over there, over there,
O think of the friends over there.

3 My Saviour is now over there;
There my kindred and friends are at rest:
Then away from my sorrow and care,
Let me fly to the land of the blest.
Over there, over there,
My Saviour is now over there.

4 I'll soon be at home over there,
For the end of my journey I see;
Many dear to my heart over there,
Are watching and waiting for me.
Over there, over there,
I'll soon be at home over there.
D. W. C. HUNTINGTON.

699 The Beautiful River.

SHALL we gather at the river
Where bright angel feet have trod;
With its crystal tide forever
Flowing by the throne of God?

CHO.—Yes, we'll gather at the river,
The beautiful, the beautiful river
Gather with the saints at the river
That flows by the throne of God.

2 On the margin of the river,
Washing up its silver spray,
We will walk and worship ever,
All the happy golden day.

3 Ere we reach the shining river,
Lay we every burden down;
Grace our spirits will deliver,
And provide a robe and crown.

4 Soon we'll reach the silver river,
Soon our pilgrimage will cease;
Soon our happy hearts will quiver
With the melody of peace.
ROBERT LOWRY.

700 What Shall the Harvest Be?

SOWING the seed by the daylight fair,
Sowing the seed by the noonday glare,
Sowing the seed by the fading light,
Sowing the seed in the solemn night:
O what shall the harvest be?

CHO.—Sown in the darkness or sown in the light,
Sown in our weakness or sown in our might,
Gathered in time or eternity,
Sure, ah! sure will the harvest be.

2 Sowing the seed by the wayside high,
Sowing the seed on the rocks to die,
Sowing the seed where the thorns will spoil,
Sowing the seed in the fertile soil:
O what shall the harvest be?

3 Sowing the seed with an aching heart,
Sowing the seed while the tear-drops start,
Sowing in hope till the reapers come,
Gladly to gather the harvest home:
O what shall the harvest be?
MRS. EMILY S. OAKEY.

701 Shall We Know Each Other?

WHEN we hear the music ringing
In the bright celestial dome,
When sweet angel voices, singing,
Gladly bid us welcome home
To the land of ancient story,
Where the spirit knows no care,
In that land of light and glory,
Shall we know each other there?

2 When the holy angels meet us,
As we go to join their band,
Shall we know the friends that greet us
In the glorious spirit-land?
Shall we see the same eyes shining
On us as in days of yore?
Shall we feel their dear arms twining
Fondly round us as before?

3 Yes, my earth-worn soul rejoices,
And my weary heart grows light;
For the sweet and cheerful voices,
And the forms so pure and bright,
That shall welcome us in heaven,
Are the loved of long ago;
And to them 'tis kindly given,
Thus their mortal friends to know.

4 O ye weary, sad, and tossed ones,
Droop not, faint not by the way:
Ye shall join the loved and just ones
In the land of perfect day.
Harp-strings touched by angel fingers,
Murmured in my raptured ear—
Evermore their sweet song lingers—
We shall know each other there.
                                    UNKNOWN.

702 Here and Yonder.

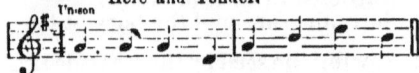

HERE we are but straying pilgrims,
Here our path is often dim;
But to cheer us on our journey,
Still we sing this wayside hymn:

CHO.—Yonder, over the rolling river,
Where the shining mansions rise,
Soon will be our home forever,
And the smile of the blessed Giver
Gladden all our longing eyes.

2 Here our feet are often weary,
On the hills that throng our way;
Here the tempest darkly gathers,
But our hearts within us say:

3 Here our souls are often fearful
Of the pilgrim's lurking foe;
But the Lord is our defender,
And he tells us we may know:

4 Here our shadowed homes are transient,
And we meet the stranger's frown;
So we'll sing with joy while going,
E'en to death's dark billow down:
                                    I. N. CARMAN.

703 The Ninety and Nine.

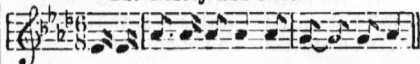

THERE were ninety and nine that
    safely lay
In the shelter of the fold,
But one had wandered far away,
In the desert so lone and cold—
Away on the mountains wild and bare,
Away from the Shepherd's tender care.

2 Shepherd, hast thou not here thy
    ninety and nine?
Are they not enough for thee?
But the Shepherd replied, "This one
    of mine,
Has wandered away from me;
The way may be wild, and rough, and
    steep,
I go to the desert to find my sheep."

3 But none of the ransomed ever knew
How deep were the waters crossed,
Nor how dark was the night the Lord
    passed through
Ere he found the sheep that was lost;
Away in the desert he heard its cry,
So feeble, and helpless, and ready to die.

4 And afar up the mountain, thun-
    der-riven,
And along the rocky steep,
There arose the glad song of joy to
    heaven,
"Rejoice: I have found my sheep!"
And the angels echoed around the
    throne,
"Rejoice: for the Lord brings back
    his own!"
                            ELIZABETH C. CLEPHANE.

704 Rest for the Weary.

IN THE Christian's home in glory
There remains a land of rest;
There my Saviour's gone before me,
To fulfill my soul's request.

CHO.—There is rest for the weary,
There is rest for the weary,
There is rest for the weary,
There is rest for you;
On the other side of Jordan,
In the sweet fields of Eden,
Where the tree of life is blooming,
There is rest for you.

2 He is fitting up my mansion,
Which eternally shall stand;
For my stay shall not be transient
In that holy, happy land.

3 Pain or sickness ne'er shall enter,
Grief nor woe my lot shall share;
But in that celestial center
I a crown of life shall wear.

4 Death itself shall then be vanquished,
And his sting shall be withdrawn:
Shout for gladness, O ye ransomed;
Hail with joy the rising morn.
J. Y. HARMER.

705 Yield not to Temptation.

YIELD not to temptation:
For yielding is sin;
Each victory will help you
Some other to win:
Fight manfully onward,
Dark passions subdue,
Look ever to Jesus:
He'll carry you through.

CHO.—Ask the Saviour to help you,
Comfort, strengthen, and keep you;
He is willing to aid you,
He will carry you through.

2 Shun evil companions,
Bad language disdain,
God's name hold in rev'rence
Nor take it in vain;

Be thoughtful and earnest,
Kind-hearted and true,
Look ever to Jesus:
He'll carry you through.

3 To him that o'ercometh
God giveth a crown;
Through faith we shall conquer,
Though often cast down;
He who is our Saviour
Our strength will renew:
Look ever to Jesus:
He'll carry you through.
H. R. PALMER.

706 Almost Persuaded.

"ALMOST persuaded" now to believe;
"Almost persuaded" Christ to receive.
Seems now some soul to say,
"Go, Spirit, go thy way,
Some more convenient day
On thee I'll call."

2 "Almost persuaded," come, come to-day;
"Almost persuaded," turn not away.
Jesus invites you here,
Angels are lingering near;
Prayers rise from hearts so dear:
O wanderer, come!

3 "Almost persuaded," harvest is past;
"Almost persuaded," doom comes at last;
"Almost" can not avail;
"Almost" is but to fail—
Sad, sad the bitter wail—
"Almost, but lost!"
P. P. BLISS.

707 Beautiful Zion.

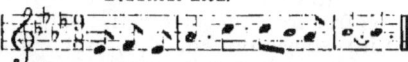

BEAUTIFUL Zion, built above—
Beautiful city that I love;
Beautiful gates of pearly white;
Beautiful temple—God its light!
He who was slain on Calvary
Opens those pearly gates to me.

2 Beautiful heaven, where all is light;
Beautiful angels, clothed in white;
Beautiful strains that never tire,
Beautiful harps through all the choir!
There shall I join the chorus sweet,
Worshiping at the Saviour's feet.

3 Beautiful crowns on every brow,
Beautiful palms the conquerors show,
Beautiful robes the ransomed wear,
Beautiful all who enter there!
Thither I press with eager feet;
There shall my rest be long and sweet.

4 Beautiful throne for Christ our King;
Beautiful songs the angels sing;
Beautiful rest—all wanderings cease;
Beautiful home of perfect peace!
There shall my eyes the Saviour see:
Haste to this heavenly home with me.
UNKNOWN.

708 Home of the Soul.

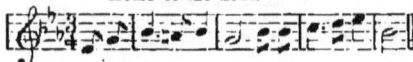

I WILL sing you a song of that beautiful land,
The far-away home of the soul,
Where no storms ever beat on the glittering strand,
While the years of eternity roll.

2 O that home of the soul, in my visions and dreams,
Its bright, jasper walls I can see,
Till I fancy but thinly the vail intervenes
Between the fair city and me.

3 There the great Tree of Life in its beauty doth grow,
And the River of Life floweth by;
For no death ever enters that city, you know,
And nothing that maketh a lie.

4 O how sweet it will be in that beautiful land,
So free from all sorrow and pain,
With songs on our lips, and with harps in our hands,
To meet one another again!
UNKNOWN.

709 Waiting at the Door.

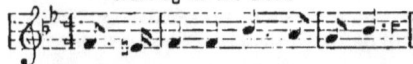

I AM waiting for the Master,
Who will rise and bid me come
To the glory of his presence,
To the gladness of his home.

CHO.—They are watching at the portal,
They are waiting at the door,
Waiting only for my coming—
All the loved ones gone before.

2 Many friends that traveled with me
Reached that portal long ago;
One by one they left me battling
With the dark and crafty foe.

3 O how soon shall I be with them,
And shall join their glorious throng,
There to mingle in their worship,
And to swell their mighty song!

4 Yet, O Lord, I wait thy pleasure,
For thy time and ways are best:
Hear me, Lord, for I am weary;
O, my Father, bid me rest.
KATE M. REASONER.

710 Safe within the Vail.

"LAND ahead!" Its fruits are waving
O'er the hills of fadeless green;
And the living waters laving
Shores where heavenly forms are seen.

CHO.—Rocks and storms I'll fear no more,
When on that eternal shore:
Drop the anchor; furl the sail:
I am safe within the vail.

2 Onward, bark: the cape I'm rounding:
See the blessèd wave their hands;
Hear the harps of God resounding
From the bright immortal bands.

3 Now we're safe from all temptation,
All the storms of life are past:
Praise the Rock of our salvation:
We are safe at home at last.
UNKNOWN.

711 Doxology.

[Inserted by request.]

PRAISE God, from whom all blessings flow;
Praise him, all creatures here below;
Praise him above, ye heavenly host;
Praise Father, Son and Holy Ghost.
THOS. KEN.

INDEX OF SUBJECTS.

All the hymns in this book are here arranged under the following general heads. Appropriate sub-heads will be found under the more important.

INDEX OF SUBJECTS.

INDEX OF SUBJECTS.

INDEX OF TUNES.

We have given notice of "copyright" or "by permission" when requested to do so; but many of the tunes in this collection are copyright property that are not so marked.

304

INDEX OF FIRST LINES.

306

INDEX OF FIRST LINES.

INDEX OF FIRST LINES.

INDEX OF FIRST LINES.